CHANGE YOUR JOB
CHANGE YOUR LIFE

Careering and Re-Careering in the New Boom/Bust Economy

9th Edition

Ron Krannich, Ph.D.

IMPACT PUBLICATIONS
Manassas Park, Virginia

Ninth Edition. Originally published in 1983 as *Re-Careering in Turbulent Times*.

Library of Congress Cataloging-in-Publication Data

Krannich, Ron
    Change your job, change your life: careering and re-careering in the new boom/bust economy / Ron Krannich.—9th ed.
        p. cm.
    Includes bibliographical references and index.
    ISBN 1-57023-220-2 (alk. paper)
      1. Vocational guidance—United States. 2. Career development—United States. 3. Career changes—United States. I. Title.
HF5382.5.U5K69   2004
650.14—dc21   2004111030

Publisher: For information on Impact Publications, including current and forthcoming publications, authors, press kits, online bookstore, and submission requirements, visit Impact's website: www.impactpublications.com.

Publicity/Rights: For information on publicity, author interviews, and subsidiary rights, contact the Public Relations Department: Tel. 703-361-7300, Fax 703-335-9486, or e-mail: info@impactpublications.com.

Sales/Distribution: All bookstore sales are handled through Impact's trade distributor: National Book Network, 15200 NBN Way, Blue Ridge Summit, PA 17214, Tel. 1-800-462-6420. All other sales and distribution inquiries should be directed to the publisher: Sales Department, IMPACT PUBLICATIONS, 9104 Manassas Drive, Suite N, Manassas Park, VA 20111-5211, Tel. 703-361-7300, Fax 703-335-9486, or e-mail: info@impactpublications.com.

Contents

Part II
DEVELOP POWERFUL CAREERING
AND RE-CAREERING SKILLS

Part III
CREATE YOUR OWN OPPORTUNITIES

Part IV
TAKE ACTION TO IMPLEMENT YOUR GOALS

Preface

ELCOME TO THE NINTH edition of *Change Your Job, Change Your Life*. In the seventh edition, written in 1999 during a period of major economic expansion and optimism, I began this Preface with these cautionary and now prophetic words:

> We enter the 21st century with lots of trendy and chauvinistic theories about the end of inflation, unemployment, and jobs based on nearly nine consecutive years of unprecedented American economic growth. We should be so fortunate, and perhaps naive, especially since we're surrounded by a world that is still trying to recover from a major economic bust that began in 1997.

Elsewhere I challenged the "end of the boom/bust economy" theory:

> The roaring 90s showed signs of re-entering a traditional boom/bust cycle at the beginning of the 21st century. A turbulent international environment and "unique events" seemed to be better guides to the future than this trendy low inflation theory. Boom and bust cycles seemed well and alive, although temporarily residing abroad, and would most likely affect future jobs and careers in America . . . . The bust side of another boom/bust cycle did not seem far away.

A New Economy and Job Market

Sixteen months later the highly over-valued stock market and shaky dot-com economy crashed and unemployment increased significantly. One of the most important "unique events" in American history took place on September 11, 2001 with simultaneous deadly terrorist attacks on New York City and Washington, DC. An already ailing "New Economy" officially went into recession and unemployment continued to increase as the luster came off this over-hyped economy. Major business scandals left over from the go-go days of the late 90s once again revealed a boom/bust economy which also had become a cowboy/casino economy – a place where lots of people ponyed up to get rich quick on risky "New Economy" schemes and scams. In the process, many people lost their jobs and personal insecurity increased accordingly. By mid-2004, the economy appeared to be gradually recovering from the 2001 recession. However, it was a rather anemic recovery characterized by a great deal of Wall Street hype countered by evidence of a jobless recovery. While the economy showed increased signs of strength, largely due to a booming housing sector, low interest rates, and high levels of consumption/indebtedness, few new jobs were being created in this recovering economy. Indeed, the low rate of job growth was largely due to two related developments – increases in workplace productivity and the offshoring of jobs to cheap labor markets. The boom side of this New Economy generated few new jobs, and what jobs it did create were disproportionately low-wage jobs for people without a four-year degree. This new trend had important implications for individuals who would increasingly face difficulties in finding good-paying jobs in the decade ahead. For them, careering and re-careering would play an important role in their future.

> By 2004, the boom side of this New Economy generated few new well-paying jobs.

As we go to press in late 2004, the economy appears weak, job growth modest and mysterious, and offshoring remains an important economic and political issue in a volatile presidential election year. At the same time, the economy and job market operate in the shadow of a war on terrorism and limited, high cost world oil supplies. What used to appear as "unique events" that could unexpectedly alter the economy and job market now seem to be predictable events. One important lesson learned since 2001 is that a major act of terrorism can fundamentally alter the economy and thus the job market. In fact, Americans live in a new era of uncertainty where major global events can have a significant impact on the jobs and careers of individuals.

The Book

This book was originally published in 1983 as *Re-Careering in Turbulent Times*. It has been periodically updated to reflect changes in the economy, job market, and employment scene. Many of the predictions and principles I outlined in the original book, as well as in subsequent editions under the title *Careering and Re-Careering*, remain true today. Above all, this is a book about empowerment – taking charge of your own career destiny. Unlike other career planning and job search books, I've purposely placed individual-level strategies and techniques within the larger context of a turbulent economy where the best laid plans often go awry because of unanticipated events. The process I call **careering and re-careering** for uncertain economic times is as true today as it was 23 years ago. Indeed, I continue to hear from readers who have successfully used the book in planning their careers and changing jobs.

This book has benefitted from over two decades of observations and analyses of the changing U.S. economy and employment scene. What has emerged during that time is a highly competitive, talent-driven economy that requires new skill sets that did not exist two decades ago. In this fascinating economy and its rapidly changing job market, a clear pattern for career success is evident: the best jobs go to those who are well educated, skilled in the new economy, work hard, behave like savvy entrepreneurs, and know when to stay and when to leave.

Since jobs change, so must you. Today's economy continues to transform the nature of work and the workplace with lightning speed. The skills you acquired recently may soon become obsolete. Not surprisingly, the job you have today may disappear tomorrow. One thing is certain: we live in a highly volatile economy where jobs are constantly created and destroyed in response to the changing nature of work and the workplace. If left to the winds of change, your future will be very uncertain. The job you possess today will not be the one you possess five years from now. And the job you'll have in five years may pay less than the one you have today.

The Possible New You

So where are you going with the rest of your life? Do you have the power to shape your future and change your life, or do you feel powerless – a passive recipient of changes initiated by others?

If you want to change your life, you first must possess the power to change your job and your career direction. For the power to change jobs and chart new careers is also the power to potentially change your life.

Whether you are starting your first job or changing jobs or careers, you're joining millions of other people who redefine their lives by changing what they do. Possessing this **power to change** is one of the most important assets for determining what you will do with the rest of your life.

Change your job and you'll probably change your life too! Never has this dictum been truer than in today's economy. The job you occupy today will most likely be radically different from the one you will perform 10 or 20 years from now. Like it or not, you **will** pursue careers that never existed 10 or 20 years ago. You will probably seek jobs and careers that are most compatible with your work-life goals. When given the choice, you will change jobs, because you want to change your life. If you're smart about your future, you will pursue jobs fit for you rather than try to fit your interests and skills into existing jobs.

While many successful people acknowledge a mixture of serendipity, excellent connections, sound planning, and smart decisions for their career fortunes, few people are fortunate to see their career and lifestyle dreams come true. Only some people are lucky enough to find a job they really love going to each day. Buffeted by the winds of change, many people feel they lack the power to shape their lives. Indeed, most people fall into jobs by chance, fail to examine many job and career alternatives suitable for their interests and skills, and pursue careers that are less than fully rewarding. After a few years of work experience, they wish they had better planned their careers as well as their lives. But by then many feel it is too late to make fundamental changes in their career direction. Their jobs lock them into particular lifestyles which appear increasingly difficult to change. Facing the realities of family, home ownership, mortgages, and the high cost of daily living, they either don't dream or they feel limited in their ability to make their dreams come true by taking the risks necessary for changing jobs and careers. They accept their present work and life pattern as inevitable rather than something they can shape in the future. Like millions of others, they feel stuck in what appears to be a career rut. Only if they lost their present job would they be forced into making some major changes in how they approach the world of work and their lives.

Many people do lose their jobs; the fortunate ones see such a loss as a wake-up call, re-examine their lives, and move on to more rewarding work. Others are less fortunate.

If you are not doing what you really love to do, if you're unsure what you might do better, if you are interested in exploring new career possibilities, or if you are interested in creating a work-life that is compatible with a desirable lifestyle, then this book is for you. If followed closely, it will help you give renewed direction to your career as well as chart a clear course for doing what you really want to do with the rest of your life.

This book is all about how to better experience serendipity, plan your career, and make intelligent job moves. It's a very different book for individuals interested in finding jobs and planning their futures. Unlike other career books, this one focuses on the **processes** of careering and re-careering within the **context** of an economy and society undergoing fundamental restructuring. Given this context, job search skills alone are not enough for long-term job and career success. Individuals must learn to career and re-career several times during their work lives. This means continuously acquiring new work-content skills, making strategic career moves, and relocating to communities which offer better job and career opportunities. They must be open, adaptive, and mobile.

With vision, determination, and a well organized plan of action, you should do well in finding rewarding jobs and careers in the decade ahead. But if you lack the necessary knowledge, skills, and motivation, you could well repeat past patterns as well as find yourself in a dead-end job which offers few rewards and a less than promising future.

If you are unemployed or about to experience a major career transition, this may be the best time to seriously consider acquiring new skills and relocating to communities offering more promising job and career opportunities. For what will certainly emerge in the decade ahead is a restructured job market in which the best jobs go to those who have the requisite education, training, and retraining capabilities demanded by employers in the new and rapidly changing job market. The worst jobs – those offering limited opportunities for career advancement and few financial rewards – will go to those who fail to take initiative to acquire the necessary education, training, and retraining to get ahead in this job market.

Dealing With Uncertainty

What should you do in the face of an uncertain job future? Are you prepared to take fundamental control of your job and your life?

If you feel your job is a life sentence, if you dread going to work, if your work is unfulfilling, if you think you're inadequately compensated, or if you're not doing what you really love to do, consider changing your job – and your life. You'll never regret having taken a risk to create a better life for you and those around you.

I know, because I and millions of others have successfully careered and re-careered. Thousands of others do so each year. We've discovered the secrets to changing our lives by changing our jobs. We've decided to risk discovering new jobs and careers that are right for us.

One thing has not changed in this new edition – the underlying philosophy of this book. It's very simple, real, and achievable: you are responsible for your own employment fate. And you must become even more responsible for your employment in the decade ahead, a revolutionary period of major economic restructuring both at home and abroad. No one is responsible for giving you a job or keeping you on the job indefinitely. While the government operates many different employment programs, these are primarily designed for people who lack basic work skills and initiative. They help train people for an uncertain and unpredictable job market affected by a larger, yet equally uncertain and unpredictable, economy which is responsible for both creating and destroying jobs. On the other hand, employers spend over $300 billion each year on training and retraining programs for ensuring a competent and competitive workforce.

You should put your employment fate in your own hands by learning how to operate in the job markets of today and tomorrow. In other words, the philosophy here is one of **individual responsibility and empowerment** – empower yourself to make things happen your way rather than in response to the wishes and whims of others as well as the boom and bust cycles of the economy. Today's 8 million unemployed merely testify to the validity of this philosophy. Many wish they had taken better care of their jobs and careers prior to receiving the shocking news that they were dismissed. And millions of others seek more rewarding jobs.

While I focus primarily on the individual, I'm also aware of the importance of other forces and actors affecting jobs and careers. Consequently, the first part of this book places the individual within the larger context of today's changing economy. There I analyze the present economy and employment situation as well as identify trends and make predictions for the future that have particular relevance for individuals. For the remaining 80 percent of the book, I return to you, the individual, who must operate within this larger organizational and societal context.

No one is responsible for giving you a job or keeping you on the job indefinitely.

Acknowledgments

I again wish to thank my many readers, from book reviewers and career counselors to students, professionals, and job seekers, who found the first eight editions of this book both useful and usable. Their many letters, phone calls, and e-mail have helped further strengthen this present edition.

Special thanks goes to Caryl Rae Krannich, who encouraged me to take on the subject, provided invaluable suggestions, contributed most of the section on interviewing, and spent numerous hours editing the manuscript. Her sense of form, style, and quality are found throughout the book. My frequent reference to "we" indicates our joint effort and ongoing partnership.

I also wish to thank my trusted editor, Mardie Younglof, for her great attention to detail in correcting my bad habits and helping further strengthen the final product.

Take Charge of Your Future

We wish you well as you navigate your career through this exciting and challenging decade. If you put into practice much of the advice found in the following chapters, you will begin reshaping your career – and your life – in the direction of your major interests, skills, and goals. Most important, you will be able to make critical job and career changes when necessary, despite the state of the economy or what others may tell you to the contrary. You will be able to do what we hope you will now do best – take charge of your own future. You can change your life because you have the power to change your job!

Ron Krannich

krannich@impactpublications.com

1

Prepare for an Uncertain Future

AFTER 11 YEARS OF UNPRECEDENTED economic expansion and employment growth, the U.S. economy returned to basics in 2001 – the economy went into another recession. Despite optimistic and trendy theories to the contrary, the boom/bust economy was well and alive. By 2004, the bust side of an anemic economy showed signs of gradual recovery. However, this appeared to be a very different type of recovery from previous decades. A so-called "jobless recovery," characterized by slow job growth and the increased offshoring of good paying service and high-tech jobs, characterized a New Economy that would predictably generate many low-wage jobs in the decade ahead. Accordingly, college graduates and professionals faced an increasingly difficult job market despite the growing economy. The job future, however, looked especially promising for people without a four-year degree and those with low-wage expectations.

Lessons Learned

For a generation of Americans who never experienced an economic downturn, layoffs, or difficulties in finding employment, a recession followed by a slow job growth recovery would teach important lessons about how one should take better care of his or her career and work life. The September 11, 2001 terrorist attacks on New York City and Washington, DC also would forever alter the way many people thought about their personal and professional goals. A new sense of job insecurity, uncertainty, pessimism, and anger arose

1

in what had become the promised land for millions of people. As many Americans found themselves experiencing important transitions, the need to change one's job as well as one's life took on renewed meaning. Indeed, business began to lose its luster as government, nonprofits, and voluntary organizations became more respectable and meaningful arenas for employment.

It's a New Job Economy

The past decade has been a turbulent one for jobs and careers in America. A recurring boom/bust economy created millions of new jobs as well as witnessed the disappearance of millions of other jobs. Some jobs and their occupants became victims of **structural unemployment** (permanent displacement of Old Economy jobs due to technological advances that make industries and skills obsolete, such as slide-rule, VCR, and film camera makers) while others experienced **cyclical unemployment** (temporary business downturns that rebound with improved economic conditions, such as real estate and automobile manufacturing). And still others have became unemployed due to the **outsourcing and offshoring** of jobs to cheaper labor markets at home and abroad. One result of these changes is what many observers optimistically refer to as the New Economy – an unpredictable high-tech driven economy that is constantly evolving within a rapidly changing global economy.

One of the major implications of today's uncertain New Economy is clearly expressed in a key question millions of individuals ask themselves:

> How should I prepare for the future when I don't know what the good jobs will look like in the future? After all, a so-called "hot job" today could well become another victim of structural, cyclical, or outsourced unemployment within the next decade!

This question becomes increasingly important in what was termed a "jobless recovery" in the highly charged political environment of 2003-2004 – economic growth accelerated due to increased productivity, but this growth was not part of the traditional pattern of cyclical unemployment. Jobs that normally would return to the American economy were, instead, outsourced to other countries. According to Goldman Sachs (*Forbes*, April 12, 2004: 98), between 2001 and 2003 nearly 400,000 service jobs and 1 million manufacturing jobs in the U.S. were lost to offshoring. Between 2004 and 2013, another 3.3 million white-collar jobs ($136 billion in wages) are expected to be offshored. Many of these jobs used to be considered hot growth jobs within the U.S. that required various levels of higher education – engineer, radiologist, software designer, and accountant. Now, these jobs can be offshored to

Bangalore, Shanghai, Hong Kong, Manila, Singapore, Kuala Lumpur, and Penang.

Offshoring of white-collar jobs, many of which require a college degree, appears to be a new and perhaps permanent pattern of employment change in America. This new phenomenon has developed in response to structural changes in the global economy brought about by the convergence of eight important developments:

1. Improved Internet connections
2. Increased bandwidth
3. Powerful fiber optic cable
4. Cheap international telecom prices
5. Large pool of well-educated and trained English-speaking workers in several developing countries
6. Efficient international transportation links and delivery services
7. Enhanced global organization and management systems
8. Multinational corporate structures with global-reach capabilities

White-collar jobs that were once part of cyclical unemployment were increasingly absorbed into a new form of structural unemployment – the geographic shift of jobs to cheaper labor markets. Creation of new jobs to replace what were once attractive value-added jobs supporting the middle and upper-middle classes in the American economy perplexed many politicians, economists, and employment specialists who seemed to be at a loss to identify new and better paying jobs that normally replaced the ones lost to outsourcing and offshoring. Instead, many of tomorrow's **safe jobs** are low- wage face-to-face jobs in the food, entertainment, health care, hospitality, transportation, and personal services industries or minimum-wage part-time and temporary jobs. Requiring only a high school education, many of these jobs offer limited benefits and little career advancement.

What Employers Want

You may or may not be prepared for what lies ahead in the world of work. Despite both optimistic and pessimistic economic projections, most job seekers face an increasingly tough and demanding employment arena:

Job seekers are required to come to the employment table with the latest marketable skills; a predictable pattern of work behavior; a willingness to take initiative, learn, and be a team player; and an entrepreneurial and positive attitude that contributes to the employer's bottom line.

Above all, they must demonstrate that they are really good at what they say they can and will do. And regardless of how good they are, once hired, they may receive small salary increments as well as become displaced workers if their employer decides to downsize, outsource, or offshore jobs. If they want to significantly increase their incomes and alter their lifestyle, they may need to find a new employer or become their own employer by changing jobs or careers.

Seeking to recruit employer-centered rather than self-centered individuals, today's employers want more performance and value from their workforce. And they are prepared to reward performance in many different ways. They simply have no choice to expect less in an economy that gives the competitive edge to companies that can recruit and retain a top quality workforce.

The New World of Work

You've seen the headlines and perhaps contemplated how they may best relate to your future:

- ▶ The recession is over, but the economy is experiencing a new jobless recovery.

- ▶ Unemployment remains stuck at 5.6 percent.

- ▶ Despite optimistic economic growth indicators, workers remain worried and angry about their future.

- ▶ Most new jobs in the decade ahead will be relatively low-wage jobs for people without a four-year degree.

- ▶ Companies lose their competitive edge due to increased problems in recruiting and retaining skilled workers.

- ▶ Today's talent-driven economy favors young, recently trained, and energetic individuals who are skilled in using today's newest technologies.

- ▶ Electronic resumes sent via e-mail and through employment websites continue to replace conventional paper resumes.

- ▶ Few job seekers know how to write an employer-centered resume for today's new job market.

► Job security and loyalty are all but disappearing in today's highly competitive and demanding workplace.

► Employers increasingly conduct situation- and behavior-based interviews and engage in rigorous psychological testing and screening.

► Employers can't afford to make the same old hiring mistakes.

► Compensation becomes a major issue in today's highly competitive job market.

► Savvy employers increasingly hire slow and fire fast.

► Between 2004 and 2013, another 3.3 million white-collar jobs ($136 billion in wages) are expected to be offshored.

► Workers over 40, who appear over-compensated and under-skilled, experience difficulties in changing jobs and careers.

► Retraining and continuing education become major issues in today's rapidly changing economy.

► Lifestyle issues, from childcare to flextime and eldercare, are increasingly important to today's workforce.

► Most employers are under-compensated by 10 percent.

► Employees need to think and behave like entrepreneurs and consultants in today's new workplace – their employer is their client.

► We're in the midst of a profound and unpredictable revolution in the world of work.

► Jobs in today's new economy have become increasingly demanding and stressful.

At the same time, employers are becoming more savvy at hiring and retaining key personnel. They know how costly hiring mistakes and losing talented employees can be. Indeed, their hiring and retention reading list now includes these popular book titles:

- ▸ *Finding and Keeping Great Employees*
- ▸ *Smart Hiring*
- ▸ *Hire With Your Head*
- ▸ *Winning the Talent Wars*
- ▸ *96 Great Interview Questions to Ask Before You Hire*
- ▸ *Love 'Em or Lose 'Em: Getting Good People to Stay*
- ▸ *Verify Those Credentials*
- ▸ *Don't Hire a Crook!*

Most of these headlines and book titles reflect a new and unsettling set of work and job search issues that were largely absent from our career vocabulary and bookshelves 10 years ago. During the past decade, numerous companies have "reinvented" themselves in terms of their goals, markets, and operations. They have merged, developed new operations, experimented with innovative management approaches, and made CEOs more accountable for performance. In their drive to increase productivity as well as avoid the trauma of a recession, they've restructured their workforces through downsizing and outsourcing. Such restructuring continues to accelerate even in a boom economy.

> **Today's talent-driven economy has created a new set of opportunities and challenges.**

Today's talent-driven economy, with its increased focus on high-tech skills, productivity, entrepreneurism, and hiring and retention issues, has created a new set of opportunities and challenges for workers. They may affect you in more ways than you have ever known. At the very least, they present a situation in which increased career choices also mean greater uncertainty, insecurity, and unpredictability in the world of work.

Power of Choice, Promise of Persistence

For the moment, let's forget about what's going on in the larger economy, the workplace, and among employers, and simply focus on your choices, for, in the end, you are the one who makes choices. It's really up to you to shape your future.

What do you really do well and enjoy doing? What's your purpose in life? Do you have a clear vision of what you want to do the rest of your life? Is your career the center of your life, or do you work so you can have a fulfilling life? Are you doing what you really love to do or are there other things you would rather be doing with your life?

A job should not become a life sentence. It should give you the freedom to do what you do well and enjoy doing. It should fit right. A job that doesn't fit right can be miserable. It can make life more difficult than it need be – unless you take action. Changing that job may forever change your life. But you must first acquire the power to make the necessary changes. That's what this book is all about – acquiring the power to take charge of your job, and your life!

Jobs and life need not be difficult if you possess the power of choice and persist in pursuing your goals. Your job should make life easier for you and those around you. You will know if your job is a good fit: it will feel good and be a rewarding experience. You'll enjoy going to work where you can fully use your knowledge, skills, and abilities and be rewarded accordingly.

Since you're reading this book, we assume you're sufficiently motivated to do something about your job and your life. If not, the following pages may help motivate you to take the necessary actions to change your life.

Welcome to the Rest of Your Life

So you're thinking of taking a major risk – seeking a job or pursuing a new career that may put you on the road to renewed success in the decade ahead.

But what exactly do you want to do with the rest of your life? How will you go about turning your dreams into realities over the next few weeks or months? Do you have goals and hidden talents that could be best directed elsewhere than in your present job or career?

Let's examine these and many other important questions for taking charge of your career today, tomorrow, and in the decade ahead. For in answering these questions, you will begin acquiring key skills and using effective strategies for shaping your future in the direction of your dreams.

Shape Your Future

Charting your career future through the power of choice and the promise of persistence is the subject of this book. Not everyone has the luxury of choice. Many people lose their jobs to the winds of economic change or to the whims of organizational politics. Recessions, layoffs, failed businesses, organizational changes, and on-the-job conflicts daily force thousands of people into unemployment lines. Indeed, millions of Americans lose their jobs each year. And millions of others quit their jobs for opportunities elsewhere.

Whatever your situation – forced or shaped by choice – the most important decision is how and what you choose to do **now** with your life. If you focus on your future in a disciplined and thoughtful manner, rather than dwell on past negatives or adopt a "can't do" attitude, you will begin turning your dreams into new realities.

The future is something we all would like to better know and control. Most people prefer to plan their future rather than wait to see what tomorrow will bring. But how do you plan effectively for tomorrow when much of life seems to be beyond one's control?

While the future may not be predictable, it is something you can and should shape for yourself. To do so requires vision, determination, and a well organized plan of action. You must first know where you are at present and then develop a clear vision of where you want to go in the future. But most important of all, you should develop and implement a plan of action for making your dreams come true.

> *The future may not be predictable, but it is something you can shape for yourself.*

Without an analysis of your present, a vision of the future, and a plan of action, your future will most likely be a repeat performance of your past patterns of behavior. You will be blown by the winds of change and whims of chance rather than direct and control your own destiny.

Beyond "Getting"

This book is all about taking better charge of your future in one of the most important areas of your life – your career. Few people actually plan their lives. Instead, they seem to be buffeted by forces beyond their control. Usually on the receiving end of life, they are great "getters": they get an education; they get married and get a family; they get a house; they get a job; they get taxed; and they get buried. If they are lucky – as Andy Warhol would have us remember – they may even get famous for 15 minutes sometime during their lives. While they may plan for some major events in their lives, few people consciously shape their future through deliberate action on an ongoing basis.

A career is something you **can** shape if you plan properly and have the requisite motivation and skills and use effective strategies to make it happen. However, the popular notion that all you need to do is get a good education that will lead to a good job and career, after which you live happily ever after, has been eroded in a society that has undergone rapid changes in education, training, occupations, and the workplace. The *"one job, one career, one work life"* phenomenon has all but ended for most occupations. The *"15 jobs, 5 careers, 10 geographic moves, and many work lives"* phenomenon is now upon us in a new careering and re-careering era. As such, the future becomes synonymous with change. Therefore, you are well advised to anticipate, plan, and manage changes to your advantage.

Examine the Evidence

The past two decades have been an extremely turbulent and rewarding period for many workers. Millions of individuals first entered the rapidly expanding workforce. At the same time, millions of these and other workers experienced unemployment brought on by larger structural changes taking place in both the international and domestic economies. Rapid technological changes made many skills increasingly obsolete for the jobs of today and tomorrow. While many of the unemployed expected to return to work once the economy improved, many would not because their skills were no longer appropriate for the job market. Unfortunately, they were not likely to acquire the necessary skills because they failed to take initiative, and neither the public nor private sectors were preparing them for new jobs. In the meantime, unemployment existed in the midst of major labor shortages.

> *No one owes anyone a job or career, and few people have valid excuses for not acquiring the necessary education and training.*

We are in the midst of a profoundly revolutionary period which will require individuals to change jobs and careers several times during their work lives. Knowing job search skills alone will be insufficient to function effectively in the rapidly changing job markets of the future. Job search skills must accompany concrete work-content skills. Individuals must continually update their present skills as well as acquire new skills in order to adjust to changing job market realities.

Empower Yourself

This book is all about empowerment – developing your ability to take charge of your future. It is designed to fill the need for an expanded perspective on jobs and careers for the decade ahead, since the problem of jobs, careers, and employment needs to be addressed with the larger future in mind. Many so-called experts tend to "stand where they sit" as well as "major in their own problems." Educators, for example, believe people need to come to them and their institutions for training when, in fact, highly bureaucratized educational institutions are more often part of the problem rather than the solution, and educators continue to face significant employment problems themselves. Politicians and bureaucrats tend to do what they do best – think in narrow policy terms: create another "innovative" government program which they hope "this time" will produce results. And career experts and futurists seem unprepared to provide practical guidance, especially on relocation and self-employment, to unemployed workers in communities that simply lack enough jobs to go around.

The perspective presented in this book synthesizes important skills training and job search approaches in relation to a society undergoing major social, economic, and political restructuring. This is a "no excuses" book that stresses the importance of individual choices relating to goals, organization, discipline, and sheer tenacity. It places full responsibility for employment on the shoulders of the individual, many of whom have a history of making bad personal and professional choices. No one owes anyone a job or career, and few people have valid excuses for not acquiring the education and training necessary to function effectively in today's job market. Therefore, you must be responsible for your own employment fate. You shape your own future by the decisions you made yesterday and make today as well as by those you will make tomorrow. This book is designed to help prepare you for turbulent times by providing you with the necessary knowledge and skills to make informed choices about your future. It's all about making better choices to take charge of your future.

Organize and Discipline Your Thinking

This book should become a flexible guide to your future which you can use over and over again in the coming years. The 17 chapters that follow move from description and explanation to prediction and prescription. Since chapters are related to one another, it's best to read each section and chapter in sequence. However, you may wish to read them in a different order, or go directly to the chapters that are of greatest interest.

If, for example, you are interested in moving to another community, go directly to Chapter 16 for tips on how to relocate and conduct a long-distance job search. If you are scheduled for a job interview in a few days, examine Chapter 13 on how to conduct an effective interview. And if you are curious about the future, browse through Chapter 3, which briefly examines 35 likely changes in the decade ahead.

The book is purposefully designed to be a comprehensive, flexible, and usable guide for readers with different interests and goals. Each part, as well as most chapters, can stand alone in addressing important issues of concern to millions of individuals.

Part I sketches the larger context within which individuals make career choices. It sets the stage for subsequent how-to chapters by analyzing industries and occupations, explaining the educational and job markets, and predicting future changes in occupations and employment. Taken together, these chapters develop a vision of what the future may look like for making career decisions. If read in sequence, this section will help you better understand the strategies and tactics outlined in Parts II and III. But if such contextual descriptions, explanations, analyses, and predictions are of peripheral interest to you, skip this section and proceed to the remaining chapters that offer practical careering and re-careering advice.

If you are mainly interested in prescriptions for finding a job, then go directly to Chapter 5. This chapter provides an important introduction and transition to the seven how-to chapters in Part II. These practical chapters focus on how to develop and implement an effective job search, from specifying a job objective to writing resumes, networking, conducting research, interviewing, and negotiating salaries.

Part III addresses important careering and re-careering opportunities you can create for yourself, from advancing on the job to relocating to another community or starting your own business. Many readers have found this section most instructive because it includes important career and lifestyle issues normally absent in other career planning and job search books.

Part IV addresses the key issue of implementation. It presents practical exercises for translating this book into action.

Select the Right Resources

We wish you well as you take this journey into an exciting and sometimes confusing world of self-discovery and action. We are primarily concerned with relating key job and career issues to your situation – from understanding the nature of the job market to developing job search skills, acquiring work-content skills, relocating to other communities, and translating this book into action. Many of these issues, which also are job search steps, are outlined in our other books: *Discover the Best Jobs for You!, High Impact Resumes and Letters, The Savvy Resume Writer, Dynamite Resumes, Dynamite Cover Letters, 201 Dynamite Job Search Letters, Savvy Interviewing, Interview for Success, Nail the Job Interview!, The Savvy Networker, Dynamite Salary Negotiations, No One Will Hire Me!,* and *Job Interview Tips for People With Not-So-Hot Backgrounds.* We also address particular jobs and career fields in the following books: *The Best Jobs for the 21st Century, America's Top 100 Jobs for People Without a Four-Year Degree, The Complete Guide to Public Employment, Find a Federal Job Fast, The Complete Guide to International Jobs and Careers, International Jobs Directory, Jobs for Travel Lovers,* and *Military Resumes and Cover Letters.* Our Internet job search books assist individuals in using the Internet to conduct an effective job search: *America's Top Internet Job Sites* and *The Directory of Websites for International Jobs.* While available in many bookstores and libraries, these and many other job search books also are available directly from Impact Publications. For your convenience, you can order them by completing the order form at the end of this book.

Impact Publications also publishes several career catalogs and numerous specialty flyers of additional job and career resources. Their catalogs and flyers can be downloaded from their main website: www.impactpublications.com. To receive a free copy of their "What's New and Hot" flyer, send a self-addressed stamped envelope (#10 business size) to:

IMPACT PUBLICATIONS
ATTN: What's New and Hot
9104 Manassas Drive, Suite N
Manassas Park, VA 20111-5211

You also may want to visit their websites, which include an online career bookstore for a complete listing of career resources and advice on finding jobs and advancing careers:

www.impactpublications.com
www.winningthejob.com

Redirect and Re-Energize Your Life

The processes we call **careering** and **re-careering** emphasize the need to prepare for an uncertain employment future. They require linking work-content skills to job search skills and relocation issues within the context of a rapidly changing economy character-ized by periodic boom/bust cycles. These economic cycles often witness the fundamental restructuring of busi-nesses, jobs, and the job market.

> *This is all about empowerment – you have within you the power to shape your own destiny.*

The chapters that follow are all about **empowerment** – you have within you the power to shape your own destiny. As such, the remaining 18 chapters reveal how you can redirect your life through new and exciting opportunities in the world of work.

Join us as we take you on a powerful journey of self-discovery. We'll share with you proven strategies for turning dreams into new realities. It's an exciting and challenging journey that may well change your life forever. Our goal is simple – to show you how to make a habit of careering and re-careering success.

Part I

Prepare for Turbulence and New Opportunities

2

Career and Re-Career in a Boom/Bust Economy

L ET'S EXPLORE THE FUTURE in order to better understand where you may want to go with your career and your life. Your vision of the future largely determines how you will approach the future. Without such a vision, you may assume tomorrow will be like today and yesterday and thus you will continue doing what you have always done – going with the flow. But if you believe tomorrow may be different, you may want to change your plans and your behavior. Let's start with some basic orientation questions before we look into the future.

You've come a long way, but you still have many years ahead. What exactly are your goals? What do you want to do with the rest of your life? Where do you see your career and lifestyle five, ten, or 20 years from now? Are your goals realistic given your interests, skills, motivations, and image of the future? What types of jobs and careers will you choose? Will these choices be the right ones for you? How will they affect your lifestyle? How much control do you want over your life? What are you willing to risk in the decade ahead?

Work and Meaningful Lifestyles

The beginnings and endings of decades are times for reflection, assessment, and redirection. They also are often times for recurring recessions in a boom/bust economy. Like the 1980s, the decade of the 1990s was a turbulent period for jobs, careers, and lifestyles. The best laid plans were subjected to unprecedented changes as millions of Americans first entered the job market, experienced unemployment, or changed jobs and careers several times. Many

15

people attempted to develop lifestyles in the face of a turbulent economic world where jobs and careers were as unpredictable as the economy. In general, however, the 1990s turned out to be one of the best periods for economic growth and employment in the history of the United States.

At the beginning of the 1990s, a highly predictable recession took a major toll on businesses and employees alike, as more than 12 million Americans joined the unemployment rolls. Millions of others became discouraged and abandoned their job search altogether. A deficit-ridden and anemic economy gradually turned around and expanded into one of the greatest boom economies of the 20th century while much of the rest of the world experienced recessions and economic crises. By 1999 unemployment in the U.S. had plunged to a low of 4.2 percent. In the meantime, companies continued to both downsize and upsize; millions of jobs were lost forever while millions of other jobs were created as the U.S. economy underwent major restructuring. It seemed as if the good times might last forever, as least it looked that way to many young workers who had never experienced a recession.

> *Despite trendy theories about a New Economy, the end of recessions, and perpetual prosperity, by 2001 this booming cowboy economy went into a relatively predictable recession.*

Despite trendy theories about a New Economy, the end of recessions, and perpetual prosperity, by 2001 this booming cowboy economy went into a relatively predictable recession as many of the much-hyped dot-coms collapsed, bankruptcies reached new highs, the over-heated stock market hit new lows, and corporations laid off thousands of workers each week. As major energy and telecommunication firms, such as Enron and Global Crossing, went bust and revealed in their aftermath an often troubled corporate world, much of the luster surrounding corporate America seemed to wear thin.

Unemployment in the U.S. climbed to nearly 6 percent by February 2002, exacerbated by the shocking terrorist events of September 11, 2001. As the economy officially went into recession, more and more companies shed jobs. In this tough job market individuals expanded their average job search time from three months to over six months. By mid-2004 unemployment had receded to 5.6 percent and the economy appeared to be well on its way to a recovery. However, this did not appear to be a traditional economic recovery followed by steady job gains. Instead, the economy grew at a much faster pace than the number of new jobs. Called a "jobless recovery," this newly emerging economy was noted for major productivity gains and the offshoring of jobs. While new jobs were being created, a disproportionate number of them were low-wage face-to-face jobs for people without a four-year degree. In fact, the U.S. Department of Labor's job forecasts for the coming decade indicated that the fastest growing jobs would be low-wage service jobs (see the charts in Chapter 4).

One thing was certain: the boom days and economic excesses of the 1990s were over, as more and more individuals were learning to play an employment game that was largely forgotten during the boom years of the 1990s – they would need to constantly career and re-career in the years ahead as more unique events and recurring recessions would most likely create greater uncertainty and turbulence in an increasingly unpredictable job market. While a college degree was still important for entry and advancement to the best-paying jobs, especially managerial and professional positions, the largest number of job opportunities in the coming decade would be in the service industries, and most of these jobs would be for people without a four-year degree. Accordingly, the ranks of the working poor were expected to expand.

Working in a Boom/Bust Economy

For many Americans, the 1990s were best approached as another turbulent decade for the economy and employment but with one new twist – the economy had experienced one of the longest periods of economic expansion in history. Economists and political pundits speculated what this meant for the future of employment. Maybe it was a new pattern or just an end-of-the-century anomaly. By 1997 some economists and financial analysts concluded, based on three years of low inflation and high employment, that the traditional boom/bust economy and its attendant recessions and unemployment cycles were over; the economy had now reached a new level of unprecedented growth characterized by full employment and a booming international economy. In fact, by 2000 the economy had experienced ten consecutive years of growth, low inflation, strong stock market fundamentals, and low unemployment. Even though the international economy went "south" in the latter half of 1997, the U.S. economy seemed destined to boom onward and upward.

Futurists and financial gurus had a field day. The theory of the "great boom ahead" became popularized in 1998 with such books as Harry S. Dent, Jr.'s *The Roaring 2000s*, Knight Kiplinger's *World Boom Ahead: How Business and Consumers Will Prosper*, and James Glassman's *Dow 36,000*. However, few people were willing to bet their futures on such an overly optimistic theory. Indeed, the roaring 90s showed signs of re-entering a traditional boom/bust cycle at the beginning of the 21st century. A turbulent international environment and "unique events" seemed to be better guides to the future than this trendy low-inflation theory. Boom-and-bust cycles seemed well and alive, although temporarily residing abroad; they would most likely affect future jobs and careers in America.

Facing a New Cowboy/Casino Economy

By 2000, an extremely over-valued stock market appeared to be on the verge of a major correction. Viewed by some realists as a cowboy/casino economy – brash and risky – the previous five years had witnessed unprecedented speculation in the stock market; a major infusion of venture capital into start-up companies of marginal performance but which managed to quickly go public; and a great deal of hype about high-tech industries and the "new frontier" of dot-com business opportunities on the Internet that threatened traditional "bricks and mortar" retail businesses. Viewed as part of the so-called "New Economy," these were, in many respects, bad ideas whose time had come in a new cowboy/casino economy. They quickly faced basic economic realities in 2001 and crashed accordingly.

Much of what passed for the "New Economy" at the turn of the century were some bad ideas whose time had come in what had essentially become an excessive cowboy/casino economy.

The bust side of another boom/bust cycle did not seem far away. Many economists began comparing this period with similar excesses of the 1980s and early 1990s, when real estate and junk bond speculation drove the memorable boom/bust cycles.

Depending on the level of economic growth, unemployment over the next decade is likely to fluctuate between four and eight percent. Millions of Americans will enter the job market for the first time; millions of others will experience unemployment; and millions more will change jobs and careers. As more companies realize productivity gains and offshore jobs, individuals will face an uncertain future requiring greater initiative to regularly acquire new skills, change jobs and careers, develop greater financial security, and relocate to growing communities.

Public opinion polls toward the end of the 1990s noted disturbing new perceptions arising during this decade of change and uncertainty: while unemployment was at an all-time low and job changing had not significantly increased during the decade, the rate of unemployment and the degree of individual job insecurity were perceived as high. This gap between objective and subjective reality for individuals had continued to grow throughout the turbulent 1990s. It became objective reality in 2001 when unemployment increased by nearly 2 percent.

Perceptions are reality for most people. If we learned anything about economics and employment during the past decade, it was this:

We live in a highly complex society with an unpredictable and risky marketplace where even the best laid plans go awry due to numerous changes beyond one's control. Since economic and employment futures are unpredictable, one is well advised to develop flexible job and career strategies for dealing with uncertainty.

At the very least these strategies must address the issues of skills, lifestyles, opportunities, and risk-taking at the most significant level in society – the individual. In other words, you are on your own in a sea of change, so you had better take initiative in shaping and securing your own economic and employment future. No one else, nor trendy theory, will do this for you.

Employment in a Dual Society

Employment in the United States is closely tied to an economic restructuring process taking place at the international, national, and local levels. During the past two decades the United States rapidly moved from a primarily industrial and technological society to one based on high technology, energy, services, and export-oriented manufacturing. It also moved from a credit nation to a debtor nation – fueling the

You are on your own in a sea of change, so you had better take initiative in shaping and securing your own future. No one else, nor trendy theory, will do this for you.

international economy with its high level of spending and consumption but positioning itself for even more vulnerable economic times ahead.

The signs of an economy and job market undergoing major restructuring are especially apparent when examining the paradoxical unemployment/labor shortage problem: unemployment exists in the midst of major labor shortages. As millions of Americans become unemployed, millions of jobs also go unfilled at the two extreme ends of the job market: those requiring high-level skills and those requiring low-level skills. Many unemployed individuals lack the necessary skills to function in a post-industrial, high-tech society; refuse to take low-paying service jobs; or do not know how to find a job appropriate for their level of skills and experience. Like the dual societies of Third World countries – one rural/agricultural and another urban/industrial – America is a dual society of a different type. This dual society is defined by the skilled "haves" and the unskilled "have-nots." Its talent-driven, value-added economy favors well educated and skilled individuals who are rewarded with the best-paying jobs with a career future. The same economy discriminates against those who lack appropriate education and skills.

Following a pattern developed during the past two decades, the coming decade will most likely be a period of accelerated structural unemployment. The dual issues of productivity and competitiveness tied to an increasingly internationalized economy and a newly shaping world political order are forcing corporate America to apply the latest cost-saving technology to the workplace. Protectionist labor unions are correct in their analysis of the problem: increases in productivity displace high-cost labor, which, in turn, erodes union membership. But at the same time, nearly 3 million new jobs are created each year to absorb many of the structurally unemployed. And without industry's ability to remain competitive in a global marketplace, those jobs and the businesses will both be lost.

The major issue for the first decade of the 21st century began in the 1980s: how to retrain and relocate an increasing number of structurally unemployed individuals in a relatively unplanned and unpredictable economy subject to a highly volatile international arena that is likely to make and break millions of jobs. Assuming continuing public policy failures to deal with economic and employment problems, individuals in the decade ahead must develop their own strategies for navigating their careers in tomorrow's boom-and-bust economy.

Take Re-Careering Initiatives

In the decade ahead, millions of workers will continue to be displaced due to the continuing transformation of the economy and workplace. But few people, especially displaced workers facing structural unemployment, are taking the initiative to provide or acquire the necessary skills training and retraining – and for good reasons. The tax, unemployment insurance, health care, and pension systems were designed for a different era when structural unemployment was not a major issue. Such systems have yet to adjust to the employment realities of a profoundly different society which is based upon high-technology and service industries and which experiences structural unemployment.

The tax, unemployment insurance, health care, and pension systems provide few incentives for retraining, relocation, and job search. Few employers, for example, receive tax incentives to retrain or outplace displaced workers. The unemployment insurance system is designed to give temporary income support for individuals facing cyclical unemployment. It does little to encourage the structurally unemployed to seek retraining, develop job search skills, or relocate to other communities. And the limited portability of most health care and pension systems discourages individuals from changing jobs and relocating.

As structural unemployment becomes more pervasive, the problem will be what to do with millions of unemployed workers who have limited educations and obsolete skills. Some analysts believe a major national training and retraining program is desperately needed. The relatively new Work Force Investment Act is supposed to address this crisis. Others see this as nearly impossible to implement given the highly decentralized and fragmented nature of policy-making and implementation.

What will displaced workers do – many of whom are highly skilled in older technologies? What actions can be taken now, and by whom, to make a positive transition to the job market of the high-tech and service society?

The answers to these questions primarily lie with the **individual** rather than with government or corporations. Indeed, one of our major purposes in writing this book is to urge you to become **self-reliant and effective** in your career. While government and the private sector may provide incentives and opportunities as well as a few limited-scale programs, the individual ultimately must be responsible for his or her own employment fate. We assume that both government and the private sector will be slow in responding to the retraining, relocation, and

> *The tax, unemployment insurance, health care, and pension systems were designed for a different era when structural unemployment was not a major issue.*

job search needs of individuals and society. Therefore, it is incumbent upon you to take initiative to acquire the necessary skills for success in the job markets of today and tomorrow. No one will do this for you.

Predict and Prepare for Uncertainty

Seven major developments in the decade ahead could have important implications for the employment futures of most Americans:

PREDICTION 1: The restructuring of the world political and economic order creates new opportunities and challenges for jobs relating to a more export-oriented economy.

IMPLICATION: While new international job and career opportunities will arise in the decade ahead, domestic jobs will become increasingly dependent on U.S. trade initiatives abroad. Great job opportunities will be available with U.S. companies doing business in Asia, Europe, and Latin America.

PREDICTION 2:   Boom/bust economic cycles, along with several "unique events," continue as the economy experiences a combination of good times and bad times which, in turn, create a great deal of uncertainty for planning careers and lifestyles.

IMPLICATION: You need to acquire the necessary work-content and job search skills for quickly changing jobs and careers. Also, be prepared to relocate to more prosperous communities as well as develop greater financial security to bridge the bust/boom cycles.

PREDICTION 3:   Millions of jobs will be created and eliminated in the decade ahead. New jobs will be created at the rate of 2 to 3 million each year. At the same time, nearly 2 million jobs will be eliminated annually. In the midst of these changes nearly 15 million Americans will experience unemployment each year; between 5 and 10 million Americans will be unemployed each day.

IMPLICATION: While you have a high probability of experiencing unemployment or a change of employment in the decade ahead, new opportunities for careering and re-careering will abound for those who know the "what," "where," and "how" of finding jobs and changing careers.

PREDICTION 4:   The rapidly expanding service sector will create the largest number of new jobs. These will be disproportionately found at the two extreme ends of the job market – high-paying jobs requiring high-level skills and low-paying face-to-face jobs requiring few specialized skills.

IMPLICATION: You should focus on acquiring specialized education and skills for the high-end of the job market. Many of your skills also should be sufficiently general and marketable so you can easily make job and career transitions without becoming a victim of structural unemployment and boom/bust cycles.

PREDICTION 5:   **Structural unemployment will accelerate due to a combination of business failures in the boom/ bust economy and continuing productivity improvements in both the manufacturing and service sectors as new technology and improved decision-making and management systems are introduced to the workplace. Structural unemployment also will be exacerbated by the increased movement of both manufacturing and service jobs offshore to low-wage countries in Asia, the Caribbean, and Central and Latin America.**

IMPLICATION: You need to acquire the necessary skills to adjust to the coming changes in the workplace and job market. Careering and re-careering should become your central focus in deciding which skills to acquire.

PREDICTION 6:   **Thousands of stagnant communities and inner-city neighborhoods will generate too few jobs to provide sufficient careering and re-careering opportunities. "Welfare-subsidy" communities, as well as those lacking a diversified service economy, will provide few job opportunities in the decade ahead.**

IMPLICATION: Individuals in stagnant communities must find ways to create their own employment or relocate to communities offering long-term careering opportunities. The most likely candidates will be growing metropolitan areas with diversified suburban economies.

PREDICTION 7:   **Public policy failures to resolve education, training, and unemployment problems – as well as initiate effective job generation, relocation, and job search approaches for promoting a**

more employable society – will continue in the decade ahead.

IMPLICATION: Given the highly decentralized and fragmented governmental and policy systems in the United States, politicians and public policy relevant to promoting full employment will remain relatively inert. Since most politicians will continue to be preoccupied with form and style rather than with substance and results in dealing with pressing economic and employment issues, individuals must take their own initiative in acquiring skills, finding jobs, changing careers, and relocating to communities offering better job opportunities.

These predictions form a set of assumptions for proposing strategies to manage your career(s) in the decade ahead. Our approach is especially relevant to a job market undergoing the types of turbulent changes we foresee for the coming decade.

Whether our predictions turn out to be 30, 70, or 100 percent accurate is beside the point. What is important is that you be aware, anticipate, and prepare for change. In so doing, you will be ready to seize new opportunities regardless of whatever direction the economy and employment situation takes in the decade ahead.

The changes taking place in the workplace have important implications for individuals in planning their future. As more and more jobs become obsolete and new opportunities arise in the high-tech and service economy, workers must be better prepared to function in today's evolving job market. At the very least, they must learn how to career and re-career throughout their worklife.

Beware of Incomplete Approaches

The nature of work and the process of finding employment have changed dramatically during the past few decades. For those who lived through the Great Depression, a job – indeed, any job – was something they were lucky to have. A good job – one they enjoyed and earned a good living from – was something only a few people were lucky to have. People essentially took jobs for financial security, not for personal or professional satisfaction, which appeared to be a luxury of the rich.

As white-collar employment expanded in the 1950s and 1960s, a new philosophy of work evolved with an expanded economy that generated lots of job opportunities. While financial security was still important, satisfaction became also important for selecting careers and choosing employers. Work was to be enjoyed and based upon one's strongest skills. Career counselors advised individuals not to find just any job. Rather, they should look for jobs they love to do – ones that would give them satisfaction. Books such as Marsha Sinetar's *Do What You Love, The Money Will Follow* captured this changing philosophy. Individuals also were advised to change jobs and careers when they were no longer happy with their work. Satisfied workers were also seen as productive and loyal workers – they ostensibly put their heart into their work and stayed with their employer as long as they remained satisfied.

Pioneered in the career planning methods of Dr. Bernard Haldane in the 1950s and 1960s and popularized in Richard Bolles's self-directed *What Color Is Your Parachute?* in the 1970s and 1980s, job search was placed on center stage as a skill that could be learned and applied with considerable success. Reflecting the do-your-own-thing philosophy of the 1960s and primarily emphasizing the importance of self-assessment and self-reliance, individuals were strongly advised to identify what they do well – their strengths – and enjoy doing. Based on this knowledge, they were further advised to take initiative in seeking employment outside the formal job market of classified ads and employment agencies. Known as the "hidden job market," this employment arena could be tapped by engaging in informational interviews – that is, asking people for information and advice about jobs and employment. The key principles for successful job search were the familiar sales approaches of **prospecting and networking** – methods for developing contacts and acquiring information, advice, and referrals. Changing careers primarily involved a strategy of identifying and communicating transferable skills to employers rather than acquiring new job-related skills.

> *Emphasizing process and form to the exclusion of such critical issues as job generation, relocation, and work-content skills, these approaches are at best incomplete.*

The process identified by Haldane, Bolles, and other career experts for finding employment is what Adele Scheele (*Skills for Success*) calls "successful careering." It requires the use of certain marketing skills and strategies for selling yourself. According to Scheele, these skills consist of (1) self-presentation, (2) positioning, and (3) connecting. Other writers, including ourselves, refer to these as self-promoting "entrepreneurial skills": (1) role playing, (2) risk taking, and (3) networking – key skills, principles, or strategies applicable to most analogous sales and marketing situations.

The job search skills promoted during the past three decades are based on a business-sales analogy. According to many career advisors, finding a job is like selling – you sell yourself in exchange for status, position, and money. The emphases here are on the **process of selling** and the **methods of self-presentation** – not the substance of work-content skills. Seldom, if ever, does this group of career advisors address the equally critical issues of **job generation and relocation**, or advise individuals to acquire new **work-content skills** which are more responsive to the changing job market. Doing so requires more comprehensive approaches as well as a major investment of time and effort, especially in education and training, which may seem beyond the immediate employment needs of many individuals.

As more and more jobs require technical skills, and as the job market continues to become restructured in response to the changing high-tech and service economy, the career planning approaches of the past three decades need to be reoriented in light of today's new economic realities. Emphasizing process and form to the exclusion of such critical issues as job generation, relocation, work-content skills, and talent, these approaches are at best incomplete in today's job market. Few individuals, for example, who use networking to market only such soft functional skills as reading, writing, and interpersonal communication will be successful in finding employment with a promising future. As many displaced homemakers and liberal arts students learned during the past two decades, such strategies have limitations in a job market requiring concrete technical skills applicable to specific work settings. Lacking an appropriate set of work-content skills, these individuals may become the new displaced, underemployed, and discontented workers of tomorrow.

The dual issues of job generation and relocation are critical in planning one's career future. We should never forget that people work in or from specific communities from which they rent or own property and develop particular lifestyles which may or may not be more important than their jobs or careers. If, for example, you live in an economically stagnant community that generates few job opportunities for someone with your interests and skills, using job search skills to find a great job in such a community would be frustrating, if not useless. Your options and approaches in such a situation come down to four:

1. Find a local job that may not fit well with your particular mix of interests and skills while hoping that more appropriate opportunities will eventually open for you in the future as this community generates more job and career options.

2. Commute to a job in another community within your region that offers opportunities appropriate for your interests and skills.

3. Start a business that is not dependent on local economic cycles – one that is broadly based with a diversified regional, national, or international clientele.

4. Relocate to a growing community that appears to be capable of generating many new jobs in the future. Such communities offer an ideal setting where job generation, relocation, and job search come together in providing individuals with numerous opportunities for careering and re-careering in the future.

Career and Re-Career for Today and Tomorrow

The processes we call "careering" and "re-careering" address present and future job realities and enable individuals to change their lives. Re-careering goes beyond the standard "careering" skills popularized during the past three decades, which were based upon an understanding of a job market in an industrial economy. As the job market continues to be restructured in the direction of high technology and services, a different approach to job hunting and career development – one responsive to new and uncertain economic realities – is required.

Success in tomorrow's job market will require a new breed of worker who anticipates, prepares, and eagerly adapts to change.

We anticipate a very different and intensely competitive job market in the future, with employers increasingly in control of a highly structured recruitment process. The major dynamic for restructuring the job market is the continuing growth of a high-tech and service society, increasingly dependent upon international trade, requiring highly specialized and skilled workers who are prepared for job and career changes. These workers must not be overly specialized nor too narrow in their perception of the future demand for their present skills. Instead, tomorrow's workers must be flexible in learning new skills, for their specialized jobs may become obsolete with the continuing productivity improvements in the workplace and movement of both manufacturing and service jobs offshore. Furthermore, tomorrow's workers must be adaptive to new jobs and careers. Overall, success in tomorrow's job market will require a new breed of worker who anticipates, prepares, and eagerly adapts to change. Such individuals prepare for career transitions by acquiring new skills and actively seeking new work environments through the use of effective job search strategies and relocating to new communities and work settings.

Careering is the process of preparing to enter the job market with marketable skills to land the job you want. **Re-careering** is the process of repeatedly acquiring marketable skills and changing careers in response to a turbulent job market. The standard careering process of the past three decades, therefore, must be modified with four new re-careering emphases:

1. Acquiring marketable skills through regular education and training.

2. Changing careers several times based on a combination of job search skills, new work-content skills, and relocation actions.

3. Using more efficient communication networks for finding jobs.

4. Relocating to communities experiencing long-term job growth.

Approach the Subject Differently

This book departs from much of the standard career literature of the past three decades as well as some of the newer approaches advanced for today's so-called new job market. Many such books are extremely useful yet redundant and static – largely focused on individual self-assessment within a never-changing job search process perhaps most relevant for the 1970s and 1980s. Newer approaches go to the other extreme – focus primarily on electronic techniques for navigating a job market found on the Internet or advance trendy theories about the "end of jobs" or the shape of a new "employment revolution." Preoccupied with one or two techniques, few such books relate one technique to another nor look beyond the individual in attempting to develop strategies for finding employment. Most lack a critical context and analysis. Many overstate reality in order to be different.

We offer what we believe is a realistic approach for the decade ahead. We place career planning and job search within a more comprehensive employment framework – careering and re-careering – than previously examined. In so doing, we outline effective job search strategies within the context of new job market realities. The result is a new synthesis and approach for career planning that (1) links the individual and job search strategies to larger employment issues, and (2) focuses on managing an uncertain future. We feel such an approach will better prepare individuals for finding employment and changing careers in the years ahead than a narrower approach that focuses solely on individual self-assessment within the job search process.

The following chapters address the problems of jobs and careers in the decade ahead as well as outline the necessary skills and strategies for finding jobs. Written for every working individual in the decade ahead, the book gives practical advice on how to prepare for new jobs and careers as well as how to make career changes. Individual chapters outline ways to identify and acquire marketable skills, state goals, write resumes and letters, prospect, network, interview, negotiate salaries, and advance and change careers. Special chapters address the challenges of career advancement, relocation, starting a business, and achieving results. Taken together, these chapters offer a recipe for changing your job and career, as well as your life.

Achieve Results

Our goals in writing this book are concrete, specific, and oriented toward action and results. You should acquire certain careering and re-careering skills. Upon completing this book you should be able to:

- Understand the changing nature of jobs and careers in the decade ahead and how they relate to your future.

- Identify desirable jobs and careers you may wish to pursue.

- Assess your goals in relation to your values and the demands of the job market.

- Identify your present interests and skills as well as the skills you can best transfer to other jobs and careers.

- Specify your need for skills training as well as know how to acquire the necessary training.

- Communicate your goals, skills, and qualifications to employers.

- Conduct targeted research on alternative jobs, careers, organizations, and communities.

- Write different types of resumes and job search letters.

- Prospect and network for job information, advice, referrals, and job leads.

- Conduct informational and job interviews.

- Negotiate salaries and the terms of employment.

- Advance your career.

- Relocate to other communities.

- Start your own business.

- Implement your plan of action.

- Identify and use additional resources for careering and re-careering.

In the end, our goal is to get you to take actions that will have a positive impact on your future. While most of this book focuses on understanding concepts, following processes, and developing effective job search strategies, the real rewards of this book come when you put these concepts and processes into practice by implementing a realistic plan of action. We'll return to this key issue of **implementation** in Chapter 18. In the meantime, get ready to put together a realistic plan that will give you the power to change both your job and your life.

3

35 Coming Changes Affecting Your Career

W HETHER OR NOT WE REALIZE IT, we all have some image of the future that influences important decisions in our lives. You would not, for example, purchase a new home, relocate to another community, or change jobs unless you first projected what the future might hold for you over the next three, five, or ten years. You want to predict your future to some degree. To help you do this, let's take a look at what the future may bring in the world of work.

Images of the Future

Individuals orient themselves to the future in different ways. Some people always view the future pessimistically. They find numerous reasons for not taking risks. Others fantasize about the future and "hope" that prosperity will come to them without their taking action or risking the unknown. And still others set goals and work toward achieving a positive future.

Finding employment and charting careers in the job markets of today and tomorrow require strategies based on an understanding of new realities as well as a different image of the future. But few people know how to plan for uncertainty. Denying new realities, many continue to operate on old assumptions. Not surprisingly, they experience difficulty adjusting to change.

Turn Turbulence Into New Opportunities

How do you anticipate the future and plan accordingly? During relatively stable times, planning proceeds along a relatively predictable path: the assumption that the future will be very similar to the past and present. Therefore, a good plan is one that is based on an analysis of historical patterns – you follow the lessons of the past in charting your future.

But during turbulent times, planning based on historical patterns is a problem. Peter Drucker's timely observations on planning for turbulent times are especially relevant for the decade ahead. Traditional planning:

> assumes a high degree of continuity. Planning starts out, as a rule, with the trends of yesterday and projects them into the future – using a different "mix" perhaps, but with very much the same elements and the same configuration. This is no longer going to work. The most probable assumption in a period of turbulence is the unique event, which changes the configuration – and unique events cannot, by definition, be "planned." But they can often be foreseen. This requires strategies for tomorrow, strategies that anticipate where the greatest changes are likely to occur and what they are likely to be, strategies that enable a business – or a hospital, a school, a university – to take advantage of new realities and to convert turbulence into opportunity. (from *Managing in Turbulent Times*)

Turbulent times often become difficult times for people who fail to anticipate and adjust to new changes. Assuming continuity, or a return to previous times, they engage in wishful thinking. Many of these people are today's victims of structural unemployment. For others, who take action based upon an understanding of coming realities, turbulent times can offer new and exciting opportunities. These people anticipate where the greatest changes will take place and accordingly adapt to change as they advance with the new jobs and careers of tomorrow.

The economic transformation of American society has far reaching implications which you should be aware of in planning your future. Over the past two decades, the projected changes have been discussed at length by Toffler (*The Third Wave*), Naisbett (*Megatrends* and *Megatrends 2000*), Ferguson (*The Aquarian Conspiracy*), Cetron (*Jobs of the Future*), Feingold and Atwater (*New Emerging Careers*), Bridges (*Job Shift*), and Harkness (*The Career Chase*). Our major concern is not in predicting the future with precision. Rather, we are concerned with formulating an image of the future and outlining the implications of turbulent times for jobs, careers, and you.

The major question we need to address here is this:

What future should you prepare for in the world of work?

Based on an understanding of new trends in the workplace and anticipating the impact of unique events on the economy, we believe you can develop strategies for converting turbulence into new opportunities.

Two powerful currents – one demographic and another technical – are converging at present in the workplace and affecting the future of work in America. These changes, in turn, are precipitating the emergence of 35 new trends for careering and re-careering in the 21st century.

Face New Demographics

The paradox of major labor shortages in the midst of high unemployment amongst certain sectors of the population is partly due to the impact of demographic changes in today's labor market. For the American population is undergoing fundamental changes at the same time the economy shifts from an industrial to a high-tech and service base.

The major demographic changes characterizing today's labor force are found at the entry level: fewer young people are filling entry-level jobs while more females, minorities, and immigrants are entering the job market.

These changes imply continuing labor shortages for entry-level jobs in high-tech and service industries as well as the inability to recruit experienced technical personnel. However, the labor shortage/unemployment paradox may continue if millions of displaced workers are not retrained for new jobs.

Forces

Two crucial demographic changes took place in the post-World War II period to help shape the present labor force. The first change was the baby-boom. As birth rates increased nearly 50 percent between 1947 and 1949, a new labor force was created for the latter part of the twentieth century. American industry in the 1960s and 1970s absorbed some of these new workers, but most were employed in the rapidly growing service sector. The U.S. economy, especially the service and high-tech sectors, was able to provide employment for 10 million new workers between 1963 and 1980 – a remarkable achievement for such a short time span. Between 1983 and 1988 the economy generated 16 million new jobs – until then the best performance in the history of the labor market. Between 1989 and 1996 the economy generated 1 to 2 million new jobs each year. From 1997 to 1999 the economy created from 2 to 3 million new jobs annually. Despite continuing downsizing, the boom economy in the second half of the 1990s was one of the greatest job generators in the 20th century.

The second major demographic change has been the rapid increase of women, minorities, and immigrants entering the labor force. This demographic current continues. For example, in 1980 over 50 percent of women worked outside the home. By 1990 more than 60 percent of women were in the labor force. Today nearly 80 percent of women are employed.

The baby-boom generation reached middle age at the turn of the new century. At the same time, the number of traditional 16- to 21-year olds entering the labor market fell dramatically during the 1990s. Today, about 80 percent of all new labor force entries are women, minorities, and immigrants. Except for women, these groups are less educated and skilled than the new workers of previous decades. For example, despite the $400 billion spent each year on education in the United States, basic literacy and skill levels remain alarmingly low for industries that must dip deeper into the entry-level labor pool. In a 1994 assessment of literacy among 21- to 25-year-olds, the U.S. Education Department found these alarming statistics:

- Only 60 percent of whites, 40 percent of Hispanics, and 25 percent of blacks can find specific information in a news article or almanac.

- Only 25 percent of whites, 7 percent of Hispanics, and 3 percent of blacks can understand a bus schedule.

Furthermore, 63 percent of white and 14 percent of black high school graduates have attained only a "basic" skill level required by the armed forces for training. There is little evidence that these numbers have changed significantly since then. Indeed, the National Institute of Literacy paints an even more alarming picture. It indicates that 21 to 23 percent of the adult population (nearly 44 million people) scored at Level 1 in literacy testing. Another 25-28 percent (45 to 50 million people) scored at Level 2. Unfortunately, adults with Level 1 and Level 2 skills (more than half of the workforce) are considered by literacy and employment experts to lack basic foundational skills to function successfully in society.

The implications of these trends are already costly for many industries, and the costs will most likely accelerate in the coming decade. Indeed, by 1998 many high-tech industries were unable to recruit and retain skilled personnel in order to grow their businesses; their opportunity costs were very high. Given rising skill requirements for entry-level jobs, coupled with the low skill levels of applicants, many other industries will experience severe labor shortages in the decade ahead. They will most likely respond to this problem by moving their operations offshore, cutting back on services and production, and/or investing more resources in educating and training what is basically an entry-level labor force ill-prepared for the jobs of today and tomorrow.

Implications

Declining birth rates since the 1960s, with America now approaching a zero-population growth rate, have important implications for the future labor market. Assuming the American economy will continue to expand, stimulated by the high-tech and service industries, labor shortages are likely to continue during the coming decade. The continuing entry of women, minorities, and immigrants into the labor force, as well as improvements in workplace productivity, will not significantly offset this labor deficiency.

Given the post-1960s decline in birth rates and the 1986 changes in immigration laws, fewer young people and immigrants are available for entry-level and low wage positions. In addition, women, who used to take part-time, low paying sales positions, are fast leaving this labor scene for better paying full-time positions. Teenagers, who make up a disproportionate share of the labor force of fast-food restaurants, are scarcer because there are fewer teenagers in the population as a whole than during the previous 30 years.

Adjustments in the changing labor force have already begun. Fast-food restaurants are employing older workers and introducing more self-service menus. Grocery stores are installing more self-service check-out counters. Many companies are replacing live schedulers and customer service representatives with the latest rules-based voice-recognition software programs. Department stores have fewer salespeople and are recruiting lower quality sales clerks – generally individuals who are less educated, skilled, stable, and responsible; training demands and customer

Mid-life crises may well disappear as more individuals experience re-careering transitions.

complaints have risen accordingly. Many small businesses, especially the "Mom and Pop" stores with fewer than five employees, are experiencing difficulty recruiting and retaining the traditional young, low-salaried entry-level workers. Instead, many businesses have been cutting back services and production as well as looking toward the elderly, particularly retired individuals, for new recruits.

The changing population structure also has important implications for the quality of the labor force. While the private sector spends over $300 billion each year on training and retraining, much of this expenditure goes to training inexperienced entry-level personnel. Given the growing shortage of this traditional labor pool, high-tech industries will be forced to recruit and then retrain displaced workers as well as offshore jobs. This will require a new emphasis on training – as well as a greater expenditure on retraining.

Other population dynamics have additional implications for the workforce of tomorrow. Minorities, especially African Americans and Hispanics, will enter the labor force at a faster rate because of their higher birth rates and immigration rates. As a result, minorities will disproportionately occupy entry-level positions. Furthermore, there will be greater pressure from minorities for advancement up the ranks, even though the upper ranks have become glutted with middle- aged managers and executives who were rapidly promoted when they were young people during the 1980s.

With the entry of more women into the labor force and the concomitant emergence of the two-career family, individuals have greater freedom of choice to change jobs or careers, take part-time positions, retire, or drop out of the labor force altogether. Job-hopping may increase accordingly. In addition, employee benefit programs, many of which are still based on the model of the traditional male head of household supporting a family, will change in response to the two-career family with few or no children.

Careering and re-careering are directly related to these changing demographics. As the workforce ages, life expectancy lengthens, the social security system changes, and labor shortages abound, fewer people will enter traditional retirement in their 60s or retire at all. An individual's work life may well become his total adult life. Re-careering will become a standard way of functioning within tomorrow's labor markets. Thus, it will not be unusual for individuals to change careers in their 40s, 50s, and 60s. Mid-life crises may well disappear as more individuals experience re-careering transitions.

Responses

Population changes also will create a more heterogeneous workforce. Along with increased minority representation in entry-level positions, more and more immigrants will come to the United States – both legally and illegally – to meet the expanding labor needs. Despite the 1986 changes in immigration laws to document illegal immigrants and stem the tide of illegal immigration into the United States – political efforts totally at odds with America's growing labor needs – nearly 600,000 immigrants enter the U.S. legally each year and another 600,000 immigrants, mainly from Mexico and the Caribbean, probably enter the U.S. illegally. Most of these people initially take low-paying, manual, and service jobs which native-born Americans avoid. Hispanic Americans now constitute nearly one-fifth of the population, or 57 million out of 285 million.

Assuming continuing low birth rates among middle class white Americans which, in turn, may contribute to labor shortages in the future, the government may be forced into a major policy reversal: relax enforcement of the 1986 immigration laws as well as open the doors to immigrants in order to alleviate the coming labor shortages. If and when this happens, training and retraining programs will become more urgently needed for the future of the high-tech and service sectors.

Peter Drucker, however, outlines another scenario which is by far one of the most interesting organizational forms for coping with the coming labor shortages in developed countries and the explosive expansion of working-age people in the less developed countries. Under a production sharing system, less developed countries with surplus labor would be responsible for labor-intensive aspects of production. Developed countries, such as the United States, would provide the needed capital, technology, and managerial skills for operating transnational companies. Such an arrangement would fully employ the surplus educated and skilled people in developing countries without experiencing the social, economic, and political dislocation attendant with large scale migration.

Production sharing forms of organization are already in place for various industries in the U.S., Japan, Singapore, Hong Kong, Malaysia, Taiwan, Korea, and Brazil – the so-called First and Second World countries. They also have developed in Third World countries, such as India, with its large labor pool of high-tech workers centered around Bangalore, and in China, with its export-oriented factories in Shenzhen. As Drucker sees this system,

> Production sharing is the best hope – perhaps the only hope – for most of the developing countries to survive without catastrophe the explosive expansion of working-age people in search of a job . . . for the standard of living of the developed world can also be maintained only if it succeeds in mobilizing the labor resources of the developing world. It has the technical resources, the entrepreneurial resources, the managerial resources – and the markets. But it lacks, and will increasingly lack, the labor resources to do the traditional stages of production.

Whether or not production sharing becomes a predominate organizational form, the changing population dynamics over the next two decades provide further evidence of the need for major skills training and retraining of the American labor force. Population dynamics undoubtedly will be a major force affecting the turbulent employment environment.

Experience the Impact of New Technologies

The second major current transforming the American workplace is technical in nature. The electronics revolution began in 1948 in Western Electric Company's Allentown, Pennsylvania manufacturing plant. There, the transistor was produced, and it began an electronics revolution which has continued to evolve into even more revolutionary forms since the invention and application of the microprocessor in the 1970s. The end of this revolution is nowhere in sight. Indeed, we may be at the initial stages of a profound transformation which will sweep across society during the next two decades.

Evidence of a coming transformation began in the 1950s as white-collar workers began to outnumber blue-collar workers. The electronics revolution helped initiate an information and communication revolution. In 1950, for example, approximately 17 percent of the population worked in information-related jobs. Today this proportion has increased to over 50 percent. During the 1970s, when nearly 19 million new jobs were created, only 16 percent were in the manufacturing and goods-producing sector.

As John Naisbett (*Megatrends*) and other futurists have noted, during the 1980s we began to move full-force into the second stage of technological development – the application of technology to old industrial tasks. Recognizing the urgent need to increase productivity in order to become more competitive in international markets, manufacturing industries have made major efforts to retool their plants with the latest labor-saving technologies and have thereby displaced workers skilled in the technologies of previous decades. Today, America's manufacturing plants are second to none in terms of technological adaptation.

Movement into third-stage technological development – innovation, making new discoveries with second-stage technologies – should proceed throughout the next decade. Within the past few years, many American manufacturing and service industries have been significantly transformed by second- and third-stage technological developments. Not surprisingly, entry into the labor market in the year 2000 required a much higher level of education and skills than in the 1980s. Those who will be in the best position to advance into the best jobs in the decade ahead will be those who seriously focus on careering and re-careering issues by:

- acquiring new work-content skills through regular training and retraining

- developing effective job search skills

- relocating when necessary

The impact of the high-tech revolution, and especially the Internet, is structural in nature. As computers, fiber optics, robotics, and genetic engineering generate new businesses and integrate into everyday life, the economy and workplace will be fundamentally altered. For example, fiber optics, which makes copper wire obsolete, is further revolutionizing communication. Genetic engineering will create major changes in agriculture and medicine. The mainframe computer, which was developed for practical use in 1945, in the form of today's microcomputer is now a common tool in most workplaces. The Internet also is playing a key role in many businesses. With the continuing impact of fiber optics and new generation microprocessing chips – not to mention some still unknown technological breakthroughs – computers with vastly expanded capabilities will become commonplace tools in homes over the next decade. Powerful laptop computers will increasingly displace standard desktop computers. And the continuing innovations and adaptation of the Internet may well transform the whole software industry within the next few years. Indeed, long-distance carriers such as AT&T and MCI, are in a race for survival as the Internet transforms long distance communications. Many in this industry predict that all long-distance phone calls will be free in the not-too-distant future as telephone companies increasingly compete to become business service providers.

The microprocessor has dramatically altered the workplace – from robots replacing assembly line workers to word processors displacing traditional typists. Office automation has transformed many secretaries into area managers, who are now in charge of coordinating workflows and managing equipment. Factory workers either become displaced or are retrained to deal with the new technology. Unfortunately, many displaced workers who have not been retrained, have become permanently displaced or have moved into lower paying, high-turnover, unskilled service jobs – the negative unemployment and underemployment consequences of structural changes.

Many futurists have predicted what seems to be an even more radical transformation of the workplace – the emergence of the electronic cottage and telecommuting. According to these predictors, computers create a decentralized workplace where individuals can work from their homes on assignments received and processed via computer terminals. The electronic cottage, in turn, will alter family relationships, especially child rearing practices, and the structure of the traditional central business district. Many workers no longer will need to commute to the office, face traffic jams, and experience the accompanying office stress. Such changes, however, do not bode well for owners of downtown office buildings, parking lots, and businesses frequented by the noontime employee-shopper. The communication revolution may be the final death blow for some cities hoping to revitalize their downtown areas. In fact, the fastest growing business sector today is the home-based business which now employs over 25 million individuals. With the emergence of the Internet as a new business arena for budding entrepreneurs who see their future in e-commerce, these numbers will probably accelerate in the decade ahead. While only talked about as a future reality 15 to 20 years ago, today the electronic cottage has become a reality for millions of individuals in the space of only a decade.

These technological changes, coupled with the demographic currents, are transforming the nature of jobs. Yesterday's and today's workers are increasingly being displaced in an environment which is ill-equipped to help them gain advantages in tomorrow's high-tech society. Instead, a new class of individuals, skilled in the technology of previous decades, may become permanently displaced in the turbulent job market of tomorrow. Their major hope for career success is to become savvy in new technologies for tomorrow.

Prepare for 35 Coming Changes

Several additional trends are evident, and they will affect both the work force and the workplace in years ahead. These trends are mainly stimulated by the larger demographic and technological changes taking place within society. We see 35 changes emerging in the areas of job creation, youth, elderly, minorities, women, immigrants, part-time employment, service jobs, education and training, unions and labor-management relations, urban-rural shifts, regionalism, small businesses and entrepreneurship, compensation, advancement opportunities, and relocation. Together these changes point to both dangers and new opportunities.

TREND 1: **A shortage of competent workers, with basic literacy and learning skills, creates serious problems in developing a 21st century economy.**

Given the double whammy of nearly 25 million functionally illiterate adults – or one-sixth of the potential labor force unable to read, write, or perform simple computations – and the availability of fewer easily trainable young entry-level workers, a large portion of the workforce is destined to remain at the lowest end of the job market despite the fact that nearly 3 million new jobs are created each year. Most of these adults will remain permanently unemployed or underemployed, contributing little to economic growth, while major labor shortages exist. As skill requirements rise rapidly for both entering and advancing within the workforce, the nation's economic development will slow due to the lack of skilled workers. Both public and private sector worker literacy, basic education, and training programs will continue to expand, but their contribution to improving the overall skill levels of the workforce will be minimal. The American economy and workforce increasingly show classic signs of Second and Third World economies – potential economic performance outstrips the availability of a skilled workforce.

TREND 2: **A renewed and strong U.S. manufacturing sector will create few new jobs; service industries will be responsible for most job growth in the decade ahead.**

Despite popular notions of the "decline" of American manufacturing industries, these industries are following the model of American agriculture – increased productivity accompanied by the increased displacement of workers. American manufacturing industry is becoming one of the strongest economic sectors in terms of production output but the weakest sector in terms of its contribution to job growth and job creation. At the same time, American manufacturing has already moved in the direction of Drucker's "production sharing system" by exporting the remaining high-cost, labor-intensive aspects of the industries. As large manufacturing companies rebounded in recent years by becoming more productive with smaller and more highly skilled workforces, most new manufacturing jobs will continue to develop among small manufacturing "job shops" employing fewer than 50 workers. The service industries, especially those in finance, retail, food, and health care, will continue to expand their workforces in the decade ahead. These industries also will experience major "productivity" and "management" improvements, much of which took place in other industries that "reinvented" themselves in the previous decade, due to (1) major labor shortages, (2) increased competition, (3) greater emphasis on customer service, and (4) the adaptation of new technology to what had become increasingly inefficient, high-cost, labor-intensive service industries, especially in the retail and health care industries.

TREND 3: Unemployment remains cyclical, fluctuating between a low of 4 percent and a high of 8 percent.

These fluctuations are attributed to a combination of boom-and-bust cycles in the economy as well as the persistence of structural unemployment exacerbated by millions of functionally illiterate adults on the periphery of the economy. In addition, millions of other Americans will be underemployed in low-paying entry-level positions which offer little or no career advancement.

TREND 4: Government efforts to stimulate employment growth continue to be primarily concentrated at the periphery of the job market.

Most government programs aimed at generating jobs and resolving unemployment problems will be aimed at the poor and unskilled. These groups also are the least likely to relocate, use job search skills, develop standard work habits, or be trained in skills for tomorrow's job market. Given the mixed results from such programs, the government eventually develops government-sponsored workfare programs as well as contracts out this class of unemployed to government contractors who will provide them with education and training along with work experience.

TREND 5: While the U.S. regained its competitive international trade position in the later half of the 1990s, it is in danger of losing its dominant position in the first decade of the 21st century.

International and domestic issues become closely tied to employment issues. Emphasis shifts to issues of economic growth, unemployment, productivity, population, consumption, and regional conflicts in Eastern Europe, the independent states of the former Soviet Union, the Middle East, Asia, and other Third and Fourth World countries that threaten the stability of international markets and thus long-term economic and employment growth in the U.S. New regional trading blocs play a central role in redefining the international economy. Economic, trade, and employment issues take center stage in restructuring a highly unstable international arena. More and more jobs in the U.S. are increasingly tied to the vicissitudes of the global economy.

TREND 6: A series of domestic and international crises – shocks and "unique events" – emerge in the early 21st century to create new boom-and-bust cycles contributing to unemployment.

The most likely sources for the international crises will be problems developing among former communist regimes and poor Third and Fourth World nations: the disintegration of the nation-states in the former Soviet Union and a few former communist regimes in Eastern Europe; energy and precious metals shortages due to a depletion of current stocks and regional military conflicts; the collapse of financial markets due to default on international debts; and dislocation of lucrative resource and consumption markets due to continued wars in the Middle East, Africa, and South Asia. The most likely domestic crises center on financial markets, real estate, energy, water, and the environment. Crises in the banking, energy, and telecommunications markets once again create major debt, credit, and bankruptcy problems for the economy. An energy crisis creates a new boom for the economies of Texas, Colorado, and Alaska. A new crisis – water shortages – in the Southwest, further slows employment growth in Southern California and Arizona. Environmental issues, such as acid rain and air and water pollution, emerge as important international and domestic crises.

TREND 7: **New jobs will be created at the rate of 1 to 2 million each year, with some boom years resulting in the creation of more than 3 million jobs annually.**

The good news is that employment will increase in most occupations in the decade ahead with export-oriented industries leading the way toward economic growth. Economic expansion in the service sector, coupled with the low productivity and low cost of labor in many parts of the service sector, contributes over 90 percent of all new jobs. Large scale manufacturing experiences labor declines while small scale manufacturing "job shops" contribute most of the minimal job growth in the manufacturing sector. The labor declines will be offset by increases in related service jobs, especially in manufacturing sales and marketing.

TREND 8: **Major shortages of skilled craftspeople will create numerous production, distribution, and service problems in the coming decade.**

During the past two decades the number of apprenticeship programs declined significantly; fewer individuals received training in blue-collar occupations; and interest among the young in blue-collar trades declined markedly. The impact of these changes will continue to be felt in the early 21st century as production and service industries requiring critically skilled craftspeople experience labor shortages; distribution of products and services will be uneven. Despite government efforts to revitalize apprenticeship programs, expect to personally encounter the effects of such labor shortages – long waits for servicing your automobile and for repairing your home and major appliances as well as very expensive charges for such services.

TREND 9: As the baby-boomers reach middle age and as the birth rate continues at a near zero-population growth rate, fewer young people within the U.S. will be available for entry-level positions in the coming decade.

Businesses will recruit and train more of the hard-core unemployed, unskilled, the elderly, and people with disabilities; they will automate; and/or they will contract for cheap offshore labor for everything from accounting, marketing, and computing services to manufacturing jobs. As a result, more stopgap job opportunities will be available for individuals losing their jobs or wishing to change jobs or careers.

TREND 10: Retirement practices continue to be transformed. More job and career choices will be available for the elderly who are either dissatisfied with traditional retirement or who no longer can afford the high costs of retirement.

As the workforce increasingly ages, traditional retirement practices will change. Many people will never retire, preferring instead part-time or self-employment in their later years. Others will retire from one job and then start new careers after age 50. A continuing financial crisis in the Social Security system results in declining Social Security benefits. Fewer Social Security benefits and higher costs of retirement will further transform retirement practices and systems in the decade ahead. Expect to see more elderly working in the McDonald's and 7-Eleven stores of tomorrow.

TREND 11: More minorities – especially those with disproportionately high birth rates, low education and skill levels, and poor economic status – will enter the job market.

A large proportion of minorities will occupy the less skilled entry-level, service positions where they will exhibit marked language, class, and cultural differences. Upwardly mobile minorities may find advancement opportunities blocked because of the glut of supervisors, managers, and executives already in many organizations.

TREND 12: Women will continue to enter the labor market, accounting for nearly 90 percent female participation in the labor force. More and more women will enter nontraditional occupations, such as engineering, construction, high-tech, and sports, which have largely been the preserves of men.

The entry of women into the workforce will continue to accelerate in the decade ahead. This will be due less to the changing role of women than to the economic necessity of women to generate family income in order to survive in an expensive consumer-oriented society. Women will account for two-thirds of the growth in all occupations. They will continue to expand into nontraditional jobs, especially production and management positions. Both men and women in a growing number of two-career families will have greater flexibility to change jobs and careers frequently.

TREND 13: More immigrants will enter the U.S. – both documented and undocumented – to meet labor shortages at all levels.

Despite major efforts of the Department of Homeland Security (INS) to stem the flow of illegal immigrants, labor market demands will require more immigrants to occupy low-paying, entry-level service jobs in the decade ahead. The brain drain of highly skilled scientific and technical workers from developing countries to the U.S. will accelerate. Unskilled immigrants will move into service positions vacated by upwardly mobile Americans.

TREND 14: Part-time and temporary employment opportunities will increase.

With the increase in two-career families, home-based businesses, and the smaller number of retirees, part-time and temporary employment will become a more normal pattern of employment for millions of Americans. More women, who wish to enter the job market but not as full-time employees, will seek new part-time employment opportunities. Temporary employment services will continue to experience a boom in business as more and more companies attempt to lower personnel costs as well as achieve greater personnel flexibility by hiring larger numbers of temporary employees.

TREND 15: Part-time and contingency workers will constitute a recognized and desirable class of workers.

The number of contingency workers – part-time, temporary, or contract workers – will continue to increase in the decade ahead as more and more businesses cut back costly full-time employees, eliminate generous benefit packages, and seek greater flexibility in hiring and firing employees. Given economic uncertainties, high costs of hiring, and advantages of working with employment firms that manage contingency workers, more and more employers will replace full-time employees with contingency workers. Many businesses employing 100 or fewer employees will routinely use contingency workers to staff at least 30 percent of their positions.

TREND 16: White-collar employment will continue to expand in the fast-growing service sector.

Dramatic growth in service jobs will take place in response to new information technology. The classification of workers into blue- and white-collar occupations, as well as into manufacturing and service jobs, will become meaningless in a service economy dominated by white-collar workers.

TREND 17: The need for a smarter workforce, with specific technical skills, will continue to impact on the traditional education system as both businesses and parents demand greater job and career relevance in educational curricula.

Expensive and overly bureaucratized, many traditional four-year colleges and universities will face stable to declining full-time enrollments as well as the flight of quality faculty to more challenging and lucrative jobs outside academia. Declining enrollments will be due to their slow response to the educational and training skill requirements of the high-tech society; increased competition from private training firms, online training technology, and distance learning groups; and the demographics of fewer numbers in the traditional 18-21 year-old student age population. The flight of quality faculty will be replaced by less qualified and inexpensive part-time faculty. Most community colleges, as well as specialized private vocational-technical institutions, will adapt to the changing demographics and labor market needs and flourish with programs most responsive to community employment needs. More and more emphasis will be placed on providing efficient short-term, intensive skills-training programs, many of which will be delivered as computer-based and Internet-based individualized training, than on providing traditional degree programs. Career planning will become a major emphasis in education programs.

TREND 18: **Union membership will continue to decline as more blue-collar manufacturing jobs disappear and interest in unions wanes among both blue- and white-collar employees.**

Given declining union membership, unions continue to find themselves on the defensive, with little choice other than to agree to management demands for greater worker productivity. In the long run, labor-management relations will shift from the traditional adversarial relationship to one of greater cooperation and participation of labor and management in the decision-making process. Profit sharing and employee ownership will become prominent features of labor-management relations. These changes will contribute to the continuing decline, and eventual disappearance, of traditional unions in many industries.

TREND 19: **The population will continue to move into suburban and semi-rural communities as high-tech industries and services move in this direction.**

Large and older central cities will continue to bear disproportionate welfare, tax, and criminal justice burdens due to their declining industrial bases, deteriorating infrastructures, relatively poor and unskilled populations, and high rates of crime. Urban populations will continue to move into suburban and semi-rural communities. Developing their own economic base, these communities will provide employment for the majority of local residents rather than serve as bedroom communities from which workers commute to the central city. With few exceptions, and despite noble attempts to "revitalize" downtown areas with new office, shopping, and entertainment complexes, most large central cities will continue to decline as their upwardly mobile residential populations move to the suburbs where they are able to find better jobs, housing, and education; enjoy attractive lifestyles; and experience lower crime rates.

TREND 20:   **The population, as well as wealth and economic activity, will continue to shift into the Northwest, Southwest, and Florida at the expense of the Northeast and North Central regions.**

Nearly 60 percent of the U.S. population now resides in the South and West. These areas also are home for the nation's youngest population. Florida, Georgia, Texas, Colorado, Arizona, Nevada, Utah, and Washington will continue to be the growth states for the decade ahead; construction and local government in these states will experience employment increases. Many states in the Northeast and Midwest, and parts of the South, will experience slow growth due to their declining industrial base, excessive welfare burdens, older population, aging infrastructure, and shrinkage of non-cyclical economic sectors – services, retail trade, and public employment. However, some Midwest states (Ohio, Indiana, Illinois, Wisconsin) will experience strong growth due to important linkages developing between their exceptionally well developed higher educational institutions and high-tech industries which depend on such institutions. Many manufacturing industries in the Midwest, especially auto, will continue to expand as they play an increasingly important role in the expanding U.S. export economy.

TREND 21:   **The number of small businesses will continue to increase as new opportunities for entrepreneurs arise in response to the high-tech, Internet, and service revolutions and as more individuals find new opportunities to experiment with changing careers.**

Over 900,000 new businesses will be started each year during the coming decade. These businesses will generate 90 percent of all new jobs created each year. The number of business failures will increase accordingly, especially during the bust cycles of the boom/bust economy. Increases in self-employment and small businesses will not provide many new opportunities for career advancement. The small promotion hierarchies of these businesses will help accelerate increased job-hopping and career changes. This new entrepreneurship is likely to breed greater innovation, competition, and productivity.

TREND 22: **As large companies continue to downsize, most job growth will take place among small companies and millions of new start-up businesses.**

Large Fortune 500 companies will further downsize their operations in the decade ahead. Firms with fewer than 500 employees should generate the most new job growth. Some of the best job opportunities will be with growing companies employing fewer than 50 employees. Large Fortune 500 companies, especially those in service industries, will

> *The best employment opportunities will be found among growing companies employing fewer than 50 employees.*

continue to cut jobs as they attempt to survive intense competition from smaller and more innovative companies, many of which pioneered new forms of e-commerce that threaten traditional "bricks and mortar" businesses. Cutbacks will further lower the morale of remaining employees who will seek new job and career opportunities; many will start their own businesses in competition with their former employers.

TREND 23: **Opportunities for career advancement will be increasingly limited within most organizations.**

Organizations will have difficulty providing career advancement for employees due to (1) the growth of small businesses with short advancement hierarchies, (2) the postponement of retirement, (3) the continuing focus on non-hierarchical forms of organization, and (4) the tendency to hire managers from outside the organization. In the future, many of today's managers will have to find non-managerial positions. Job satisfaction will become less oriented toward advancement up the organizational ladder and more toward such organizational benefits and perks as club memberships, sabbaticals, vacations, retraining opportunities, flexible working hours, family services, and health care packages.

TREND 24: **Job satisfaction will become a major problem as many organizations will experience difficulty in retaining highly qualified personnel.**

Greater competition, fewer promotions, frustrated expectations, greater discontent, and job-hopping will arise in executive ranks due to limited advancement opportunities. As middle-management positions continue to be eliminated as part of overall downsizing efforts, managerial and executive turnover will increase accordingly. The problem will be especially pronounced for many women and minorities who have traditional aspirations to advance to the top but will be blocked by the glut of managers and executives from the baby-boom generation who are trying to survive at both the middle and top of their organizations. Many of these frustrated individuals will become entrepreneurs by starting their own businesses in competition with their former employers.

TREND 25: **Many employers will resort to unorthodox hiring practices, improved working conditions, and flexible benefit packages to recruit and retain critical personnel.**

Hiring and retention of a talented workforce become critical issues for most employers who face an increasingly competitive business arena in the decade ahead. Facing increased competition for skilled workers, employers will use new and more effective ways of finding and keeping personnel: Internet recruitment; job fair weekends; headhunters and executive search firms; temporary employment services; raids of competitor's personnel; bonuses to current employees for finding needed personnel; entry-level hiring bonuses for new recruits; stock options; attractive profit-sharing packages for long-term commitments; vacation and travel packages; relocation and housing services; flex-time and job-sharing; home-based work; and daycare services.

TREND 26: **Job-hopping will increase as more and more individuals learn how to change careers.**

As more job and career opportunities become available for the skilled and savvy worker, as pension systems become more portable, as more individuals use the Internet to browse job opportunities, and as job search and relocation techniques become more widely known, more and more individuals will change jobs and careers in the decade ahead. The typical employee will work in one job and organization for two ro three years and then move on to a similar job in another organization. Within 12 years this individual will have acquired new interests and skills and thus decide to change to a new career. Similar three- and 12-year cycles of job and career changes will be repeated by the same individual. Job-hopping will become an accepted and necessary way of getting ahead in the job and career markets of tomorrow.

TREND 27: **Geographic relocation will accelerate as more and more individuals become drawn to growing communities offering attractive job opportunities.**

A favorable real estate market provides incentives to pull up stakes in one community to relocate to another. More and more people will move into the Southeast and West in pursuit of better job and career opportunities.

TREND 28: **The hot jobs in the decade ahead – those offering excellent pay, advancement, and security – will be in health care and high-tech service industries.**

These jobs will require substantial amounts of education, training, and retraining. They also will command top salaries and benefits as well as offer attractive advancement opportunities and numerous career options for individuals interested in careering and re-careering.

TREND 29: **Except for IT workers, salaries will only incrementally increase in the decade ahead. In many organizations, executive-level compensation will actually decline as well as be more closely tied to productivity indicators.**

Salary increments will more and more be tied to annual performance evaluations which link pay raises to quantifiable performance indicators. More attractive and portable benefit packages will be offered by organizations seeking to recruit and retain highly skilled workers.

TREND 30: **Benefit packages will undergo increased scrutiny as more and more organizations cut back on personnel expenses.**

Traditional high-cost health insurance and pension plans will be reassessed by employers and subject to cutbacks. More and more employers will require employees to make significant contributions to health insurance and retirement plans. While most employers will offer some form of health insurance, fewer employers will provide company-sponsored retirement plans. Workers can expect to contribute at least 20 percent to the cost of health insurance as well as develop their own retirement plans which will include little or no contribution from employers. More and more employers will opt to hire contingency workers whose benefits are handled by contractors.

TREND 31: **Apprenticeship programs will increase in number as the nation attempts to train and retrain a skilled labor pool for high-demand service industries.**

The coming shortage of skilled labor to service everything from air conditioners to automobiles is directly related to the decline of apprenticeship programs and the lack of interest in pursuing careers in the trades. The government in cooperation with industry will make a major effort to revitalize such programs. Individuals not pursuing higher education degrees will find excellent career opportunities available through such programs.

TREND 32: **More and more skilled and high-tech service jobs will move offshore as U.S. businesses take advantage of both cheap skilled labor and high-speed communications.**

The next decade will be the decade of the global job market for both skilled and unskilled labor. The stereotypical manufacturing sweatshops with cheap and relatively unskilled labor producing garments, footwear, and toys in China, Indonesia, and India will give way to more high-tech sweatshops in these and many other countries. However, the high-tech sweatshops will focus more and more on the service industries and use skilled labor in Third World countries. For example, given inexpensive high-speed communications, many businesses can now export their accounting, design, telemarketing, and data management functions to India, the Philippines, Mexico, and countries in the Caribbean via the Internet, faxes, and special two- and three-day delivery services (DHL, UPS, Federal Express). Skilled cheap labor will pose a new challenge to the U.S. labor market. While it will help relieve some labor shortages, it also will compete directly with high-wage skilled workers in the U.S.

TREND 33: The fastest growing jobs in the decade ahead will be for people without a four-year degree.

A disproportionate number of opportunities will be low-wage, dead end jobs in the service industries, such as janitors, cafeteria workers, home health aides, security guards, and groundskeepers. Most of these will be face-to-face jobs that cannot be automated nor offshored. While individuals with only a high school diploma and basic literacy skills will find many job opportunities, they also will join the growing ranks of the working poor.

TREND 34: Professional and managerial jobs will continue to grow in the decade ahead and represent some of the best career opportunities available.

At the other end of the job spectrum, the number of well paying professional and managerial jobs, especially for lawyers, engineers, and nurses, is expected to accelerate in the decade ahead. These jobs require a great deal of education, training, and certification beyond a basic four-year degree. Individuals in these jobs should experience long-term job security as well as advance into well-paying positions. However, many of these people also will experience job burnout and explore more personally rewarding career alternatives.

TREND 35: Fewer people will be obsessed with chasing traditional careers. More and more people want satisfying jobs that enable them to pursue interesting lifestyle goals.

The concept of a "career" is deeply rooted in the post-World War II era of big corporations. Until the 1990s, many individuals pursued careers, often within a single organizational setting. Given the changing structure of the job market, the decline of traditional career paths, and the increased interest in pursuing satisfying lifestyles, the future will witness the gradual erosion of careers. More and more individuals today and in the decade ahead will be interested in finding specific jobs which may or may not be related to careers.

Be Realistic

While many individuals look toward the future with unquestioned optimism, there are good reasons to be cautious and less than enthusiastic. The decade ahead may be the worst of times for many people. Take several examples which indicate a need to be cautiously optimistic. Displaced workers who remain unemployed after five years will have received an occupational death sentence of continuing unemployment, underemployment, or socio-economic decline. Many of the nation's poor, with high birth rates and low levels of education, are destined to remain at the bottom of society; their children may fare no better. And we should not forget that America has not solved its energy and environmental problems, and a boom/bust economy may still be well and alive.

In the turbulent society, many people experience both the best and the worst of times at the same time.

The best of times are when you are gainfully employed, enjoy your work, and look to your future with optimism. In the turbulent society, people experience both the best and worst of times at the same time. Those who are unprepared for the growing uncertainty and instability of the turbulent society may get hurt.

We lack a healthy sense of reality in facing change. Indeed, the future is seldom what we think it is. Only recently have we begun to take a second look at the high-tech and service revolutions and raised some sobering questions about their impact on work and the workplace. We have not fully explored unanticipated consequences of new structural changes on individuals and society.

The 35 changes we forecast will create dislocations for individuals, groups, organizations, communities, and regions. These dislocations will require some form of public-private intervention. For example, the question of renewable energy resources has not been adequately dealt with in relation to the high-tech revolution. Many of the key metals for fueling the high-tech economy are located in politically unstable regions of Africa and the former Soviet Union. Such resources must be secured or substitutions found in order for the revolution to proceed according to optimistic predictions. Capital formation, investment, and world markets must also be secure and stable. New management systems must evolve in response to the changes. In other words, these key factors are variables or "if's" – not the constants underlying most predictions of the future. As such, they are unpredictable.

The clearer picture of unanticipated consequences of technological changes is already evident on the changing assembly lines, in the automated offices, and in the electronic cottages of today. While automation often creates more jobs as it displaces workers – usually at higher skill levels – the jobs may be psychologically and financially less rewarding. Supervising robots eight hours a day can be tedious and boring work with few on-the-job rewards. The same is true for the much touted "office of the future." Interacting with a computer terminal eight hours a day is tedious, tiring, and boring work for many people, and job burnout may accelerate.

The electronic cottage has similar unanticipated consequences. Many people may miss the daily interaction with fellow workers – the gossip, the politics, the strokes. Instead of being rewarding, work at home can become drudgery and low paying work, a 21st century version of the sweatshop.

The optimists often overlook the fact that the nature of work itself provides rewards. Many people intrinsically enjoy the particular job they perform. Furthermore, many rewards are tied to the human dimension of work – the interaction with others. Thus, the high-tech and service society will have to deal with serious management and motivational problems arising from the changing nature of work and the workplace.

Many workers may need to re-career in order to overcome the boredom and burnout accompanying many of the new jobs or work situations of tomorrow. And even if the high-tech and service society does not emerge in the form outlined by us and other forecasters, the need to re-career will become necessary given the job and career uncertainty of a turbulent society largely shaped by a cyclical boom/bust economy and affected by international events.

4

The Best and Worst Jobs for the Future

W HERE ARE THE JOBS, and how do I get one? These are the first two questions most people ask when seeking employment. But one other equally important question should precede these traditional questions:

"**What** are the jobs of tomorrow?"

For the nature of jobs is changing rapidly in response to (1) technological innovations, (2) the development and application of new technology to the workplace, and (3) the demand for a greater variety of consumer services. Today's job seeker needs answers to the "what," "where," and "how" of jobs for today and tomorrow.

Many jobs in the decade ahead will look very different from those of yesterday. Indeed, if we project present trends into the future and believe what futurists tell us about emerging new careers, the 21st century will offer unprecedented and exciting careering and re-careering opportunities.

But such changes and opportunities have costs. The change in jobs and occupations will be so rapid that skills learned today may become obsolete in another five to ten years. Therefore, knowing what the jobs are becomes a prerequisite to knowing how to prepare for them, find them, and change them in the future.

Beware of Changing Occupational Profiles

A few words of caution are in order on how you should and should not use the information in this chapter. If you wish to identify a growing career field to plan your own career, do so only **after** you identify your interests, skills, and abilities – the subjects of Chapters 6, 7, and 8. You need to know if that career field is appropriate for you and vice versa. Furthermore, you need to determine if you have the proper skills or aptitude and interests to acquire the necessary skills. The next step is to acquire the training before conducting a job search. Only then should you seriously consider pursuing what appears to be a growing field.

At the same time, you should be aware that the statistics and projections on growing industrial and occupational fields may be inaccurate. First, they are based on traditional models and economic studies conducted by the U.S. Department of Labor, Bureau of Labor Statistics. The Bureau conducts "empirical studies" which assume a steady rate of economic growth. Such occupational projections are nothing more than "best guesses" based upon a traditional model which assumes continual, linear growth. This planning model does not deal well with the realities of cyclical changes and unique events that can significantly alter future projections.

Second, during a period of turbulent change, occupational profiles may become quickly outdated. Training requirements change, and thus individuals encounter greater uncertainty in career choices.

Expect Job Growth for Most Occupations

The growth in jobs has been steady during the past three to four decades. From 1955 to 1980, for example, the number of jobs increased from 68.7 to 105.6 million. This represented an average annual increase of about 1.5 million new jobs. During the 1970s the number of jobs increased by over 2 million per year. And between the years 1983 and 1994 the number of jobs increased by 24.6 million, a strong growth rate of 24 percent over an 11-year period or over 2 million new jobs each year. Between 1995 and 1999, jobs grew by over 2 million each year. By the year 2012 employment is expected to increased from 144 million in 2002 to 165 million in 2012, or by 14.8 percent.

If you wish to identify a growing career field to plan your own career, do so only after you identify your interests, skills, and abilities.

Highlighting these patterns of job growth are 16 forecasts, based on U.S. Department of Labor data and projections and other recent analyses, which represent the recent confluence of demographic, economic, and technological changes in society:

1. **Growth of the labor force slows.**

    The growth in the labor force will slow to 162.3 million by the year 2012 – a 17.4 percent increase from the year 2002. The U.S. population is expected to increase by 24 million over the 2002-12 period, which is slower than in the two previous decades.

2. **The labor force will be racially and ethnically more diverse.**

    The U.S. workforce will be more diverse by 2012. White, non-Hispanic persons will continue to make up a decreasing share of the labor force, falling from 71.3 percent in 2002 to 65.5 percent in 2012. White, non-Hispanics will remain the largest group in the labor force in 2012. Hispanics are projected to account for an increasing share of the labor force by 2012, growing from 12.4 to 14.7 percent. By 2012, Hispanics will constitute a larger proportion of the labor force than will blacks, whose share will grow from 11.4 percent to 12.2 percent. Asians will continue to be the fastest growing of the four labor force groups.

3. **Fewer young people will enter the job market.**

    The youth labor force, aged 16 to 24, is expected to slightly decrease its share of the labor force to 15 percent by 2012 or just over 24 million. Businesses depending on this age group for students, recruits, customers, and part-time workers – especially colleges, the armed forces, eating and drinking establishments, and retail stores – must draw from a smaller pool of young people. Competition among young people for entry-level jobs will decline accordingly.

4. **The workforce will continue to gray as it becomes older.**

    The number of workers 55 and older will increase substantially by the year 2012. This group is expected to increase from 14.3 percent to 19.1 percent of the labor force between 2002 and 2012, due to the aging of the baby-boom generation.

5. **Women will continue to enter the labor force in growing numbers.**

    The male labor force is projects to grow by 10 percent from 2002 to 2012, compared with 14.3 percent for women. Men's share of the labor force is expected to decrease from 53.5 to 52.5 percent, while women's share is expected to increase from 46.5 to 47.5 percent. By the year 2012, four out of five women ages 25-54 will be in the labor force.

6. **Education requirements for most new jobs will rise.**

Most new jobs will require strong basic education skills, such as reading, writing, oral communication, and math. Many of these jobs will include important high-tech components, which will require specialized education and training as well as the demonstrated ability to learn and acquire nontraditional education and training to continuously re-tool.

7. **The fastest growing occupations will be in executive, managerial, professional, and technical fields – all requiring the highest levels of education and skill.**

Three-quarters of the fastest growing occupational groups will be executive, administrative, and managerial; professional specialty; and technicians and related support occupations – occupations that require the highest levels of education and skill. Few opportunities will be available for high school dropouts or those who cannot read or follow directions. A combination of greater emphasis on productivity in the workplace, increased automation, technological advances, innovations, changes in consumer demands, and import substitutions will decrease the need for workers with little formal education and few skills – helpers, laborers, assemblers, machine operators.

8. **Employment will continue to increase for most occupations.**

As the population continues to grow and become more middle-aged and affluent, demands for more services will increase accordingly. Except in the cases of agriculture, mining, and traditional manufacturing, the past decade has seen a steady to significant job growth in all occupations. Over 21 million jobs will be added to the U.S. economy between the years 2002 and 2012. However, new jobs will be unevenly distributed across major industrial and occupational groups due to the restructuring of the economy and the increased education and training requirements for most jobs. Professional and related occupations will grow the fastest and add more new jobs than any other major occupational group.

9. **The greatest growth in jobs will take place in service industries and occupations as the long-term shift from goods-producing to**

service-providing employment continues.

Over 90 percent of all new jobs in the 1990s were in the service-producing industries with services such as legal, business (advertising, accounting, and computer support), and healthcare leading the way. The number of jobs in the service-producing industries is expected to account for approximately 20.8 million of the 21.6 million new wage and salary jobs generated over the 2002-2012 period.

10. **Education and health services will add more jobs than any other industry supersector.**

This industry supersector is expected to grow by 31.8 percent during the 2002-2012 period. About one out of every four new jobs created in the U.S. economy will be in either the healthcare and social assistance or private education services sector.

11. **Government employment will increase at different rates for different levels of government as well as for governmental units in different regions of the country.**

Between 2002 and 2012, government employment, including public education and hospitals, is expected to increase by 11.8 percent, from 21.5 million to 24 million jobs. Growth in government employment will be fueled by growth in state and local educational services and the shift of responsibilities from the federal government to the state and local governments. Local government education services is projected to increase 17.5 percent, adding over 1.3 million jobs. State government education services also are projected to grow 17.5 percent, adding 388,000 jobs. Federal government employment, including the Postal Service, is expected to increase by less than 1 percent as the federal government continues to contract out many government jobs to private companies.

12. **Employment growth in education at all levels will be incremental.**

Private educational services will grow by 28.7 percent and add 759,000 new jobs through 2012. Rising student enrollments at all levels of education will create demand for educational services. Job opportunities should increase for teachers, teacher aides, counselors, and administrative staff.

13. **Jobs in manufacturing will continue to decline.**

Manufacturing jobs are expected to decline by 1 percent, or 157,000 jobs, in the period 2002-2012. Most of the decline will affect production jobs; professional, technical, and managerial positions in manufacturing will increase. These declines will be due to productivity gains achieved through automation and improved management as well as the closing of less efficient plants. However, employment in plastics and rubber products manufacturing and machinery manufacturing is expected to grow by 138,000 and 120,000 jobs, respectively. Due to an aging population and increasing life expectancies, pharmaceutical and medicine manufacturing is expected to grow by 23.2 percent and add 68,000 jobs through 2012.

14. **Employment in agriculture, forestry, fishing, and mining jobs will continue to decline.**

Employment in agriculture, forestry, and fishing is expected to decline by 2 percent from 2002 to 2012, due to advancements in technology. The only supersector expected to grow is support activities for agriculture and forestry, which includes farm labor contractors and farm management services. This industry is expected to grow by 18.4 percent and add 17,000 new jobs. Strong growth will take place in agricultural services industries, especially landscape, horticultural, and farm management services. Much of the self-employment decline in agriculture will be due to the closing of lucrative export markets as the productivity of agriculture abroad improves and new hybrid crops are introduced from genetic engineering breakthroughs to solve many of the world's food problems.

15. **Glamorous new occupations, responding to new technological developments and consumer demands, will offer exciting new opportunities for job seekers who are well educated and skilled in the jobs of tomorrow.**

New occupations, created through a combination of technological innovations and new service demands, will provide excellent career opportunities for those who possess the necessary skills and drive to succeed in the decade ahead. New occupations with such names as bionic-electronic technician, holographic inspector, cryonics technician, and aquaculturist will enter our occupational vocabulary during the coming decade.

16. **The hottest career fields for the first decade of the 21st century will be in science, engineering, computer technology, and health services.**

Look for these jobs to be the highest demand and highest paying jobs for the coming decade: biological scientist, physician, mechanical engineer, chemical engineer, computer scientist, computer engineer, materials engineer, medical technologist. Demand also will be high for these less well paid jobs: special education teachers, personal and home care aides, home health aides, and physical therapists.

Examine Growing and Declining Occupations

The U.S. Department of Labor divides occupations into 16 broad groups based on the Standard Occupational Classification, the classification system used by all government agencies for collecting occupational information:

- Executive, administrative, and managerial occupations
- Engineers, scientists, and related occupations
- Social science, social service, and related occupations
- Teachers, librarians, and counselors
- Health-related occupations
- Writers, artists, and entertainers
- Technologists and technicians
- Marketing and sales occupations
- Administrative support occupations, including clerical
- Service occupations
- Agricultural and forestry occupations
- Mechanics and repairers
- Construction occupations
- Production occupations
- Transportation and material moving occupations
- Handlers, equipment cleaners, helpers, and laborers

Every two years the department's Bureau of Labor Statistics updates its employment outlook for the coming decade and publishes the results in the November issue of the *Monthly Labor Review* as well as the latest edition of the biannual *Occupational Outlook Handbook*. For the latest statistics and projections relating to several tables presented in this chapter, please visit the Bureau of Labor Statistics' website: http://stats.bls.gov. You also can access online the complete text of the popular *Occupational Outlook Handbook*:

www.bls.gov/oco

Assuming a moderate rate of economic growth in the decade ahead – not boom-and-bust cycles – the U.S. Department of Labor in projects an average growth rate of nearly 15 percent for all occupations in the coming decade. Technical and service occupations will grow the fastest:

Fastest Growing Occupations, 2002-2012
(Numbers in thousands of jobs)

Occupational Title	Employment 2002	2012	Percent Change	Postsecondary Education or Training
▪ Medical assistants [3]	365	579	59	Moderate-term on-the-job training
▪ Network systems and data communications analysts [1]	186	292	57	Bachelor's degree
▪ Physician assistants [3]	63	94	49	Bachelor's degree
▪ Social and human service assistants [3]	305	454	49	Moderate-term on-the-job training
▪ Home health aides [4]	580	859	48	Short-term on-the-job training
▪ Medical records and health information technicians [3]	147	216	47	Associate degree
▪ Physical therapist aides [3]	37	54	46	Short-term on-the-job training
▪ Computer software engineers, applications [1]	394	573	46	Bachelor's degree
▪ Computer software engineers [1]	281	409	45	Bachelor's degree
▪ Physical therapist assistants [2]	50	73	45	Associate degree
▪ Fitness trainers and aerobics instructors [3]	183	264	44	Postsecondary vocational award
▪ Database administrators [1]	110	159	44	Bachelor's degree
▪ Veterinary technologists and technicians [3]	53	76	44	Associate degree
▪ Hazardous materials removal workers [2]	38	54	43	Moderate-term on-the-job training
▪ Dental hygienists [1]	148	212	43	Associate degree
▪ Occupational therapist aides [3]	8	12	43	Short-term on-the-job training
▪ Dental assistants [3]	266	379	42	Moderate-term on-the-job training

▪ Personal and home care aides [4]	608	854	40	Short-term on-the-job training
▪ Self-enrichment education teachers [2]	200	281	40	Work experience in a related occupation
▪ Computer systems analysts [1]	468	653	39	Bachelor's degree
▪ Occupational therapist assistants [2]	18	26	39	Associate degree
▪ Environmental engineers [1]	47	65	38	Bachelor's degree
▪ Postsecondary teachers [1]	1,581	1,284	38	Doctoral degree
▪ Network and computer systems administrators [1]	251	345	37	Bachelor's degree
▪ Environmental science and protection technicians, including health [2]	28	38	37	Associate degree
▪ Preschool teachers, except special education [4]	424	577	36	Postsecondary vocational award
▪ Computer and information systems managers [1]	284	387	36	Bachelor's or higher degree, plus work experience
▪ Physical therapists [1]	137	185	35	Master's degree
▪ Occupational therapists [1]	82	110	35	Bachelor's degree
▪ Respiratory therapists [2]	86	116	35	Associate degree

[1] Very high average annual earnings ($42,820 and over)
[2] High average annual earnings ($27,500 to $41,780)
[3] Low average annual earnings ($19,710 to $27,380)
[4] Very low average annual earnings (up to $19,600)

Occupations With the Largest Job Growth, 2002-2012
(Numbers in thousands of jobs)

Occupational Title	Employment		Percent Change	Postsecondary Education or Training
	2002	2012		
▪ Registered nurses [1]	2,284	2,908	27	Associate degree
▪ Postsecondary teachers [1]	1,581	2,184	38	Doctoral degree
▪ Retail salespersons [4]	4,076	4,672	15	Short-term on-the-job training
▪ Customer service representatives [3]	1,894	2,354	24	Moderate-term on-the-job training

■ Combined food preparation and service workers, including fast food [3]	1,990	2,444	23	Short-term on-the-job training
■ Cashiers, except gaming [4]	3,432	2,886	13	Short-term on-the-job training
■ Janitors and cleaners, except maids and housekeeping cleaners [4]	2,267	2,681	18	Short-term on-the-job training
■ General and operations managers [1]	2,049	2,425	18	Bachelor's or higher degree + experience
■ Waiters and waitresses [4]	2,097	2,464	18	Short-term on-the-job training
■ Nursing aides, orderlies, and attendants [3]	1,375	1,718	25	Short-term on-the-job training
■ Truck drivers, heavy and tractor-trailer [2]	1,767	2,104	19	Moderate-term on-the-job training
■ Receptionists and information clerks [3]	1,100	1,425	29	Short-term on-the-job training
■ Security guards [4]	995	1,313	32	Short-term on-the-job training
■ Office clerks, general [3]	2,991	3,301	10	Short-term on-the-job training
■ Teacher assistants [4]	1,277	1,571	23	Short-term on-the-job training
■ Sales representative, wholesale and manufacturing, except technical and scientific products [1]	1,459	1,738	19	Moderate-term on-the-job training
■ Home health aides [4]	580	859	48	Short-term on-the-job training
■ Personal and home care aides [4]	608	854	40	Short-term on-the-job training
■ Truck drivers, light or delivery services [3]	1,022	1,259	23	Short-term on-the-job training
■ Landscaping and groundskeeping workers [3]	1,074	1,311	22	Short-term on-the-job training
■ Elementary school teachers, except special education [2]	1,467	1,690	15	Bachelor's degree
■ Medical assistants [3]	365	579	59	Moderate-term on-the-job training
■ Maintenance and repair workers, general [2]	1,266	1,472	16	Moderate-term on-the-job training
■ Accountants and auditors [1]	1,055	1,261	19	Bachelor's degree
■ Computer systems analysts [1]	468	653	39	Bachelor's degree

▪ Secondary school teachers, except special and vocational education [1]	988	1,167	18	Bachelor's degree
▪ Computer software engineers [1]	394	573	46	Bachelor's degree
▪ Management analysis [1]	577	753	30	Bachelor's or higher degree, plus work experience
▪ Food preparation workers [4]	850	1,022	20	Short-term on-the-job training
▪ First-line supervisors/ manager of retail sales workers [2]	1,798	1,962	9	Work experience in a related occupation

[1] Very high average annual earnings ($42,820 and over)
[2] High average annual earnings ($27,500 to $41,780)
[3] Low average annual earnings ($19,710 to $27,380)
[4] Very low average annual earnings (up to $19,600)

Fastest Growing Industries, 2002-2012
(Numbers in thousands of jobs)

Industry Description	Jobs		Percent Change	Average annual rate of change
	2002	2012		
▪ Software publishers	256.0	429.7	173.7	5.3
▪ Management, scientific, and technical consulting services	731.8	1,137.4	405.6	4.5
▪ Community care facilities for the elderly and residential care facilities	695.3	1,077.6	382.3	4.5
▪ Computer systems design and related services	1,162.7	1,797.7	635.0	4.5
▪ Employment services	3,248.8	5,012.3	1,763.5	4.4
▪ Individual, family, community, and vocational rehabilitation services	1,238.8	1,866.6	597.3	3.9
▪ Ambulatory health care services except offices of health practitioners	1,443.6	2,113.4	669.8	3.9
▪ Water, sewage, and other systems	48.5	71.0	22.5	3.9

▪ Internet services, data processing, and other information services	528.8	773.1	244.3	3.9
▪ Child day care services	734.2	1,050.3	316.1	3.6

20 Jobs With High Median Earnings and a Significant Number of Job Openings, 2002-2012

Occupation	Average Annual Projected Job Openings, 2002-2012	Median Earnings 2002
▪ Registered nurses	110,119	$48,090
▪ Postsecondary teachers	95,980	$49,090
▪ General and operations managers	76,245	$68,210
▪ Sales representatives, wholesale and manufacturing, except technical and scientific products	66,239	$42,730
▪ Truck drivers, heavy and tractor-trailer	62,517	$33,210
▪ Elementary school teachers, except special education	54,701	$41,780
▪ First-line supervisors or managers of retail sales workers	48,645	$29,700
▪ Secondary school teachers, except special education	45,761	$43,950
▪ General maintenance and repair workers	44,978	$29,370
▪ Executive secretaries and administrative assistants	42,444	$33,410
▪ First-line supervisors or managers of office and administrative support workers	40,909	$38,820
▪ Accountants and auditors	40,465	$47,000
▪ Carpenters	31,917	$34,190
▪ Automotive service technicians and mechanics	41,887	$30,590
▪ Police and sheriff's patrol officers	31,290	$42,270
▪ Licenses practical and licensed vocational nurses	29,480	$31,440
▪ Electricians	28,485	$41,390
▪ Management analysts	25,470	$60,340

■ Computer systems analysts	23,735	$62,890
■ Special education teachers	23,297	$43,450

Certain patterns are clearly evident from the U.S. Department of Labor's employment projections for the coming decade:

1. The hot occupational fields are in health care and computers and involve increased technical education and training on an on-going basis.

2. Education is closely associated with earnings – the higher the education, the higher the average annual earnings.

3. Many of the fastest growing jobs require short- or moderate-term education.

4. Two-year associate degrees in several medical-related fields offer some of the best paying jobs.

5. Nearly 50 percent of the fastest growing jobs that generate relatively high median earnings, such as carpenters, truck drivers, repair workers, and auto mechanics, do not require a four-year degree.

Determine the "Best" Jobs for You

The fastest growing occupational fields are not necessarily the best ones to enter. The best job and career for you will depend on your particular mix of skills, interests, and work and lifestyle values. Money, for example, is only one of many determiners of whether or not a job and career are particularly desirable. A job may pay a great deal of money, but it also may be very stressful, insecure, or found in an undesirable location. The "best" job for you will be one you find rewarding in terms of your own criteria and priorities.

Periodically some observers of the labor market attempt to identify what are the best, the worst, the hottest, the most lucrative, or the most promising jobs and careers of the decade. One of the most ambitious attempts to assemble a list of the "best" jobs in America is presented in the *Jobs Rated Almanac*. Similar in methodology to *Places Rated Almanac* for identifying the best places to live in America, the latest edition (2002) of this book evaluates and ranks 250 jobs in terms of six primary "job quality" criteria: income, stress, physical demands, environment, outlook, and security. According to this analysis, the 20 highest ranking ("best") jobs by accumulated score of these criteria are:

The Best Jobs in America

Job title	Overall rank
Biologist	1
Actuary	2
Financial planner	3
Computer system analyst	4
Accountant	5
Software engineer	6
Meteorologist	7
Paralegal assistant	8
Statistician	9
Astronomer	10
Mathematician	11
Parole officer	12
Hospital administrator	13
Architectural drafter	14
Physiologist	15
Dietician	16
Website manager	17
Physicist	18
Audiologist	19
Agency director (nonprofit)	20
Industrial designer	21
Chemist	22
Medical laboratory technician	23
Archeologist	24
Economist	25

The 20 worst jobs, or those that rank at the very bottom of the list of 250, include the following:

The Worst Jobs in America

Job title	Overall rank
Fisherman	250
Roustabout	249
Lumberjack	248
Cowboy	247
Ironworker	246
Garbage collector	245
Construction worker (laborer)	244
Taxi driver	243
Stevedore	242
Welder	241
Roofer	240
Dancer	239
Firefighter	238

- Dairy Farmer   237
- Seaman   236
- Farmer   235
- Boilermaker   234
- Carpenter   234
- Sheet metal worker   232
- Butcher   231

For the relative rankings of all 250 jobs as well as the ratings of each job on individual criterion, consult the latest edition of the *Jobs Rated Almanac*, which should be available in your local library or bookstore.

One of the most recent examinations of the best jobs in the decade ahead – those offering high pay, fast growth, and the most new jobs – is found in Ferguson's *25 Jobs That Have It All* (Chicago, IL: Ferguson Publishing Co.). They identify these 25 jobs as the top ones:

- Advertising account executives
- Business managers
- College professors
- Computer network administrators
- Computer systems programmers/analysts
- Database specialists
- Dental hygienists
- Graphic designers
- Health care managers
- Management analysts and consultants
- Medical record technicians
- Occupational therapists
- Paralegals
- Pharmacy technicians
- Physician assistants
- Police officers
- Public relations specialists
- Registered nurses
- Secondary school teachers
- Software designers
- Software engineers
- Special education teachers
- Speech-language pathologists and audiologists
- Technical support specialists
- Writers and editors

Look for Exciting New Occupations

In the early 1980s the auto and related industries – steel, rubber, glass, aluminum, railroads, and auto dealers – accounted for one-fifth of all employment in the United States. Today that percentage continues to decline as service occupations further dominate America's occupational structure.

New occupations for the decade ahead will center around information, energy, high-tech, healthcare, and financial industries. They promise to create a new occupational structure and vocabulary relating to computers, the Internet, robotics, biotechnology, lasers, and fiber optics. By 1999, for example, the Internet reportedly was responsible for 1.3 million new jobs within a four-year period that generated more than $300 billion in business. And as these fields begin to apply new technologies to developing new innovations, they in turn will generate other new occupations in the 21st century. While most new occupations are not major growth fields – because they do not initially generate a large number of new jobs – they will present individuals with fascinating new opportunities to become leaders in pioneering new fields and industries.

Futurists agree that most new occupations in the coming decade will have two dominant characteristics:

- **They will generate fewer new jobs** in comparison to the overall growth of jobs in hundreds of more traditional service fields, such as sales workers, office clerks, truck drivers, and janitors.

- **They require a high level of education and skills** for entry into the fields as well as continuing training and retraining as each field transforms itself into additional growth fields.

If you plan to pursue an emerging occupation, expect to first acquire highly specialized skills which may require years of higher education and training.

Implications of Future Trends for You

Most growth industries and occupations require skills training and experience. Moving into one of these fields will require knowledge of job qualifications, the nature of the work, and sources of employment. Fortunately, the U.S. Department of Labor publishes several useful sources of information available in most libraries to help you. These include the _O*NET Dictionary of Occupational Titles_, which identifies over 1,100 job titles (reduced from 13,000 titles found in the old _Dictionary of Occupational Titles_). The _Occupational Outlook Handbook_ provides an overview of current labor market conditions and projections, as well as discusses nearly 250 occupations that account for 107 million jobs, or 87 percent of the nation's total jobs, according to several useful informational categories: nature of work; working conditions; employment; training, other qualifications, and achievement; job outlook; earnings; related occupations; and sources of additional information.

During the past eight years, the U.S. Department of Labor overhauled its traditional job classification system which was based on an analysis of the U.S. job market of the 1960s, 1970s, and 1980s. This system had generated over 13,000 job titles as outlined in the *Dictionary of Occupational Titles* and numerous related publications. Known as the O*NET project (The Occupational Information Network), this new occupational classification system more accurately reflects the structure of today's new job market; it condenses the 13,000+ job titles into over 1,100 job titles. The new system is being gradually introduced into career education to replace the job classification system that has defined most jobs in the U.S. during the past four decades.

Anyone seeking to enter the job market or change careers should initially consult the U.S. Department of Labor publications as well as access information on the new O*NET (www.onetcenter.org). The Department of Labor only makes this data available online (www.online.onetcenter.org). A commercial version of this system, published in book form, also is available. You should be able to find it in your local library. If not, the *O*NET Dictionary of Occupational Titles* can be ordered from Impact Publications by completing the form at the end of this book or through Impact's online bookstore: www.impactpublications.com.

However, remember that labor market statistics are for industries and occupations **as a whole**. They tell you little about the shift in employment emphasis **within the industry**, and nothing about the outlook of particular jobs for you, **the individual**. For example, employment in agriculture was projected to decline by 14 percent between 1985 and 2000, but the decline consisted of an important shift in employment emphasis within the industry: there would be 500,000 fewer self-employed workers but 150,000 more wage and salary earners in the service end of agriculture. The employment statistics also assume a steady state of economic growth with consumers having more and more disposable income to stimulate a wide variety of service and trade industries.

Therefore, be careful in how you interpret and use this information in making your own job and career decisions. If, for example, you want to become a college teacher, and the data tells you there will be a 10-percent decline in this occupation during the next 10 years, this does not mean you would not find employment, as well as advance, in this field. It merely means that, on the whole, competition may be keen for these jobs, and that future advancement and mobility in this occupation may not be very good – **on the**

whole. At the same time, there may be numerous job opportunities available in a declining occupational field as many individuals abandon the field for more attractive occupations. In fact, you may do much better in this declining occupation than in a growing field depending on your interests, motivations, abilities, job search savvy, and level of competition. And if the decade ahead experiences more boom-and-bust cycles, expect most of these U.S. Department of Labor statistics and projections to be invalid for the economic realities of this decade.

Use this industrial and occupational data to expand your awareness of various job and career options. By no means should you make critical education, training, and occupational choices based upon this information alone. Such choices require additional types of information – subjects of the next six chapters – about you, the individual. If identified and used properly, this information will help clarify exactly which jobs are best for you.

5

Myths, Competencies, and Your Success

AKING FUTURE OCCUPATIONAL projections and knowing "what" jobs are available and "where" to find them in general tells you little about the critical "how" to find a job for your situation. Answers to general "what" and "where" questions may be interesting in describing and explaining reality, but they may or may not be useful in developing specific action strategies.

If you are to be effective in the job markets of the decade ahead, you must link the "how" to the "what" and "where." At the very least, you must plan and organize specific activities in relation to your future goals.

Careering and Re-Careering Prerequisites

Achieving job and career success in the decade ahead will depend on how well you understand and implement key processes for planning your future. Directly related to on-going job market realities, these processes constitute a set of **how-to strategies** for developing an effective job search, organizing specific job search activities, and achieving success. Examined separately, they are important prerequisites for developing effective careering and re-careering skills. Taken together, they constitute a well-organized framework for achieving successful careering and re-careering today and tomorrow.

This chapter relates our previous overview of careering and re-careering to the practical aspects of planning and implementing an effective job search. Here we examine the basic prerequisites for launching a successful job search. Each constitutes a skill that you can learn and apply:

74

- Understand job market realities
- Develop a well-organized job search
- Identify your careering and re-careering competencies
- Seek assistance when necessary
- Manage your time effectively
- Organize a plan of action
- Follow principles for achieving success
- Take risks
- Handle rejections
- Form a support group

Above all, you must organize and implement to achieve success. You must translate your understanding of problems, approaches, and solutions into concrete action steps for achieving results.

Understand Key Myths and Realities

What do you know about the job market? Is it a place that has jobs for you? Where do you start? How will you approach it? What do you do when you get there? Whom do you talk to? What do you say?

The job market is anything but organized, centralized, and coherent. It is more an abstraction than a set of well defined and related structures.

The abstract notion of a "job market" generates several images of structures, processes, decision points, and outcomes. In one sense it appears to be well structured for dispensing job information and assistance. After all, you will find various elements that supposedly make up the structure of the job market: online employment sites with job listings and resume databases; classified ads listing job vacancies; personnel offices with vacancy announcements; employment agencies and electronic databases linking candidates to job openings; and a variety of helpers known as career counselors, coaches, employment specialists, and executive recruiters who make a living by serving as gatekeepers to the "job market." At the same time, we know various processes are key to making this job market function: self-assessment, objective setting, research, applications, resume and letter writing, networking, interviewing, negotiating, and hiring. You need to become very familiar with each process as well as integrate each into a coherent job search.

Understanding the job market is like the blind person exploring an elephant: you may recognize a trunk, a leg, and a tail, but you're not sure what it is as a whole. As we will see shortly, the job market is anything but organized, centralized, and coherent. It is more an abstraction, or convenient short hand way of talking about finding jobs, than a set of well defined and related structures.

Most people have an image of how the job market works as well as how they should relate to it. This image is based upon a combination of facts, stereotypes, and myths learned from experience and from the advice of well-meaning individuals. It's an unfortunate image when it guides people into unproductive job search channels by advising them to spend most of their time responding to vacancy announcements and waiting to hear from employers. In so doing, it reconfirms the often-heard lament of the unsuccessful job searcher – *"What more can I do? There are no jobs out there for me."*

Let's examine 32 myths about jobs, careers, and the job search before you proceed to organize yourself for today's and tomorrow's employment realities. These myths illustrate important points, or basic principles, for organizing and implementing your job search:

MYTH 1:   Nearly 85 percent of Americans are unhappy with their jobs. They would change jobs if only they felt they could.

REALITY: This is one of those phoney statistics thrown out by so-called career specialists who want to make themselves and their services highly visible. Unfortunately, such false assertions get quoted by others as employment "facts" and evidence of a job "crisis" in America. The truth, based upon numerous yearly studies of worker attitudes, is that over 80 percent of workers are relatively happy with their jobs. Less than 15 percent report they may be interested in making a job change. Half of that number indicate they are unhappy with their current jobs. The statistical distribution of these supposedly happy/unhappy workers has been very consistent over the past three decades.

MYTH 2:   We are now in a revolutionary period where we are witnessing the end of jobs.

REALITY: Let's not get carried away with another trendy concept based on a skewed, anecdotal view of the job market. Jobs are here to stay and in a very big way. However, careers are clearly disappearing for many people. They are careers, not jobs, that may become obsolete. While traditional manufacturing jobs have been transformed in terms of skills required, jobs are still the basic activities by which work gets organized and accomplished. Employers still fill **positions** which consist of various assigned duties and responsibilities that define particular jobs. Certain jobs in certain industries, especially those using nontraditional organizational forms, have become less well defined and thus do not conform to the traditional concept of an assigned job. But such changes are no reason for thinking that jobs are ending. What is ending is the notion of a career. Individuals entering the job market today expect to have many different jobs throughout their worklife. These jobs may or may not constitute a well-defined career.

MYTH 3: Your employment future and income look uncertain because more and more jobs, both manufacturing and service, are being offshored to cheap labor markets abroad.

REALITY: While many such jobs are being offshored, this is merely a trend that has existed for decades. Indeed, within the United States, millions of jobs have moved from expensive labor markets in high-cost metropolitan areas to cheaper labor markets within the country during the past 50 years. Known as "outsourcing," this is not a new nor alarming phenomenon. Outsourcing or offshoring of jobs tends to cut production costs and thus make businesses more efficient and competitive in the long run. While some people will lose their jobs to outsourcing, many others will be hired to manage the growth of such companies. Since many jobs require face-to-face relationships, outsourcing only affects certain types of jobs. Your best insurance against long-term job loss and declining income is education and training.

MYTH 4: Anyone can find a job; all you need to know is how to find a job.

REALITY: This classic "form versus substance" myth is often associated with popular career planning exhortations that stress the importance of having a positive attitude and self-esteem, setting goals, dressing for success, and using interpersonal strategies for finding jobs. While such approaches may work well in an industrial society with low unemployment, they constitute myths in a post-industrial, high-tech society which requires employees to demonstrate both **intelligence and concrete work skills** as well as a **willingness to relocate** to new communities offering greater job opportunities. For example, many of today's unemployed are highly skilled in the old technology of the industrial society, but they live and own homes in communities that offer few rewarding job and career opportunities. These people lack the necessary **skills and mobility** required for getting jobs in high-tech, growth communities. Knowing job search skills alone will not help these people. Indeed, such advice and knowledge will most likely frustrate such highly motivated and immobile individuals who possess skills of the old technology.

MYTH 5: The best way to find a job is to respond to classified ads, use employment agencies, and submit applications to personnel offices.

REALITY: Except for certain types of organizations, such as government, these formal application procedures are not the most effective ways of finding jobs. Such approaches assume the presence of an organized, coherent, and centralized job market – but no such thing exists. The job market is highly decentralized, fragmented, and chaotic. Classified ads, employment agencies, and personnel offices tend to list low-paying, yet highly competitive jobs or high-paying, highly skilled positions that are hard to fill.

> *Despite attempts to organize it electronically, the job market remains highly decentralized, fragmented, and chaotic.*

Most jobs are neither listed nor advertised; they are most likely discovered through word-of-mouth contacts. Your most fruitful strategy will be to conduct research and informational interviews on what career counselors call the "hidden job market."

MYTH 6: Few jobs are available for you in today's job market.

REALITY: This may be true if you lack marketable skills and insist on applying for jobs listed in newspapers, employment agencies, personnel offices, or online (the Internet). Competition in the advertised job market usually is high, especially for jobs requiring few skills. Numerous jobs with little competition are available on the hidden job market. Jobs requiring advanced technical skills often go begging. Little competition may occur during periods of high unemployment, because many people quit job hunting after a few disappointing weeks of concentrating job search efforts on working the advertised job market.

MYTH 7:   You know how to find a job, but there are no oppor-
                tunities for you.

REALITY: Most people don't know the best way to find a job, or they lack
                marketable job skills. They continue to use ineffective job
                search methods, such as only responding to classified ads with
                resumes and cover letters. Opportunities are readily available
                for individuals who understand the structure and operation of
                the job market, have appropriate work-content skills, and use
                job search methods designed for the hidden job market. They
                must learn to develop an effective networking and information-
                al interviewing campaign for uncovering promising job leads.
                And they must persist in prospecting for new job leads as well
                as learn to handle rejections. In fact, many job seekers are their
                own worst enemy and thus they turn this myth into a self-
                fulfilling prophecy. They make numerous mistakes that can be
                easily corrected given some basic information on effective job
                search strategies. We address this issue at length in *No One
                Will Hire Me! Avoid 15 Mistakes and Win the Job* (Impact
                Publications, 2004).

MYTH 8:   We are over-qualified in the eyes of many employers. They
                don't want to hire over-qualified individuals.

REALITY: Yes, if you're seeking a $40,000 a year job but you have
                experience and qualifications for an $80,000 a year job! Why
                would you even want to consider such a job? Who wants to hire
                someone who is over-qualified and thus likely to leave for
                greener pastures once they get their wake-up call that they are
                under-employed and under-compensated? This is the classic
                self-fulfilling prophecy of many career changers who don't know
                how to best communicate their qualifications to prospective
                employers. Being over-qualified for a job raises a big red flag in
                the eyes of the employer. You're never over-qualified if you seek
                jobs for your level of skills and experience. Employers who view
                you as over-qualified are the wrong employers to whom to
                apply. They do you a favor by not giving you a job. Thank them
                for being so discriminating. They serve as your wake-up call.
                You need to get a better sense of where you fit into the job
                market. Stop under-selling yourself and thus contributing to
                this over-qualification myth. You need some job market smarts
                before you approach any more employers.

MYTH 9:   Employers are in the driver's seat; they have the upper hand with applicants.

REALITY: Most often no one is in the driver's seat since both the employer and the job seeker have a problem to solve. Not knowing what they want, many employers make poor hiring decisions. They frequently let applicants define their hiring needs. If you can define employers' needs as your skills, you might end up in the driver's seat!

MYTH 10:   Employers hire the best qualified candidates. Without a great deal of experience and qualifications, you don't have a chance.

REALITY: Employers hire people for all kinds of reasons. Most rank experience and qualifications third or fourth in their pecking order of hiring criteria. Employers seldom hire the best qualified candidate, because "qualifications" are difficult to define and measure. Employers normally seek people with the following characteristics: competent, intelligent, honest, enthusiastic, and likable. "Likability" tends to be an overall concern of employers – will you "fit in" and get along well with your superiors, co-workers, and clients? Employers want **value** for their money. Therefore, you must communicate to employers that you are such a person. You must overcome employers' objections to any lack of experience or qualifications. But never volunteer your weaknesses. The best qualified person is the one who knows how to get the job – convinces employers that he or she is the **most** desirable for the job.

MYTH 11:   It is best to go into a growing field where jobs are plentiful.

REALITY: Be careful in following the masses to the "in" fields. First, many so-called growth fields can quickly become no-growth fields, such as aerospace engineering, nuclear energy, defense contracting, and nursing. Second, by the time you acquire the necessary skills, you may experience the "disappearing job" phenomenon: too many people did the same thing you did and thus glutted the job market. Third, since many people leave no growth fields, new opportunities may arise for you. Fourth, if you go after a growth field, you will try to fit into a job rather than find a job fit for you. If you know what you do well and enjoy doing (Chapters 6 and 7), and what additional training you may need, you should look for a job or career conducive to your particular mix of skills, interests, and motivations. In the long run you will be much happier and more productive finding a job fit for you. If you find a job you really love, you will be better compensated emotionally than if you only focus on finding a job that pays a high salary.

> *If you go after a growth field, you will try to fit into a job rather than find a job fit for you.*

MYTH 12:   People over 40 have difficulty finding a good job; employers prefer hiring younger and less expensive workers.

REALITY: Yes, if they apply for youth jobs. Age should be an insignificant barrier to employment if you conduct a well organized job search and are prepared to handle this potential negative with employers. Age should be a positive and must be communicated as such. After all, employers want experience, maturity, and stability. People over 40 generally possess these qualities. As the population ages and birth rates decline, older individuals should have a much easier time changing jobs and careers.

MYTH 13:   It's best to use an employment firm to find a job.

REALITY: It depends on the firm and the nature of employment you are seeking. Employment firms that specialize in your skill area may be well worth contacting. For example, many law firms use employment firms to hire paralegals rather than directly recruit such personnel themselves. Many employers now use temporary employment firms to recruit both temporary and full-time employees at several different levels, from clerical to professional. Indeed, many temporary employment firms have temp-to-perm programs that link qualified candidates to employers who are looking for full-time employees. But make sure you are working with a legitimate employment firm. Such firms get paid by employers or they collect placement fees from applicants only **after** the applicant has accepted a position. Beware of firms that want up-front fees for promised job placement assistance.

MYTH 14:   You must be aggressive in order to find a job.

REALITY: Aggressive people tend to be offensive and obnoxious. They also make pests of themselves. Try being purposeful, persistent, and pleasant in all job search activities. Such behavior is well received by potential employers!

MYTH 15:   Hiring a professional to help you find a job is a waste of time and money.

REALITY: It depends on the professional. Hiring a career professional to help you with your job search can save you a great deal of time and wasted effort. A career professional should serve as a coach in helping you through a job search process. Many people can benefit from the structure, discipline, and direction provided by such a professional. If you're interested in contacting a career professional, visit the following websites, which are linked to associations of career professionals: www.nbcc.org, www.ncda.org, www.certifiedcareercoaches.com, and www.careernetwork.com.

MYTH 16:   You should not change jobs and careers more than once or twice. Job-changers are discriminated against in hiring.

REALITY: While this may have been generally true 30 years ago, it is no longer true today. America is a skills-based society: individuals market their skills to organizations in exchange for money, position, and other on-the-job rewards. Furthermore, since most organizations are small businesses with limited advancement opportunities, careers quickly plateau for most people. For them, the only way up is to get out and into another organization. Therefore, the best way to advance careers in a society of small businesses is to periodically change jobs. Job-changing is okay as long as such changes demonstrate career advancement and one isn't changing jobs every few months. Most individuals entering the job market today will undergo several career and job changes regardless of their initial desire for a one-job, one-career life plan.

MYTH 17:   People get ahead by working hard and putting in long hours.

REALITY: Success patterns differ. Many people who are honest, work hard, and put in long hours also get fired, have ulcers, and die young. Some people get ahead even though they are dishonest and lazy. Others simply have good luck or a helpful mentor or patron. Moderation in both work and play will probably get you just as far as the extremes. There are other ways, as outlined near the end of this chapter, to become successful in addition to hard work and long hours.

MYTH 18: You should not try to use "connections" to get a job. You should apply through the front door like everyone else. If you're the best qualified, you'll get the job.

REALITY: While you may wish to stand in line for tickets, bank deposits, and loans – because you have no clout – standing in line for a job is not the best approach. Every employer has a front door as well as a back door. Try using the back door if you can. It works in many cases. Chapter 12 details how you can develop your contacts, use connections, and enter **both** the front and back doors.

MYTH 19: You need to get more education and training to qualify for today's jobs.

REALITY: You may or may not need more education and training, depending on your present skill levels and the needs of employers. Most employers want to recruit individuals who are intelligent, communicate well, take initiative, and are trainable. Since they train their employees to respond to the needs of their organization, they want people who can quickly learn new skills. You first need to know what skills you already possess and if they appear appropriate for the types of jobs you are seeking. Also, be sure to communicate to employers that you enjoy learning and are trainable.

MYTH 20: Once you apply, it's best to wait to hear from an employer.

REALITY: Waiting is not a good job search strategy. If you want action from employers, you must first take action. The key to getting a job interview and offer is follow up, follow up, follow up. You do this by making follow-up telephone calls as well as writing follow-up and thank you letters to employers.

MYTH 21: You don't need a resume. You can get a job based solely on your network contacts.

REALITY: While networking is one of the most effective methods for finding employment, it does not erase the need for a resume. The resume is your calling card; it provides a prospective employer with a snapshot of your background and skills. Employers often want to first see you on paper (resume) **before** meeting you in person (interview). Whether you like it or not, chances are you'll need a resume very early in your job search, especially when a contact asks you to "Send me a copy of your resume."

MYTH 22: A good resume is the key to getting a job.

REALITY: While resumes play an important role in the job search process, they are often overrated. The purpose of a resume is to communicate your qualifications to employers who, in turn, invite you to job interviews. The key to getting a job is the job interview. No job interview, no job offer.

MYTH 23: You should include my salary expectations on your resume or in your cover letter.

REALITY: You should never include your salary expectations on your resume or in a cover letter, unless specifically requested to do so. Salary should be the very last thing you discuss with a prospective employer. You do so only after you have had a chance to assess the worth of the position and communicate your value to the employer. This usually occurs at the end of your final job interview, just before or after being offered the job. If you pre-maturely raise the salary issue, you may devalue your worth.

MYTH 24: Your resume should emphasize your work history.

REALITY: Employers are interested in hiring your future rather than your past. Therefore, your resume should emphasize the skills and abilities you will bring to the job as well as your interests and goals. Let prospective employers know what you are likely to do for them **in the future**. When you present your work history, do so in terms of your major skills and accomplishments.

MYTH 25: It's not necessary to write letters to employers – just send them a resume or complete an application.

REALITY: You should be prepared to write several types of job search letters – cover, approach, resume, thank you, follow-up, acceptance, and rejection. In addition to communicating your level of literacy, these job search letters enable you to express important values sought after by employers – your professionalism, tactfulness, enthusiasm, thoughtfulness, likability, and ability to follow up. Sending a resume without a cover letter tends to devalue your resume and application.

> *Employers are interested in hiring your future.*

MYTH 26: You only need an electronic resume to land a job.

REALITY: Electronic resumes are increasingly important for job seekers and employers alike. These resumes come in two major forms: e-mail resumes and scannable resumes. More and more employers request that resumes be sent to them by e-mail. Therefore, you need to create an e-mail version of your resume. Large employers also use the latest resume scanning technology to quickly screen hundreds of resumes. Therefore, it's also in your interest to write a "computer friendly" resume based on the principles of electronic resumes. These are very different resumes compared to conventional resumes. Structured around "keywords" or nouns which stress capabilities, electronic resumes are ideally suited for scanners. Keep in mind that electronic resumes are primarily written for electronic scanners and high-tech distribution systems rather than for human beings. Since human beings interview and hire, you should first create a high impact resume that follows the principles of human communication and intelligence.

MYTH 27: Individuals who post their resumes to online resume databases, such as www.monster.com, www.hotjobs.yahoo.com, and www.careerbuilder.com, are more likely to get high-paying jobs than those who don't.

REALITY: Don't get carried away in your job search with all the bells, whistles, and hype of the many Internet employment sites that offer resume databases and thousands of job postings. Basically operated for their paying customers – employers – these are largely high-tech classified ad operations that also enable employers to search thousands of online resumes by keywords. There is nothing magical about this search and retrieval media. Indeed, there is no evidence that individuals who conduct an online job search find better jobs than those who do not. In fact, the Internet is a big disappointment for many job seekers who spend a disproportionate amount of time submitting resumes to databases and applying for jobs online. Recent surveys indicate that fewer than 20 percent of candidates get jobs through their online job search efforts. While this number is increasing, the shift in emphasis for employers is from using commercial employment websites to using their own company websites to recruit candidates. While individuals are well advised to include an Internet component in their job search, especially focusing on employer websites, they also are well advised to spend most of their time engaged in job search activities that have real payoffs, such as networking for information, advice, and referrals (Chapter 12) and contacting employers by telephone and in person. For job seekers, the real power of the Internet lies in conducting research on jobs, employers, and communities and for communicating with individuals by e-mail.

> *The Internet is a big disappointment for many job seekers. In fact, recent surveys indicate that fewer than 20 percent of candidates get jobs through their online job search efforts.*

MYTH 28:   The best way to ace the job interview is to practice answers to anticipated interview questions.

REALITY: The job interview is much more than just providing canned answers to anticipated interview questions. Employers are looking for signs of likability, competence, and intelligence throughout all phases of the interview. Since over 80 percent of what's communicated in the interview is nonverbal, be sure to pay particular attention to your nonverbal behaviors, such as attire, handshake, eye contact, and vocalized pauses. Avoid memorizing answers to questions since you will more likely appear coached rather than candid. Two of the most important things you should do during the interview is (1) ask intelligent questions and (2) close the interview properly.

MYTH 29: Salaries are pre-determined by employers.

REALITY: Most salaries are negotiable within certain ranges and limits. Before you ever apply or interview for a position, you should know what the salary range is for the type of position you seek. When you finally discuss the salary question – preferably at the end of the final job interview – do so with this range in mind. Assuming you have adequately demonstrated your value to the employer, try to negotiate the highest possible salary within the range.

MYTH 30: It's better to concentrate on negotiating a gross salary figure rather than focus on benefits and perks.

REALITY: It depends on the employer and situation. Benefits and perks can translate into a significant amount of compensation. In fact, the U.S. Department of Labor reports that, on average, 43 percent of total compensation is in the form of benefits. Benefits such as stock options, profit sharing, disability insurance, and child care can add up to a significant amount of compensation. Make sure you look at the total compensation package rather than just the gross salary figure. For example, a $50,000 base salary with Employer X may actually be worth $80,000 with benefits, whereas a $60,000 base salary with Employer Y may only be worth $70,000 with benefits.

MYTH 31: It's best to relocate to a booming community.

REALITY: Similar to the "disappearing job" phenomenon for college majors, today's economically booming communities may be tomorrow's busts. It's best to select a community that is conducive to your lifestyle preferences as well as has a sufficiently diversified economy to weather boom-and-bust economic cycles.

MYTH 32: It's best to broadcast or "shotgun" your resume to as many employers as possible.

REALITY: Broadcasting your resume to employers is a game of chance in which you usually waste your time and money. It's always best to target your resume on those employers who have vacancies or who might have openings in the near future. Your single best approach for uncovering job leads will be the process called networking.

You also should be aware of several other realities which will affect your job search or which you might find helpful in developing your plan of action for finding a job or changing a career:

- **You will find less competition for high-level jobs than for middle- and low-level jobs.** If you aim high, yet are realistic, you may be pleasantly surprised with the results.

- **Human resources or personnel offices seldom hire.** They primarily screen candidates for employers who are found in operating units of organizations. Knowing this, you should focus your job search efforts on those who do the actual hiring – the hiring managers.

- **Employment firms and personnel agencies may not help you.** Most work for employers and themselves rather than for applicants. Few have your best interests at heart. Use them only after you have investigated their effectiveness. Avoid firms that require up-front money for vague promises of performance.

- **It is better to narrow or "rifle" your job search on particular organizations and individuals rather than broaden or "shotgun"** it to many alternatives. If you remain focused, you will be better able to accomplish your goals.

- **Most people can make satisfying job and career changes.** They should minimize efforts in the advertised job market and concentrate instead on planning and implementing a well organized job search tailored to the realities of the hidden job market.

- **Jobs and careers tend to be fluid and changing.** Knowing this, you should concentrate on acquiring and marketing skills, talents, and abilities which can be transferred from one job to another.

- **Millions of job vacancies are available every day** because new jobs are created, and people resign, retire, get fired, or die.

- **Most people, regardless of their position or status, love to talk about their work and give advice** to both friends and strangers. You can learn the most about job opportunities and alternative careers by talking to such people.

- **Politics are both ubiquitous and dangerous in many organizations.** If you think you are above politics, you may quickly become one of its victims. Unfortunately, you only learn about "local politics" **after** you accept a position and begin relating to players in the organization.

As you conduct your job search, you will encounter many of these and other myths and realities about how you should relate to the job market. Several people will give you advice. While much of this advice will be useful, a great deal of it will be useless and misleading. You should be skeptical of well-meaning individuals who most likely will reiterate the same job and career myths. You should be particularly leery of those who try to **sell** you their advice. Always remember you are entering a relatively disorganized and chaotic job market where you can find numerous job opportunities. Your task is to organize the chaos around your skills and interests. You must convince prospective employers that they will like you more than other "qualified" candidates.

Find Jobs and Change Careers

If you are looking for your first job, re-entering the job market after a lengthy absence, or planning a job or career change, you will join an army of millions of individuals who do so each year. Indeed, between 10 and 15 million people find themselves unemployed each year. Millions of others try to increase their satisfaction within the workplace as well as advance their careers by looking for alternative jobs and careers. If you are like most other Americans, you will make more than 10 job changes and between three and five career changes during your lifetime.

Most people make job or career transitions by accident. They do little other than take advantage of opportunities that may arise unexpectedly. While chance and luck do play important roles in finding employment, we recommend that you **plan** for future job and career changes so that you will experience even greater degrees of chance and luck!

Finding a job or changing a career in a systematic and well-planned manner is hard yet rewarding work. The task should first be based upon a clear understanding of the key ingredients that define jobs and careers. Starting with this understanding, you should next convert key concepts into action steps for implementing your job search.

A career is a series of jobs which have common skill, interest, and motivational bases. You may change jobs several times without changing careers. But once you change skills, interests, and motivations, you change careers.

It's not easy to find a job given the present structure of the job market. You will find the job market to be relatively disorganized, although it projects an outward appearance of coherence. If you seek comprehensive, accurate, and timely job information, the job market will frustrate you with its poor avenues of communication. While you will find many employment services ready to assist you, such services tend to be fragmented and their performance is often disappointing. Job search methods are controversial and many are ineffective.

> *If you seek comprehensive, accurate, and timely job information, the job market will frustrate you.*

No system is organized to give people jobs. At best you will encounter a **decentralized and fragmented system** consisting of job listings in newspapers, trade journals, employment offices, or on the Internet – all designed to link candidates to job openings. Many people will try to sell you questionable job services and information. In the end, most systems organized to help you find a job do not provide you with the information you need in order to land a job that is most related to your skills and interests.

Understand the Career Development Process

Finding a job is both an art and a science; it encompasses a variety of basic facts, principles, and skills which can be learned but which also must be adapted to individual situations. Thus, **learning how to find a job** can be as important to career success as **knowing how to perform a job**. Indeed, job finding skills are often as important to career success as job performance or work-content skills.

Our understanding of how to find jobs and change careers is illustrated on pages 91 and 92. As outlined on page 91, you should involve yourself in a four-step career development process as you prepare to move from one job to another:

The Career Development Process

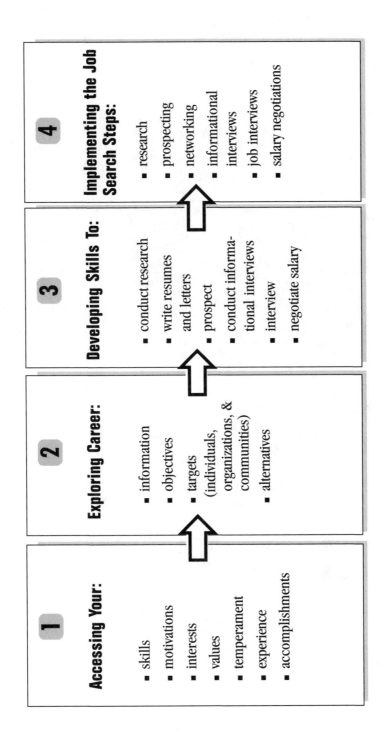

1

Accessing Your:

- skills
- motivations
- interests
- values
- temperament
- experience
- accomplishments

2

Exploring Career:

- information
- objectives
- targets (individuals, organizations, & communities)
- alternatives

3

Developing Skills To:

- conduct research
- write resumes and letters
- prospect
- conduct informational interviews
- interview
- negotiate salary

4

Implementing the Job Search Steps:

- research
- prospecting
- networking
- informational interviews
- job interviews
- salary negotiations

Job Search Steps and Stages

7. Negotiate salary and terms of employment

6. Manage Job Interviews

5. Conduct informational/ networking interviews

4. Produce resumes and job search letters

3. Research individuals, organizations, communities, and jobs

2. Specify a job/career objective

1. Identify motivated skills and abilities

1. Conduct a self-assessment

This first step involves assessing your skills, abilities, motivations, interests, values, temperament, experience, and accomplishments – the major concern of this book. Your basic strategy is to develop a firm foundation of information on **yourself** before proceeding to other stages in the career development process. This self-assessment develops the necessary self-awareness from which you can effectively communicate your qualifications to employers as well as focus and build your career.

2. Gather career and job information

Closely related to the first step, this second step is an exploratory, research phase of your career development. Here you need to formulate goals, gather information about alternative jobs and careers through reading and talking to informed people, and then narrow your alternatives to specific jobs.

3. Develop job search skills

The third step focuses on specific job search skills for landing the job you want. As further outlined on page 91, these job search skills are closely related to one another as a series of **job search steps**. They involve conducting research, writing resumes and letters, prospecting and networking, conducting informational interviews, interviewing for a job, and negotiating salary and terms of employment. Each of these job search skills involves well-defined strategies and tactics you must learn in order to be effective in the job market.

4. Implement each job search step

The final career development step emphasizes the importance of transforming understanding into **action**. You do this by implementing each job search step which already incorporates the knowledge, skills, and abilities you acquired in Steps 1, 2, and 3.

Organize and Sequence Your Job Search

The figure on page 92 further expands our career development process by examining the key elements in a successful job search. It consists of a seven-step process which relates your past, present, and future. We cover all of these steps in subsequent chapters which deal with skills assessment, research, resume writing, networking, interviewing, and salary negotiations.

Based on this concept, **your past** is well integrated into the process of finding a job or changing your career. Therefore, you should feel comfortable conducting your job search: it represents the best of what you are in terms of your past and present accomplishments as these relate to your present and future goals. If you base your job search on this process concept, you will communicate your **best self** to employers as well as focus on **your strengths** both during the job search and on the job.

Since the individual job search steps are interrelated, they should be followed in sequence. If you fail to properly complete the initial self-assessment steps, your job search may become haphazard, aimless, and costly. For example, you should never write a resume (Step 3) before first conducting an assessment of your skills (Step 1) and identifying your objective (Step 2). Relating Step 1 to Step 2 is especially critical to the successful implementation of all other job search steps. You **must** complete Steps 1 and 2 **before** continuing on to the other steps. Steps 3 to 6 may be conducted simultaneously because they complement and reinforce one another.

Try to sequence your job search as closely to these steps as possible. The true value of doing so will become very apparent as you implement your plan.

The processes and steps identified on pages 91 and 92 represent the careering and re-careering processes used successfully by thousands of job-seekers during the past 30 years. They are equally applicable as careering and re-careering processes for the decade ahead as long as you recognize the importance of acquiring work-content skills along with job search skills.

You must do much more than just know how to find a job. In the job markets of today and tomorrow, you need to constantly review your work-content skills to make sure they are appropriate for the changing job market. Assuming you have the necessary work-content skills, you should be ready to target your skills on particular jobs and careers that you do well and enjoy doing. You will be able to avoid the trap of trying to fit into jobs that are not conducive to your particular mix of interests, abilities, skills, and motivations.

Test Your Careering Competencies

Knowing **where** the jobs are is important to your job search. But knowing **how to find a job** is even more important. Before you acquire names, addresses, and phone numbers of potential employers, you should possess the necessary job search knowledge and skills for gathering and using job information effectively.

Answers to many of your job-related questions are found by examining your present level of job search knowledge and skills. Successful job seekers, for example, use a great deal of information as well as specific skills and strategies for getting the jobs they want.

Let's begin by testing for the level of job search information, skills, and strategies you currently possess as well as those you need to develop and improve. Identify your level of job search competence by completing the exercise on pages 96-97.

After you finish this exercise, calculate your overall careering competencies by adding the numbers you circled for a composite score. If your total is more than 75 points, you need to work on developing your careering skills. How you scored each item will indicate to what degree you need to work on improving specific job search skills. If your score is under 50 points, you are well on your way toward job search success. In either case, this book should help you better focus your job search as well as identify job search skills you need to acquire or strengthen.

Career Planning and Job Search Services

While some people can successfully conduct a job search based on the advice of books such as this, many others also need the assistance of various professional groups that offer specific career planning and job search services. These groups offer everything from testing and assessment services to offering contacts with potential employers, including job vacancy information and temporary employment services. Some do one-on-one career counseling while others sponsor one- to three-day workshops or six- to 12-week courses on the various steps in the career planning process. You should know something about these services before you invest your time and money beyond this and other career planning and job search books.

Make Wise Choices

You have two options in organizing your job search. First, you can follow the principles and advice outlined in this and many other self-directed books. Just read the chapters and then put them into practice by following the step-by-step instructions. Second, you may wish to seek professional help to either supplement or replace this book. Indeed, many people will read parts of this book – perhaps all of it – and do nothing. Lacking sufficient time or motivation, or failing to follow through, many people eventually seek professional help to organize and implement their job search. Hopefully, they will work with a career professional or career coach who can provide them with assistance in completing each step outlined in this book. Such assistance results in creating a structure for implementation.

Your Careering Competencies

INSTRUCTIONS: Respond to each statement by circling which number at the right best represents your situation.

SCALE:　　1 = strongly agree　　　4 = disagree
　　　　　　　2 = agree　　　　　　　5 = strongly disagree
　　　　　　　3 = maybe, not certain

1. I know what motivates me to excel at work.　　　1 2 3 4 5

2. I can identify my strongest abilities and skills.　　　1 2 3 4 5

3. I have seven major achievements that clarify a pattern of interests and abilities that are relevant to my job and career.　　　1 2 3 4 5

4. I know what I both like and dislike in work.　　　1 2 3 4 5

5. I know what I want to do during the next 10 years.　　　1 2 3 4 5

6. I have a well defined career objective that focuses my job search on particular organizations and employers.　　　1 2 3 4 5

7. I know what skills I can offer employers in different occupations.　　　1 2 3 4 5

8. I know what skills employers most seek in candidates.　　　1 2 3 4 5

9. I can clearly explain to employers what I do well and enjoy doing.　　　1 2 3 4 5

10. I can specify why employers should hire me.　　　1 2 3 4 5

11. I can gain the support of family and friends for making a job or career change.　　　1 2 3 4 5

12. I can find 10 to 20 hours a week to conduct a part-time job search.　　　1 2 3 4 5

13. I have the financial ability to sustain a three-month job search.　　　1 2 3 4 5

14. I can conduct library and interview research on different occupations, employers, organizations, and communities.   1 2 3 4 5

15. I can write different types of effective resumes and job search/thank you letters.   1 2 3 4 5

16. I can produce and distribute resumes and letters to the right people.   1 2 3 4 5

17. I can list my major accomplishments in action terms.   1 2 3 4 5

18. I can identify and target employers I want to interview.   1 2 3 4 5

19. I can develop a job referral network.   1 2 3 4 5

20. I can persuade others to join in forming a job search support group.   1 2 3 4 5

21. I can prospect for job leads.   1 2 3 4 5

22. I can use the telephone to develop prospects and get referrals and interviews.   1 2 3 4 5

23. I can plan and implement an effective direct-mail job search campaign.   1 2 3 4 5

24. I can generate at least one job interview for every 10 job search contacts I make.   1 2 3 4 5

25. I can follow up on job interviews.   1 2 3 4 5

26. I can negotiate a salary 10-20% above what an employer initially offers.   1 2 3 4 5

27. I can persuade an employer to renegotiate my salary after six months on the job.   1 2 3 4 5

28. I can create a position for myself in an organization.   1 2 3 4 5

TOTAL   _____

We recognize the value of professional assistance. Especially with the critical assessment and objective setting steps (Chapters 6, 7, and 8), some individuals may need more assistance than our advice and exercises provide. You may, for example, want to take a battery of tests to better understand your interests and values in relation to alternative jobs and careers. And still others, due to a combination of job loss, failed relationships, or depression, may need therapy best provided by a trained psychologist or psychiatrist rather than career testing and information services provided by career counselors. If any of these situations pertain to you, by all means seek professional help.

You also should beware of pitfalls in seeking professional advice. While many services are excellent, other services are useless and fraudulent. Remember, career planning and job assistance are big businesses involving millions of dollars each year. Many people enter these businesses without expertise. Professional certification in these areas is extremely weak to nonexistent in some states. Indeed, many so-called "professionals" get into the business because they are unemployed. In other words, they major in their own problem! Others are frauds and hucksters who prey on vulnerable and naive people who feel they need a "specialist" or "expert" to get them a job. They will take your money in exchange for promises. You will find several types of services promising to assist you in finding all types of jobs. You should know something about these professional services before you venture beyond this book.

If you are interested in exploring the services of job specialists, begin by looking in the Yellow Pages of your telephone directory under these headings: Management Consultants, Employment, Resumes, Career Planning, and Social Services. Several career planning and employment services are available, ranging from highly generalized to very specific services. Most services claim they can help you. If you read this book, you will be in a better position to seek out specific services as well as ask the right questions for screening the services. You may even discover you know more about finding a job than many of the so-called professionals!

Consider Alternative Services

At least 12 different career planning and employment services are available to assist you with your job search. Each has certain advantages and disadvantages. Approach them with caution. Never sign a contract before you read the fine print, get a second opinion, and talk to former clients about the **results** they achieved through the service. With these words of caution in mind, let's take a look at the variety of services available.

1. Public employment services

Public employment services usually consist of a state agency which provides employment assistance as well as dispenses unemployment compensation benefits. Employment assistance largely consists of job listings and counseling services. However, counseling services often screen individuals for employers who list with the public employment agency. If you are looking for an entry-level job or a job paying $18,000 to $40,000, contact this service. Most employers still do not list with this service, especially for positions paying more than $40,000 a year. Although the main purpose of these offices has been to dispense unemployment benefits, don't overlook these offices because of past stereotypes. The Workforce Development Act has re-energized such offices. Within the past three years, many of these offices have literally "reinvented" themselves for today's new job market with One-Stop Career Centers computerized job banks, counseling services, training programs, and other innovative organizational and technical approaches. Many of them offer useful employment services, including self-assessment and job search workshops as well as access to job listings on the Internet. Most of these offices are linked to America's Job Bank (www.ajb.dni.us), an electronic job bank which includes over 1 million job listings throughout the U.S. and abroad. This is one of the primier employment websites that offers a wealth of information and resources for job seekers. It's one all job seekers need to become familiar with. America's Job Bank, in turn, is linked to the U.S. Department of Labor's three other useful websites – America's CareerInfoNet (www. acinet.org), America's Service Locator (www.servicelocator.org), and Career OneStop (www.careeronestop.org). If you are a veteran, you will find many of the jobs listed with state employment offices give veterans preference in hiring. Go see for yourself if your state employment office offers useful services for you.

2. Private employment agencies

Private employment agencies work for money, either from applicants or employers. Approximately 8,000 such agencies operate nationwide. Many are highly specialized in technical, scientific, and financial fields. The majority of these firms serve the interests of employers since employers – not applicants – represent repeat business. While employers normally pay the placement fee, many agencies charge applicants 10 to 15 percent of their first year salary. These firms have one major advantage: job leads which you may have difficulty uncovering elsewhere.

Especially for highly specialized fields, a good firm can be extremely helpful. The major disadvantages are that they can be costly and the quality of the firms varies. Be careful in how you deal with them. Make sure you understand the fee structure and what they will do for you before you sign anything. The bi-annual directory *JobBank Guide to Employment Services* (Adams Media) includes data on nearly 3,000 firms.

3. Temporary staffing firms

During the past decade temporary staffing firms have come of age as more and more employers turn to them for recruitment assistance. They offer a variety of employment services to both applicants and employers who are either looking for temporary work and workers or who want to better screen applicants and employers. Many of these firms, such as Manpower (www.manpower.com), Olsten (www.olsten.com), and Kelly Services (www.kellyservices.com), recruit individuals for a wide range of positions and skill levels as well as full-time employment. Some firms, such as Robert Half International (www.rhii.com) specialize in certain types of workers, such as accounting, law, IT, and computer personnel. If you are interested in "testing the job waters," you may want to contact these firms for information on their services. Employers – not job seekers – pay for these services. While many of these firms are listed in your community Yellow Pages, most have websites. The following websites are especially popular with individuals interested in part-time, temporary, or contract work: www.net-temps.com, www.eLance.com, www. ework.com, www.guru.com, www.contractorforum.com, www.talentmarket.monster.com, and www.talentgateway.com.

4. College/university placement offices

College and university placement offices provide in-house career planning services for graduating students. While some give assistance to alumni, don't expect too much help if you have already graduated; you may, instead, need to contact the alumni office which may offer employment services. Many college placement offices are understaffed or provide only rudimentary services, such as maintaining a career planning library, coordinating on-campus interviews for graduating seniors, and conducting workshops on how to write resumes and conduct interviews. Others provide a full range of well supported services including testing and one-on-one counseling. Indeed, many community colleges offer such services to members of the community on a walk-in basis. You can use their libraries and computerized career assessment programs, take personality and interest inventories, or attend special workshops or full-semester career planning courses which will take you through each step of the career planning and job search processes. You may want to enroll in such a course since it is likely to provide just enough structure and content to assess your motivated abilities and skills and to assist you in implementing a successful job search plan. Check with your local campus to see what services you might use. Many of the college and university placement offices belong to the National Association of Colleges and Employers, which operates its own employment website: www.jobweb.com. This site includes a wealth of information on employment for college graduates (see the "Site Map" section: www. jobweb.com/search/sitemap.htm). Its "Career Library" section includes direct links to hundreds of college and university placement offices: www.jobweb.com/Career-Development/collegeres.htm. To find college alumni offices, visit the following websites: www.alumni.net, www.bc harrispub.com, and www.jobweb.com/After_College/alumni.net. Since colleges and universities tend to be very Web-savvy, you can visit hundreds of their career websites to acquire all types of useful free information on conducting an effective job search. One of our favorites is the website operated by the Career Center at the College of William and Mary (www.wm.edu/career). Indeed, searching many of these college and university websites is comparable to having your own personal career counselor – without having to go to college!

5. Private career and job search firms

Private career and job search firms help individuals acquire job search skills and coach them through the process of finding a job. They do not find you a job. In other words, they teach you much of what is outlined in this book. Expect to pay anywhere from $1,500 to $10,000 for this service. If you need a structured environment for conducting your job search, contract with one of these firms for professional assistance. One of the major such firms is BH Careers International. Many of their pioneering career planning and job search methods are incorporated in this book as well as can be found in five other key job search books: _Haldane's Best Resumes for Professionals_, _Haldane's Best Cover Letters for Professionals_, _Haldane's Best Answers to Tough Interview Questions_, _Haldane's Best Salary Tips for Professionals_, and _Haldane's Best Employment Websites for Professionals_ (Impact Publications – see the order form at the end of this book or www.impactpublications.com). You will find over 60 branches of this firm located in the United States, Canada, Australia, England, Scotland, and the United Arab Emirates. For information on the BH Careers International office nearest you, visit their website: www.bhcareers.com. Other firms offering similar services include Right Management Associates (www.right.com), R. L. Stevens & Associates (www.interviewing.com), and Lee Hecht Harrison (www.lhh.com/us).

6. Executive search firms and headhunters

Executive search firms work for employers in finding employees to fill critical positions in the $50,000 plus salary range. They also are called "headhunters," "management consultants," and "executive recruiters." These firms play an important role in linking high level technical and managerial talent to organizations. Don't expect to contract for these services. Executive recruiters work for employers, not applicants. If a friend or relative is in this business or you have relevant skills of interest to these firms, let them know you are available – and ask for their advice. On the other hand, you may want to contact firms that specialize in recruiting individuals with your skill specialty. For a comprehensive listing of these firms, see the latest annual edition of *The Directory of Executive Recruiters* (Kennedy Information, www.kennedyinfo.com; also see the order form at the end of this book and www.impactpublications. com). Several companies, such as www.resumezapper.com, www.blast myresume.com, and www.resumeblaster.com, offer e-mail resume blasting services that primarily target headhunters. For a fee, which usually ranges from $50 to $200, these firms will blast your resume to 5,000 to 10,000 headhunters. This is a quick, easy, and inexpensive way to reach thousands of headhunters and executive search firms. However, as we noted in Myth #32 (see pages 87-88), this resume distribution method also may be a waste of time and money. Approach it with a healthy sense of skepticism.

7. Marketing services

Marketing services represent an interesting combination of job search and executive search activities. They can cost $2,500 or more, and they work with individuals anticipating a starting salary of at least $75,000 but preferably over $100,000. These firms try to minimize the time and risk of applying for jobs. A typical operation begins with a client paying a $150 fee for developing psychological, skills, and interests profiles. If you pass this stage – most anyone with money does – you go on to the next one-on-one stage. At this point, a marketing plan is outlined and a contract signed for specific services. Work for the clients usually involves activities centered on the resume and interviewing. Using word processing software, the firm normally develops a slick "professional" resume and sends it by mail or e-mail, along with a cover letter, to hundreds – maybe thousands – of firms. Clients are then briefed and sent to interview with interested employers. While you can save money and achieve the same results on your own, these firms do have one major advantage: They save you **time** by doing most of the work for you. Again, approach these services with caution and with the knowledge that you can probably do just as well – if not better – on your own by following the step-by-step advice of this and other job search books.

8. Women's centers and special career services

Women's centers and special career services for displaced workers, such as 40-Plus Clubs (www.40plus.org/chapters) and Five O'Clock Clubs (www.fiveoclockclub.com), have been established to respond to the employment needs of special groups. Women's centers are particularly active in sponsoring career planning workshops and job information networks. These centers tend to be geared toward elementary job search activities, because many of their clientele consist of homemakers who are entering or re-entering the workforce with little knowledge of the job market. Special career services arise at times for different categories of employees. For example, unemployed aerospace engineers, teachers, veterans, air traffic controllers, and government employees have formed special groups for developing job search skills and sharing job leads.

9. Testing and assessment centers

Testing and assessment centers provide assistance for identifying vocational skills, interests, and objectives. Usually staffed by trained professionals, these centers administer several types of tests and charge from $300 to $800 per person. You may wish to use some of these services if you feel our activities in Chapters 6, 7, and 8 generate insufficient information on your skills and interests to formulate your job objective. If you use such services, make sure you are given one or both of the two most popular and reliable tests: *Myers-Briggs Type Indicator* and the *Strong Interest Inventory*. You should find both tests helpful in better understanding your interests and decision-making styles. However, try our exercises before you hire a psychologist or visit a testing center. If you first complete these exercises, you will be in a better position to know exactly what you need from such centers. In many cases, the career office at your local community college or women's center can administer these tests at minimum cost. At the same time, many of these testing and assessment services are now available online. Check out these popular websites: www.skillsone.com, www.self-directed-search.com, www.careerlab.com, www.personalityonline.com, www.assessment.com, and www.personalitytype.com.

10. Job fairs or career conferences

Job fairs or career conferences are organized by a variety of groups – from schools and government agencies to headhunters, employment agencies, and professional associations – to link applicants to employers. Usually consisting of one- to two-day meetings in a hotel or conference center, employers meet with applicants as a group and on a one-to-one basis. Employers give presentations on their companies, applicants circulate resumes, and employers interview candidates. Many such conferences are organized to attract hard-to-recruit groups, such as engineers, computer programmers, and clerical and service workers. These are excellent sources for job leads and information on specific employers – if you are invited to attend or if the meeting is open to the public. Employers pay for this service, although some job fairs or career conferences may charge job seekers a nominal registration fee.

11. Professional associations

Professional associations often provide placement assistance. This usually consists of listing job vacancies in publications, maintaining a resume database, and organizing a job information exchange at annual conferences. Many large associations operate their own online employment sites; members can include their resume in an electronic database and employers can access the database to search for qualified candidates. Annual conferences are good sources for making job contacts in different geographic locations within a particular professional field. But don't expect too much. Talking to people (networking) at professional conferences may yield better results than reading job listings, placing your resume in a database, or interviewing at conference placement centers. For excellent online directories of professional associations, be sure to visit these two sites: www.ipl.org/ref/AON and www.asaenet.org.

12. Professional resume writers

Professional resume writers are increasingly playing an important role in career planning. Each year thousands of job seekers rely on these professionals for assistance in writing their resumes. Many of them also provide useful job search tips on resume distribution, cover letters, and networking. Charging from $100 to $600 for writing a resume, they work with the whole spectrum of job seekers – entry-level to senior executives making millions of dollars each year. While not certified career counselors, many of these professionals have their own associations and certification groups. If you are interested in working with a professional resume writer, visit the following websites for information on this network of career professionals: www.parw.com, www.prwra.com, and www.nrwa.com. Examples of their high-end work can be found in Wendy Enelow's two books: _Best Resumes for $100,000+ Jobs_ and _Best Cover Letters for $100,000+ Jobs_ (Impact Publications – see order form at the end of this book or visit the publisher's online bookstore: www.impactpublications.com).

Choose the Best

Other types of career planning and employment services are growing and specializing in particular occupational fields. You may wish to use these services as a supplement to this book.

Whatever you do, be a smart shopper for career planning and job search services. Proceed with caution, know exactly what you are getting into, and choose the best. Remember, there is no such thing as a free lunch, and you often get less than what you pay for. At the same time, the most expensive services are not necessarily the best. Indeed, the free and inexpensive career planning services offered by many community or junior colleges – libraries, computerized career assessment programs, testing, and workshops – may be all you need. On the other hand, don't be afraid to spend some money on getting the best services. You may quickly discover that this money was well spent when you land a job that pays 20 to 40 percent more than your previous job! Whatever you do, don't be _"pennywise but pound foolish"_ by trying to do your job search on the cheap. If you have difficulty writing a first-class resume, by all means contact a resume writing pro who can put together a dynamite resume that truly represents what you have done, can do, and will do in the future.

After reading this book, you should be able to make intelligent decisions about what, when, where, and with what results you can use professional assistance. Shop around, compare services and costs, ask questions, talk to former clients, and read the fine print before giving an employment expert a job using your hard earned money!

When in Doubt, Take Purposeful Action

The old adage *"When in doubt, do something"* is especially relevant when expanded to include a thoughtful plan of action related to the job search process: *"When in doubt, engage in a concrete activity related to the sequence of job search steps."* This might include conducting research on communities, companies, positions, and salaries; surveying job vacancy announcements; writing a resume and job search letters; or contacting three employers each day.

But developing a plan and taking action are much easier said than done. If conducted properly, a job search can become an extremely time-consuming activity. It inevitably competes with other personal and professional priorities. That's why you need to make some initial decisions as to how and when you will conduct a job search. How much time, for example, are you willing to set aside each day or week to engage in each of the seven job search activities outlined at the beginning of this chapter? After you've spent numerous hours identifying your abilities and skills and formulating an objective, are you willing to commit yourself to 20 hours a week to network for information and advice? If you are unwilling to commit both your time and yourself to each activity within the process, you may remain stuck, and inevitably frustrated, at the initial stages of self-awareness and understanding. Success only comes to those who take action at other stages in the job search process.

Use Time Wisely

If you decide to conduct your own job search with minimum assistance from professionals, your major cost will be your time. Therefore, you must find sufficient time to devote to your job search. Ask yourself this question:

*"How valuable is my time in relation to finding a
job or changing my career?"*

Assign a dollar value to your time. For example, is your time worth $3, $5, $10, $25, $50, or $100 an hour? Compare your figure with what you might pay a professional for doing much of the job search work for you. Normal professional fees range from $1,500 to $10,000.

The time you devote to your job search will depend on whether you want to work at it on a full-time or part-time basis. If you are unemployed, by all means make this a full-time endeavor – 40 to 80 hours per week. If you are presently employed, we do not recommend quitting your job in order to look for employment. You will probably need the steady income and attendant health benefits during your transition period. Furthermore, it is easier to find new employment by appearing employed. Unemployed people project a negative image in the eyes of many employers – they appear to need a job. **Your goal is to find a job based on your strengths rather than your needs.**

However, if you go back to school for skills retraining, your present employment status may be less relevant to employers. Your major strength is the fact that you have acquired a skill the employer needs. If you quit your job and spend money retraining, you will communicate a certain degree of risk-taking, drive, responsibility, and dedication which employers readily seek, but seldom find, in candidates today.

Assuming you will be conducting a job search on a part-time basis – 15 to 25 hours per week – you will need to find the necessary time for these job activities. Unfortunately, most people are busy, having programmed every hour to "important" personal and professional activities. Thus, conducting a job search for 15 or more hours a week means that some things will have to go or receive low priority in relation to your job search.

This is easier said than done. The job search often gets low priority. It competes with other important daily routines, such as attending meetings, taking children to games, going shopping, watching favorite TV programs, and using the Internet. Rather than fight with your routines – and create family disharmony and stress – make your job search part of your daily routines by improving your overall management of time.

Certain time management techniques will help you make your job search a high-priority activity in your daily schedule. These practices may actually lower your present stress level and thus enhance your overall effectiveness.

Time management experts estimate that most people waste their time on unimportant matters. Lacking priorities, people spend 80 percent of their time on trivia and 20 percent of their time on the important matters which should get the most attention. If you reverse this emphasis, you could have a great deal of excess time – and probably experience less stress attendant with the common practice of crisis-managing the critical 20 percent.

Before reorganizing your time, you must know how you normally use your time. Therefore, complete the exercise on pages 108-109 to assess your time management behavior. While many of these statements are relevant to individuals in managerial positions, respond to those statements that are most relevant to your employment situation. If you answered "no" to many of these statements, you should consider incorporating a few basic time management principles and practices into your daily schedule.

Don't go to extremes by drastically restructuring your life around the "religion" of time management. If you followed all the advice of time management experts, you would probably alienate your family, friends, and colleagues with your narrow efficiency mentality! A realistic approach is to start monitoring your time use and then gradually re-organize your time according

Your Time Management Inventory

Respond to each statement by circling "yes" or "no," depending on which response better represents your normal pattern of behavior.

1. I have a written set of long, intermediate, and short-range goals for myself (and my family).   Yes   No

2. I have a clear idea of what I will do today at work and at home.   Yes   No

3. I have a clear idea of what I want to accomplish at work this coming week and month.   Yes   No

4. I set priorities and follow through on the most important tasks first.   Yes   No

5. I judge my success by the results I produce in relation to my goals.   Yes   No

6. I use a daily, weekly, and monthly calendar for scheduling appointments and setting work targets.   Yes   No

7. I delegate as much work as possible.   Yes   No

8. I get my subordinates to organize their time in relation to mine.   Yes   No

9. I file only those things which are essential to my work. When in doubt, I throw it out.   Yes   No

10. I throw away junk mail.   Yes   No

11. My briefcase is uncluttered, including only essential materials; it serves as my office away from the office.   Yes   No

12. I minimize the number of meetings and concentrate on making decisions rather than discussing aimlessly.   Yes   No

13. I make frequent use of the telephone and face-to-face encounters rather than written communications.   Yes   No

14. I make minor decisions quickly.   Yes   No

15. I concentrate on accomplishing one thing
    at a time.   Yes   No

16. I handle each piece of paper once and
    only once.   Yes   No

17. I answer most letters on the letter I receive
    with either a handwritten or typed message.   Yes   No

18. I set deadlines for myself and others and
    follow through in meeting them.   Yes   No

19. I reserve time each week to plan.   Yes   No

20. My desk and work area are well organized
    and clear.   Yes   No

21. I know how to say "no" and do so.   Yes   No

22. I first skim books, articles, and other forms
    of written communication for ideas before
    reading further.   Yes   No

23. I monitor my time use during the day by
    asking myself "How can I best use my
    time at present?"   Yes   No

24. I deal with the present by getting things
    done that need to be done.   Yes   No

25. I maintain a time log to monitor the best
    use of my time.   Yes   No

26. I place a dollar value on my time and
    behave accordingly.   Yes   No

27. I – not others – control my time.   Yes   No

28. My briefcase includes items I can work on
    during spare time in waiting rooms, lines,
    and airports.   Yes   No

29. I keep my door shut when I'm working.   Yes   No

30. I regularly evaluate to what degree I am
    achieving my stated goals.   Yes   No

to goals and priorities. This is all you need to do. Forget the elaborate flow charts that are the stuff of expensive time management workshops and consultants. Start by developing a time management log that helps you monitor your present use of time. Keep daily records of how you use your time over a two-week period. Identify who controls your time and the results of your time utilization. Within two weeks, clear patterns will emerge. You may learn that you have an "open door" policy that enables others to control your time, leaving little time to do your own work. Based on this information, you may need to close your door and be more selective about access. You may find from your analysis that you use most time for activities that have few if any important outcomes. If this is the case, then you may need to set goals and prioritize daily activities.

A simple yet effective technique for improving your time management practices is to complete a "to do" list for each day. You can purchase tablets of these forms in many stationery and office supply stores, or you can develop your own "Things To Do Today" list. This list also should prioritize which activities are most important to accomplish each day. Include at the top of your list a particular job search activity or several activities that should be completed on each day. If you follow this simple time management practice, you will find the necessary time to include your job search in your daily routines. You can give your job search top priority. Better still, you will accomplish more in less time, and with better results.

Plan to Take Action

While we recommend that you plan your job search, we also caution you to avoid the excesses of too much planning. Like time management, planning should not be all-consuming. Planning makes sense because it focuses attention and directs action toward specific goals and targets. It requires you to set goals and develop strategies for achieving the goals. However, too much planning can blind you to unexpected occurrences and opportunities – that wonderful experience called serendipity. Given the highly decentralized and chaotic nature of the job market, you want to do just enough planning so you will be in a position to take advantage of what will inevitably be unexpected occurrences and opportunities arising from your planned job search activities. Therefore, as you plan your job search, be sure you are flexible enough to take advantage of new opportunities.

Based on our previous discussion of the sequence of job search steps, we outline on page 111 a hypothetical plan for conducting an effective job search. This plan incorporates the individual job search activities over a six-month period. If you phase in the first five job search steps during the initial three to four weeks and continue the final four steps in subsequent weeks and months,

Organization of Job Search Activities

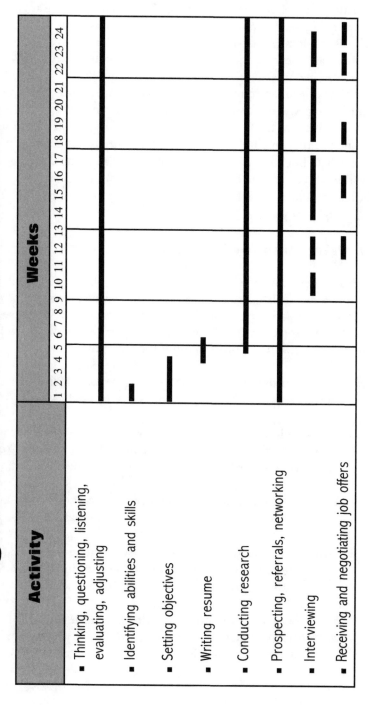

Activity	Weeks
	1 2 3 4 5 6 7 8 9 10 11 12 13 14 15 16 17 18 19 20 21 22 23 24
▪ Thinking, questioning, listening, evaluating, adjusting	
▪ Identifying abilities and skills	
▪ Setting objectives	
▪ Writing resume	
▪ Conducting research	
▪ Prospecting, referrals, networking	
▪ Interviewing	
▪ Receiving and negotiating job offers	

you should begin receiving job offers within two to three months after initiating your job search. Interviews and job offers can come anytime – often unexpectedly – as you conduct your job search. An average time is three months, but it can occur within a week or take as long as five months or more. If you plan, prepare, and persist at the job search, the pay-off will be job interviews and offers.

While three months may seem a long time, especially if you have just lost your job and you need work immediately, you can shorten your job search time by increasing the frequency of your individual job search activities. If you are job hunting on a full-time basis, you may be able to cut your job search time in half. But don't expect to get a job – especially a job that's right for you – within a week or two. Job hunting requires time and hard work – perhaps the hardest work you will ever do – but if done properly, it pays off with a job that is right for you.

20 Principles for Job Search Success

Success is determined by more than just a good plan getting implemented. We know success is not determined primarily by intelligence, time management, or luck. Based upon experience, theory, research, common sense, and acceptance of some self-transformation principles, we believe you will achieve job search success by following most of these 20 principles:

1. **You should work hard at finding a job:** Make this a daily endeavor and involve your family. Focus on specifics.

2. **You should not be discouraged by setbacks:** You are playing the odds, so expect disappointments and handle them in stride. You will get many "no's" before finding the one "yes" which is right for you.

3. **You should be patient and persevere:** Expect three to six months of hard work before you connect with the job that's right for you.

4. **You should be honest with yourself and others:** Honesty is always the best policy. But don't be naive and stupid by confessing your negatives and shortcomings to others.

5. **You should develop a positive attitude toward yourself:** Nobody wants to employ guilt-ridden people with inferiority complexes. Focus on your positive characteristics.

6. **You should associate with positive and successful people:** Finding a job largely depends on how well you relate to others. Avoid associating with negative and depressing people who complain and have a "you-can't-do-it" attitude. Run with winners who have a positive "can-do" outlook on life.

7. **You should set goals:** You should have a clear idea of what you want and where you are going. Without these, you will present a confusing and indecisive image to others. Clear goals help direct your job search into productive channels. Moreover, setting high goals will help make you work hard in getting what you want.

8. **You should plan:** Convert your goals into action steps that are organized as short-, intermediate-, and long-range plans.

9. **You should get organized:** Translate your plans into activities, targets, names, addresses, telephone numbers, and materials. Develop an efficient and effective filing system and use a large calendar to set time targets, record appointments, and compile useful information.

10. **You should be a good communicator:** Take stock of your oral, written, and nonverbal communication skills. How well do you communicate? Since most aspects of your job search involve communicating with others, and communication skills are one of the most sought-after skills, always present yourself well both verbally and nonverbally.

11. **You should be energetic and enthusiastic:** Employers are attracted to positive people. They don't like negative and depressing people who toil at their work. Generate enthusiasm both verbally and nonverbally. Check on your telephone voice – it may be more unenthusiastic than your face-to-face voice.

12. **You should ask questions:** Your best information comes from asking questions. Learn to develop intelligent questions that are non-aggressive, polite, and interesting to others. But don't ask too many questions and thereby become a bore.

13. **You should be a good listener:** Being a good listener is often more important than being a good questioner or talker. Learn to improve your face-to-face listening behavior (nonverbal cues) as well as remember and use information gained from others. Make others feel

they enjoyed talking with you, i.e., you are one of the few people who actually **listens** to what they say.

14. **You should be polite, courteous, and thoughtful:** Treat gatekeepers, especially receptionists, like human beings. Avoid being aggressive. Try to be polite, courteous, and gracious. Your social graces are being observed. Remember to send thank you letters – a very thoughtful thing to do in a job search. Even if rejected, thank employers for the "opportunity." They may later have additional opportunities, and they will remember you.

15. **You should be tactful:** Watch what you say to others about other people. Don't be a gossip, back-stabber, or confessor.

16. **You should maintain a professional stance:** Be neat in what you do and wear, and speak with the confidence, authority, and maturity of a professional.

17. **You should demonstrate your intelligence and competence:** Present yourself as someone who gets things done and achieves results – a **producer.** Employers generally seek people who are bright, hard working, responsible, communicate well, have positive personalities, maintain good interpersonal relations, are likable, observe dress and social codes, take initiative, are talented, possess expertise in particular areas, use good judgment, are cooperative, trustworthy, and loyal, generate confidence and credibility, and are conventional. In other words, they like people who score in the "excellent" to "outstanding" categories of a performance evaluation.

18. **You should not overdo your job search:** Don't engage in overkill and bore everyone with your job search stories. Achieve balance in everything you do. Occasionally take a few days off to do nothing related to your job search. Develop a system of incentives and rewards – such as two non-job search days a week if you accomplish targets A, B, C, and D.

19. **You should be open-minded and keep an eye out for "luck":** Too much planning can blind you to unexpected and fruitful opportunities. You should welcome serendipity. Learn to re-evaluate your goals and strategies. Seize new opportunities if appropriate.

20. **You should evaluate your progress and adjust:** Take two hours once every two weeks and evaluate your accomplishments. If necessary, tinker with your plans and reorganize your activities and priorities. Don't become too routinized and thereby kill creativity and innovation.

These principles should provide you with an initial orientation for starting your job search. As you become more experienced, you will develop your own set of operating principles that should work for you in particular employment situations.

Take Risks and Handle Rejections

You can approach a job or career change in various ways. Some actions have higher pay-offs than others. Many people waste time by doing nothing, reconstructing the past, worrying about the future, and thinking about what they should have done. This negative approach impedes rather than advances careers.

*Job hunting is a highly ego-involved activity. While your greatest difficulty may be in handling rejections, you must encounter rejections **before** you get acceptances.*

A second approach is to do what most people do when looking for a job. They examine classified ads, respond to vacancy announcements, put their resume online, and complete applications in personnel offices or online. While this approach is better than doing nothing, it is relatively inefficient as well as ineffective. You compete with many others who are using the same approach. Furthermore, the vacancy announcements do not represent the true number of job vacancies, nor do they offer the best opportunities. As we will see in Chapter 10, you should use this approach to some degree, but it should not preoccupy your time. Responding to vacancy announcements is a game of chance, and the odds are usually against you. It makes you too dependent upon others to give you a job.

The third approach to making a job change requires **taking creative action** on your part. You must become a self-reliant risk-taker. You identify what it is you want to do, what you can do (acquired skills and catalogued accomplishments), and organize yourself accordingly by following the methods outlined in subsequent chapters. You don't need to spend much time with classified ads, employment agencies, personnel offices, and Internet recruitment sites. And you don't need to worry about your future. You take charge of your future by initiating a job search which pays off with interviews and job offers. Your major investment is **time**. Your major risk is **rejection**.

Job hunting is a highly ego-involved activity. You place your past, abilities, and self-image before strangers who don't know who you are or what you can do. Being rejected or having someone say "no" to you will probably be your greatest job hunting difficulty. We know most people can handle two or three "no's" before they get discouraged. If you approach your job search from a less ego-involved perspective, you can take "no's" in stride; they are a normal aspect of your job search experience. Be prepared to encounter 10, 20, or 50 "no's." Remember, the odds are in your favor. For every 20 "no's" you get, you also should uncover one or two "yeses." The more rejections you get, the more acceptances you also will get. Therefore, you must encounter rejections **before** you get acceptances.

This third approach is the approach of this book. Experience with thousands of clients shows that the most successful job seekers are those who develop a high degree of self-reliance, maintain a positive self-image, and are willing to risk being rejected time after time without becoming discouraged. This approach will work for you if you follow our advice on how to become a self-reliant risk-taker in today's job market. Better yet, use the networking strategies outlined in Chapter 12 as well as more fully developed in our *Interview for Success* and *The Savvy Networker* books, and you can significantly decrease the number of "no's" you receive on your way to a job that's right for you.

Consider Forming a Support Group

We believe most people can conduct a successful job search on their own by following the step-by-step procedures of this book. We know they work because these methods have been used by thousands of successful job hunters. We also know it's difficult to become a risk-taker, especially in an area where few people have a base of experience and knowledge. Therefore, we recommend sharing the risks with others.

Our self-directed methods work well when you join others in forming a job search group or club. The group provides a certain degree of security which is often necessary when launching a new and unknown adventure. In addition, the group can provide important information on job leads. Members will critique your approach and progress. They will provide you with psychological supports as you experience the frustration of rejections and the joys of success. You also will be helping others who will be helping you. Some career counselors estimate that membership in such groups can cut one's job search time by as much as 50 percent!

You can form your own group by working with your spouse or by finding friends who are interested in looking for a new job. Your friends may know other friends or colleagues who are interested in doing the same. Some of your friends may surprise you by indicating they would like to join your group out of curiosity. If you are over 40 years of age, check to see if there is a chapter of the 40-Plus Club (www.40plus.org/chapters) or Five O'Clock Club (www. fiveoclockclub.com) in your community. These groups are organized as job search clubs.

Your group should meet regularly – once a week. At the meetings discuss your experiences, critique each other's approaches and progress, and share information on what you are learning or what you feel you need to know more about and do more effectively. Include your spouse in this group.

Professional Assistance and Honesty

One other aspect of this self-directed book should be clarified. We recommend that you first read this book **before** seeking professional assistance. A professional career counselor, for example, can provide important assistance at certain stages and depending on individual needs. Take, for example, the next chapter which focuses on skills identification. While we present the necessary

> *You must be honest with yourself before you can be honest with others.*

information for you to identify your skills, you may wish to enhance this step of the job search with the assistance of a professional career counselor who has access to more sophisticated testing instruments for meeting your assessment needs.

On the other hand, if you bring to your job search certain health and psychological problems which affect your job performance, you should seek professional help rather than try to solve your problems with this book. This is especially true for those with alcohol or drug problems who really need some form of professional therapy before putting into practice the job search steps identified here. If you are in serious financial trouble, or a separation or divorce is greatly troubling you, seek professional help. Only after you get yourself together physically and mentally will this book produce its intended results for you. Remember, no employer wants to hire alcohol, drug, mental, financial, or marital problems. They want productive, job-centered individuals who are capable of handling their personal problems.

You must be honest with yourself before you can be honest with others. The whole philosophy underlying this book is one of personal honesty and integrity in everything you do related to your job search.

Part II

Develop Powerful Careering and Re-Careering Skills

6

Identify Your Skills and Abilities

WE LIVE IN A SKILLS-BASED society where individuals market their skills to employers in exchange for money, position, and power. The ease by which they change jobs and careers is directly related to their ability to communicate their skills to employers and then transfer them to new work settings.

To best position yourself in the job markets of today and tomorrow, you should pay particular attention to refining your present skills as well as acquiring new and more marketable skills.

Identify Your Skills

But before you can refine your skills or acquire additional skills, you need to know what skills you presently possess. Unfortunately, few people can identify and talk about their skills even though they possess hundreds of skills which they use on a regular basis. This becomes a real problem when they must write a resume or go to a job interview. Since employers want to know about your specific abilities and skills, you must learn to both identify and communicate your skills to employers. You should be able to explain what it is you do well and give examples relevant to employers' needs.

What skills do you already have to offer employers? If you have just completed an educational program, the skills you have to offer are most likely related to the subject matter you studied. If you are changing jobs or careers, the skills you wish to communicate to employers will be those things you already have demonstrated you can do in specific jobs.

As we noted earlier, the skills required for **finding a job** are no substitute for the skills necessary for **doing the job**. Learning new skills requires a major investment of time, money, and effort. Nonetheless, the long-term pay-off should more than justify the initial costs. Indeed, research continues to show that well selected education and training provide the best returns on individual and societal investment.

Types of Skills

Most people possess two types of skills that define their accomplishments and strengths as well as enable them to enter and advance within the job market: work-content skills and functional skills. You need to acquaint yourself with these skills before communicating them to employers. These skills become the key language for communicating your qualifications to employers through your resumes and letters as well as in interviews. They can be expressed in the form of both verbs and nouns – an important distinction that differentiates a conventional paper resume from an electronic scannable resume.

We assume you have already acquired certain **work-content skills** necessary to function effectively in today's job market. These "hard skills" are easy to recognize since they are often identified as "qualifications" for specific jobs; they are the subject of most educational and training programs. Work-content skills tend to be technical and job-specific in nature. Examples of such skills include proficiency in designing Web pages, programming computers, teaching accounting, or operating an X-ray machine. They may require formal training, are associated with specific trades or professions, and are used only in certain job and career settings. One uses a separate skills vocabulary, jargon, and subject matter for specifying technical qualifications of individuals entering and advancing in an occupation. While these skills do not transfer well from one occupation to another, they are critical for entering and advancing within certain occupations.

At the same time, you possess numerous **functional/transferable skills** employers readily seek along with your work-content skills. These "soft skills" are associated with numerous job settings, are mainly acquired through experience rather than formal training, and can be communicated through a general vocabulary. Functional/transferable skills are less easy to recognize since they tend to be linked to certain **personal characteristics** (energetic, intelligent, likable) and the ability to **deal with processes** (communicating, problem-solving, motivating) rather than **do things** (programming a computer, building a house, repairing air-conditioners). While most people have only a few work-content skills, they may have numerous – as many as 300 – functional/transferable skills. These skills enable job seekers to more easily change jobs. But you must first be aware of your functional skills before you can relate them to the job market.

Most people view the world of work in traditional occupational job skill terms. This is a **structural view** of occupational realities. Occupational fields are seen as consisting of separate and distinct jobs which, in turn, require specific work-content skills. From this perspective, occupations and jobs are relatively self-contained entities. Social work, for example, is seen as being different from paralegal work; social workers, therefore, are not "qualified" to seek paralegal work.

On the other hand, a **functional view** of occupations and jobs emphasizes the similarity of job characteristics as well as common linkages between different occupations. Although the structure of occupations and jobs may differ, they have similar functions. They involve working with people, data, processes, and objects. If you work with people, data, processes, and objects in one occupation, you can transfer that experience to other occupations which have similar functions. Once you understand how your skills relate to the functions as well as investigate the structure of different occupations, you should be prepared to make job changes from one occupational field to another. Whether you possess the necessary work-content skills to qualify for entry into the other occupational field is another question altogether.

The skills we identify and help you organize in this chapter are the func-

> *Functional skills can be transferred from one job or career to another.*

tional skills career counselors normally emphasize when advising clients to assess their **strengths**. In contrast to work-content skills, functional skills can be transferred from one job or career to another. They enable individuals to make some job and career changes without acquiring additional education and training. They constitute an important bridge for moving from one occupation to another.

Before you decide if you need more education or training, you should first assess both your functional and work-content skills to see how they can be transferred to other jobs and occupations. Once you do this, you should be better prepared to communicate your qualifications to employers with a rich skills-based vocabulary.

Your Strengths

Regardless of what combination of work-content and functional skills you possess, a job search must begin with identifying your strengths. Without knowing these, your job search will lack content and focus. After all, your goal should be to find a job that is fit for you rather than one you think you might be able to fit into. Of course, you also want to find a job for which there is a demand. This particular focus requires a well-defined approach to identifying and communicating your skills to others. You can best do this by asking the right questions about your strengths and then conducting a systematic self-assessment of what you do best.

Ask the Right Questions

Knowing the right questions to ask will save you time and steer you into productive job search channels from the very beginning. Asking the wrong questions can leave you frustrated. The questions must be understood from the perspectives of both employers and applicants.

Two of the most humbling questions you will encounter in your job search are *"Why should I hire you?"* and *"What are your weaknesses?"* While employers may not directly ask these questions, they are asking them nonetheless. If you can't answer these questions in a positive manner – directly, indirectly, verbally, or nonverbally – your job search will likely founder and you will join the ranks of the unsuccessful and disillusioned job searchers who feel something is wrong with them. Individuals who have lost their jobs are particularly vulnerable to these questions since many have lowered self-esteem and self-image as a result of the job loss. Many such people focus on what is wrong rather than what is right about themselves. Such thinking creates self-fulfilling prophecies and is self-destructive in the job market. By all means avoid such negative thinking.

> *Employers want to hire your value or strengths – not your weaknesses.*

Employers want to hire your **value or strengths** – not your weaknesses. Since it is easier to identify and interpret weaknesses, employers look for indicators of your strengths by trying to identify your weaknesses. The more successful you are in communicating your strengths to employers, the better off you will be in relation to both employers and fellow applicants.

Unfortunately, many people work against their own best interests. Not knowing their strengths, they market their weaknesses by first identifying job vacancies and then trying to fit their "qualifications" into job descriptions. This approach often frustrates applicants; it presents a picture of a job market which is not interested in the applicant's strengths. This leads some people toward acquiring new skills which they hope will be marketable, even though they do not enjoy using them. Millions of individuals find themselves in such misplaced situations. Your task is to avoid joining the ranks of the misplaced and unhappy workforce by first understanding your skills and then relating them to your interests and goals. In so doing, you will be in a better position to target your job search toward jobs that should become especially rewarding and fulfilling.

Functional/Transferable Skills

We know most people stumble into jobs by accident. Some are in the right place at the right time to take advantage of opportunities. Others work hard at trying to fit into jobs posted on the Internet; listed in classified ads, employment agencies, and personnel offices; identified through friends and acquaintances; or found by knocking on doors. After 15 to 20 years in the work world, many people wish they had better planned their careers from the very start. All of a sudden they are unhappily locked into jobs because of retirement benefits and family responsibilities of raising children and meeting monthly mortgage payments.

Your goal should be to find a job that is fit for you rather than one you think you might be able to fit into.

After 10 or 20 years of work experience, most people have a good idea of what they don't like to do. While their values are more set than when they first began working, many people are still unclear as to what they do well and how their skills fit into the job market. What other jobs, for example, might they be qualified to perform? If they have the opportunity to change jobs or careers – either voluntarily or forced through termination – and find the time to plan the change, they can move into jobs and careers which fit their skills.

The key to understanding your non-technical strengths is to identify your transferable or functional skills. Once you have done this, you will be better prepared to identify what it is you want to do. Moreover, your self-image and self-esteem will improve. Better still, you will be prepared to communicate your strengths to others through a rich skills-based vocabulary. These outcomes are critically important for writing your resume and letters as well as for conducting informational and job interviews.

Let's illustrate the concept of functional/transferable skills for educators. Many educators view their skills in strict work-content terms – knowledge of a particular subject matter such as math, history, English, physics, or music. When looking for jobs outside education, many seek employment which will use their subject matter skills. But they soon discover non-educational institutions are not a ready market for such "skills."

On the other hand, educators possess many other skills that are directly transferable to business and industry. Unaware of these skills, many educators fail to communicate their strengths to others. For example, research shows that graduate students in the humanities most frequently possess these transferable skills, in order of importance:

- critical thinking
- research techniques
- perseverance
- self-discipline
- insight
- writing

- general knowledge
- cultural perspective
- teaching ability
- self-confidence
- imagination
- leadership ability

Most functional/transferable skills can be classified into two general skills and trait categories – organizational/interpersonal skills and personality/work-style traits:

Organizational and Interpersonal Skills

___ communicating
___ problem solving
___ analyzing/assessing
___ planning
___ decision-making
___ innovating
___ thinking logically
___ evaluating
___ identifying problems
___ synthesizing
___ forecasting
___ tolerating ambiguity
___ motivating
___ leading
___ selling
___ performing
___ reviewing
___ attaining
___ team building
___ updating
___ coaching
___ supervising
___ estimating
___ negotiating
___ administering

___ trouble-shooting
___ implementing
___ self-understanding
___ understanding
___ setting goals
___ conceptualizing
___ generalizing
___ managing time
___ creating
___ judging
___ controlling
___ organizing
___ persuading
___ encouraging
___ improving
___ designing
___ consulting
___ teaching
___ cultivating
___ advising
___ training
___ interpreting
___ achieving
___ reporting
___ managing

Personality and Work-Style Traits

___ diligent
___ patient
___ innovative

___ honest
___ reliable
___ perceptive

__ persistent	__ assertive
__ tactful	__ sensitive
__ loyal	__ astute
__ successful	__ risk-taker
__ versatile	__ easygoing
__ enthusiastic	__ calm
__ outgoing	__ flexible
__ expressive	__ competent
__ adaptable	__ punctual
__ democratic	__ receptive
__ resourceful	__ diplomatic
__ determining	__ self-confident
__ creative	__ tenacious
__ open	__ discrete
__ objective	__ talented
__ warm	__ empathic
__ orderly	__ tidy
__ tolerant	__ candid
__ frank	__ adventuresome
__ cooperative	__ firm
__ dynamic	__ sincere
__ self-starter	__ initiator
__ precise	__ competent
__ sophisticated	__ diplomatic
__ effective	__ efficient

These are the types of skills you need to identify and then communicate to employers in your resumes and letters as well as during interviews.

Identify Your Skills

If you are just graduating from high school or college and do not know what you want to do, you probably should take a battery of vocational tests and psychological inventories to identify your interests and skills. These tests are listed in Chapter 8. If you don't fall into these categories of job seekers, chances are you don't need complex testing. You have experience, you have well defined values, and you know what you don't like in a job. Therefore, we outline several alternative skills identification exercises – simple to complex – assisting you at this stage. We recommend using the most complete and extensive activity – Motivated Skills Exercise – to gain a thorough understanding of your strengths.

Use the following exercises to identify both your work-content and transferable skills. These self-assessment techniques stress your positives or strengths rather than identify your negatives or weaknesses. They should generate a rich vocabulary for communicating your "qualifications" to employers. Each exercise requires different investments of your time and effort as well as varying degrees of assistance from other people.

These exercises, however, should be used with caution. There is nothing magical nor particularly profound about them. Most are based upon a very simple and somewhat naive **deterministic theory of behavior** – your past patterns of behavior are good predictors of your future behavior. Not a bad theory for most individuals, but it is rather simplistic and disheartening for individuals who wish to, and can, break out of past patterns as they embark on a new future. Furthermore, most exercises are **historical devices**. They provide you with a clear picture of your past, which may or may not be particularly useful for charting your future. Nonetheless, these exercises do help individuals (1) organize data on themselves, (2) target their job search around clear objectives and skills, and (3) generate a rich vocabulary of skills and accomplishments for communicating strengths to potential employers.

If you feel these exercises are inadequate for your needs, by all means seek professional assistance from a testing or assessment center staffed by a licensed psychologist. These centers do in-depth testing which goes further than these self-directed skill exercises.

When using the following exercises, keep in mind that some individuals can and do change – often very dramatically – their behavior regardless of such deterministic and historical assessment devices. Much of the "motivation and success," "power of positive thinking," "thinking big," and "empowerment" literature, for example, challenges the validity of these standardized assessment tests that are used to predict or pattern future individual behavior. So be careful how you use such information for charting your career future. You **can** change your future. But at least get to know yourself before making the changes. Critiques of, as well as alternatives to, these exercises are outlined in two of our books, *Discover the Best Jobs for You* and *I Want to Do Something Else, But I'm Not Sure What It Is* (Impact Publications).

Checklist Method

This is the simplest method for identifying your strengths. Review the different types of transferable skills outlined on pages 126-127. Place a "1" in front of the skills that **strongly** characterize you; assign a "2" to those skills that describe you to a **large extent**; put a "3" before those that describe you to **some extent**. After completing this exercise, review the lists and rank order the 10 characteristics that best describe you on each list.

Skills Map

Richard N. Bolles has produced two well-known exercises for identifying transferable skills based upon John Holland's typology of work environments. Both are historical devices structured around a deterministic theory of behavior. In his book, *The Three Boxes of Life* (Ten Speed Press), he develops a checklist of 100 transferable skills. They are organized into 12 categories or types of skills: using hands, body, words, senses, numbers, intuition, analytical thinking, creativity, helpfulness, artistic abilities, leadership, and follow-through.

Bolles's second exercise, "The Quick Job Hunting Map," expands upon this first one. The "Map" is a checklist of 222 skills. This exercise requires you to identify seven of your most satisfying accomplishments, achievements, jobs, or roles. After writing a page about each experience, you relate each to the checklist of 222 skills. The "Map" should give you a comprehensive picture of what skills you (1) use most frequently and (2) enjoy using in satisfying and successful settings. While this exercise may take six hours to complete, it yields an enormous amount of data on past strengths. Furthermore, the "Map" generates a rich skills vocabulary for communicating your strengths to others. The "Map" is found in Bolles's *What Color Is Your Parachute?* and *What Color Is Your Parachute Workbook* (Ten Speed Press). These books can be ordered directly from Impact Publications by completing the order form at the end of this book.

Autobiography of Accomplishments

Write a lengthy essay about your life accomplishments. This could range from 20 to 100 pages. After completing the essay, go through it page by page to identify what you most enjoyed doing (working with different kinds of information, people, and things) and what skills you used most frequently as well as enjoyed using. Finally, identify those skills you wish to continue using. After analyzing and synthesizing this data, you should have a relatively clear picture of your strongest skills.

Computerized Assessment Systems

While the previous self-directed exercises required you to either respond to checklists of skills or reconstruct and analyze your past job experiences, several computerized self-assessment programs are designed to help individuals identify their skills. Many of the programs are available in schools, colleges, and libraries. Some of the most widely used programs include:

- *Career Navigator*
- *Choices*
- *Discover II*
- *Guidance Information System* (GIS)
- *Self-Directed Search (SDS) Form R*
- *SIGI-Plus* (System of Interactive Guidance and Information)

Most of these comprehensive career planning programs do much more than just assess skills. As we will see in Chapter 8, they also integrate other key components in the career planning process – interests, goals, related jobs, college majors, education and training programs, and job search plans. These programs are widely available in schools, colleges, and libraries across the country. You might check with the career or counseling center at your local community college to see what computerized career assessment systems are available for your use. Relatively easy to use, they generate a great deal of useful career planning information. Many will print out a useful analysis of how your interests and skills are related to specific jobs and careers.

Online Assessment

Within the past few years, several companies have developed online assessment devices which you can quickly access via the Internet 24 hours a day in the comfort of your home or office. Some of the testing devices are self-scoring and free of charge while others require interacting with a fee-based certified career counselor or testing expert. SkillsOne (www.skillsone.com), for example, is operated by the producers of the *Myers-Briggs Type Indicator®* and *Strong Interest Inventory®* – Consulting Psychologists Press. CareerLab (www.career lab.com) offers one of the largest batteries of well respected assessment tools: *Campbell Interest and Skills Survey*, *Strong Interest Inventory®*, *Myers-Briggs Type Indicator®*, *16-Personality Factors Profile*, *FIRO-B*, *California Psychological Inventory (CPI)*, *The Birkman Method*, and *Campbell Leadership Index*. The following seven websites are well worth exploring for both free and fee-based online assessments tools:

■ **SkillsOne**	www.skillsone.com
	www.cpp-db.com
■ **CareerLab.com**	www.careerlab.com
■ **Self-Directed Search®**	www.self-directed-search.com
■ **Personality Online**	www.personalityonline.com
■ **Keirsey Character Sorter**	www.keirsey.com
■ **MAPP™**	www.assessment.com
■ **PersonalityType**	www.personalitytype.com

These 18 additional sites also include a wealth of related assessment devices that you can access online:

- **Analyze My Career**   www.analyzemycareer.com
- **Birkman Method**   www.princetonreview.com/cte/quiz/quizoverview.asp
- **Career Key**   www.careerkey/prgemg;osj
- **CareerLeader™**   www.careerdiscover.com/careerleader
- **Career Services Group**   www.careerperfect.com
- **Careers By Design®**   www.careers-by-design.com
- **College Board**   www.myroad.com
- **Emode**   www.emode.com/tests/career.jsp
- **Enneagram**   www.ennea.com
- **Fortune.com**   www.fortune.com/fortune/careers
- **Humanmetrics**   www.humanmetrics.com
- **Jackson Vocational Interest Inventory**   www.jvis.com
- **My Future**   www.myfuture.com
- **People Management International**   www.sima-pmi.com
- **Personality and IQ Tests**   www.davideck.com
- **Profiler**   www.profiler.com
- **QueenDom**   www.queendom.com
- **Tests on the Web**   www.2h.com

Specify Your Interests and Values

K NOWING WHAT YOU DO well is essential for understanding your strengths and for linking your capabilities to specific jobs so that you can best target your job search and communicate your strengths to employers. However, just knowing your abilities and skills will not give your job search the direction it needs for finding the right job. You also need to know your work values and interests. These are the basic building blocks for setting goals and targeting your abilities toward certain jobs and careers.

Take, for example, individuals who type 120 words a minute or design Web pages. While these people possess highly marketable skills, if they don't regularly enjoy using these skills and are more interested in working outdoors or with people, these will not become **motivated skills**; these individuals will most likely not pursue jobs relating to word processing or the Internet. In the end, your interests and values will determine whether or not certain skills should play a central role in your job search.

Vocational Interests

We all have interests. Most change over time. Many of your interests may center on your present job whereas others relate to activities that define your hobbies and leisure activities. A good place to start identifying your interests is by examining the information and exercises found in both *The Guide to Occupational Exploration* and *The Enhanced Guide to Occupational Exploration*. Widely used by students and others first entering the job market, these are also relevant to individuals who already have work experience. These books classify all jobs in the United States into 12 interest areas. Examine the following list of interest areas. In the first column check those work areas that appeal to you. In the second column rank order those areas you checked in the first column. Start with "1" to indicate the most interesting:

Your Work Interests

Yes/No (x)	Ranking (1-12)	Interest Area
___	___	**Artistic:** An interest in creative expression of feelings or ideas.
___	___	**Scientific:** An interest in discovering, collecting, and analyzing information about the natural world, and in applying scientific research findings to problems in medicine, the life sciences, and the nature sciences.
___	___	**Plants and animals:** An interest in working with plants and animals, usually outdoors.
___	___	**Protective:** An interest in using authority to protect people and property.
___	___	**Mechanical:** An interest in applying mechanical principles to practical situations by using machines or hand tools.
___	___	**Industrial:** An interest in repetitive, concrete, organized activities done in a factory setting.
___	___	**Business detail:** An interest in organized, clearly defined activities requiring accuracy and attention to details (office settings).
___	___	**Selling:** An interest in bringing others to a particular point of view by personal persuasion, using sales and promotion techniques.

___   ___   **Accommodating:** An interest in catering to the wishes and needs of others, usually on a one-to-one basis.

___   ___   **Humanitarian:** An interest in helping others with their mental, spiritual, social, physical, or vocational needs.

___   ___   **Leading and influencing:** An interest in leading and influencing others by using high-level verbal or numerical abilities.

___   ___   **Physical performing:** An interest in physical activities performed before an audience.

The Guide to Occupational Exploration also includes other checklists relating to home-based and leisure activities that may or may not relate to your work interests. If you are unclear about your work interests, you might want to consult these other interest exercises. You may discover that some of your home-based and leisure activity interests should become your work interests. Examples of such interests include:

Leisure and Home-Based Interests

___ Acting in a play or amateur variety show.

___ Advising family members on their personal problems.

___ Announcing or emceeing a program.

___ Applying first aid in emergencies as a volunteer.

___ Building model airplanes, automobiles, or boats.

___ Building or repairing radios, televisions, or computers.

___ Buying large quantities of food or other products for an organization.

___ Campaigning for political candidates or issues.

___ Canning and preserving food.

___ Carving small wooden objects.

___ Coaching children or youth in sports activities.

___ Conducting experiments involving plants.

___ Conducting house-to-house or telephone surveys for a PTA or other organization.

___ Creating or styling hairdos for friends.

___ Designing your own greeting cards and writing original verses.

___ Developing film or producing digital photos.

___ Doing impersonations.

___ Doing public speaking or debating.

___ Entertaining at parties or other events.

___ Helping conduct physical exercises for disabled people.

___ Making ceramic objects.

___ Modeling clothes for a fashion show.

___ Mounting and framing pictures.

___ Nursing sick pets.

___ Painting the interior or exterior of a home.

___ Playing a musical instrument.

___ Refinishing or re-upholstering furniture.

___ Repairing electrical household appliances.

___ Repairing the family car.

___ Repairing or assembling bicycles.

___ Repairing plumbing in the house.

___ Speaking on radio or television.

___ Taking photographs.

___ Teaching in Sunday School.

___ Tutoring pupils in school subjects.

___ Weaving rugs or making quilts.

___ Writing articles, stories, or plays.

___ Writing songs for club socials or amateur plays.

Indeed, many people turn hobbies or home activities into full-time jobs after deciding that such "work" is what they really enjoy doing.

Other popular exercises designed to identify your work interests include John Holland's "The Self-Directed Search" which is found in his book, *Making Vocational Choices: A Theory of Careers*. It is also published as a separate testing instrument, *The Self-Directed Search – A Guide to Educational and Vocational Planning*. Developed from Holland's Vocational Preference Inventory, this popular self-administered, self-scored, and self-interpreted inventory helps individuals quickly identify what type of work environment they are motivated to seek – realistic, investigative, artistic, social, enterprising, or conventional – and aligns these work environments with lists of common occupational titles. An easy exercise to use, it gives you a quick overview of your orientation toward different types of work settings that interest you.

Holland's self-directed search is also the basic framework used in developing Bolles's "The Quick Job Hunting Map" (see discussion on page 129).

For more sophisticated treatments of work interests, which are also validated through testing procedures, contact a career counselor, women's center, or testing and assessment center for information on these tests:

- *Strong Interest Inventory™*
- *Myers-Briggs Type Indicator™*
- *Edwards Personal Preference Schedule*
- *Kuder Occupational Interest Survey*
- *Vocational Interest Inventory*
- *Career Assessment Inventory*
- *Temperament and Values Inventory*

Numerous other job and career interest inventories are also available. For further information, contact a career counselor or consult Educational Testing Service which compiles such tests. *The ETS Test Collection Catalog* (New York: Oryx Press), which is available in the reference section of many libraries, lists most of these tests. The *Mental Measurements Yearbook* (Lincoln, NE: University of Nebraska Press) also surveys many of the major testing and assessment instruments.

Keep in mind that not all testing and assessment instruments used by career counselors are equally valid for career planning purposes. While the *Strong Interest Inventory™* appears to be the most relevant for career decision-making, the *Myers-Briggs Type Indicator™* has become extremely popular during the past ten years. Based on Carl Gustav Jung's personality preference theory, the *Myers-Briggs Type Indicator™* is used extensively by psychologists and career counselors for identifying personality types. However, it is more useful for measuring individual personality and decision-making styles than for predicting career choices. It is most widely used in pastoral counseling, student personnel, and business and religious organizations for measuring personality and decision-making styles. For more information on this test, contact: Consulting Psychologists Press, Inc., 3803 East Bayshore Road, Palo Alto, CA 94303, Tel. 800-624-1765 (website: www.cpp-db.com). A version of the test is also available online through CompuServe. In the meantime, many career counselors find Holland's *The Self-Directed Search* an excellent self-directed alternative to these professionally administered and interpreted tests. This book, as well as related SDS software programs, are available through Impact Publications.

Work Values

Work values are those things you like to do. They give you pleasure and enjoyment. Most jobs involve a combination of likes and dislikes. By identifying what you both like and dislike about jobs, you should be able to better identify jobs that involve tasks that you will most enjoy.

Several exercises can help you identify your work values. First, identify what most satisfies you about work by completing the following exercise:

My Work Values

I prefer employment which enables me to:

____ contribute to society	____ be creative
____ have contact with people	____ supervise others
____ work alone	____ work with details
____ work with a team	____ gain recognition
____ compete with others	____ acquire security
____ make decisions	____ make money
____ work under pressure	____ help others
____ use power and authority	____ solve problems
____ acquire new knowledge	____ take risks
____ be a recognized expert	____ work at own pace

Select four work values from the above list which are the most important to you and list them on page 138. Include any other work values (desired satisfactions) which were not listed above but are nonetheless important to you:

1. _____

2. _____

3. _____

4. _____

Another approach to identifying work values is outlined in *The Guide to Occupational Exploration*. If you feel you need to go beyond the above exercises, try this one. In the first column check those values that are most important to you. In the second column rank order the five most important values:

Ranking Work Values

Yes/No (x)	Ranking (1-5)	Work Values
____	____	**Adventure:** Working in a job that requires taking risks.
____	____	**Authority:** Working in a job in which you use your position to control others.
____	____	**Competition:** Working in a job in which you compete with others.
____	____	**Creativity and self-expression:** Working in a job in which you use your imagination to find new ways to do or say something.
____	____	**Flexible work schedule:** Working in a job in which you choose your hours to work.
____	____	**Helping others:** Working in a job in which you provide direct services to persons with problems.
____	____	**High salary:** Working in a job where many workers earn a large amount of money.
____	____	**Independence:** Working in a job in which you decide for yourself what work to do and how to do it.

____ ____ **Influencing others:** Working in a job in which you influence the opinions of others or decisions of others.

____ ____ **Intellectual stimulation:** Working in a job which requires a great amount of thought and reasoning.

____ ____ **Leadership:** Working in a job in which you direct, manage, or supervise the activities of other people.

____ ____ **Outside work:** Working out-of-doors.

____ ____ **Persuading:** Working in a job in which you personally convince others to take certain actions.

____ ____ **Physical work:** Working in a job which requires substantial physical activity.

____ ____ **Prestige:** Working in a job which gives you status and respect in the community.

____ ____ **Public attention:** Working in a job in which you attract immediate notice because of appearance or activity.

____ ____ **Public contact:** Working in a job in which you daily deal with the public.

____ ____ **Recognition:** Working in a job in which you gain public notice.

____ ____ **Research work:** Working in a job in which you search for and discover new facts and develop ways to apply them.

____ ____ **Routine work:** Working in a job in which you follow established procedures requiring little change.

____ ____ **Seasonal work:** Working in a job in which you are employed only at certain times of the year.

____ ____ **Travel:** Working in a job in which you take frequent trips.

____ ____ **Variety:** Working in a job in which your duties change frequently.

____ ____ **Work with children:** Working in a job in which you teach or care for children.

____ ____ **Work with hands:** Working in a job in which you use your hands or hand tools.

____ ____ **Work with machines or equipment:** Working in a job in which you use machines or equipment.

____ ____ **Work with numbers:** Working in a job in which you use mathematics or statistics.

Second, develop a comprehensive list of your past and present **job frustrations and dissatisfactions**. This should help you identify negative factors you should avoid in future jobs.

My Job Frustrations and Dissatisfactions

List as well as rank order as many past and present things that frustrate or make you dissatisfied and unhappy in job situations:

Rank

1. _____ ____
2. _____ ____
3. _____ ____
4. _____ ____
5. _____ ____
6. _____ ____
7. _____ ____
8. _____ ____
9. _____ ____
10. _____ ____

Third, brainstorm a list of "Ten or More Things I Love to Do." Identify which ones could be incorporated into what kinds of work environments:

Ten or More Things I Love to Do

	Item	Related Work Environment
1.	_____	_____
2.	_____	_____
3.	_____	_____
4.	_____	_____
5.	_____	_____
6.	_____	_____
7.	_____	_____
8.	_____	_____
9.	_____	_____
10.	_____	_____

Fourth, list at least ten things you most enjoy about work and rank each item accordingly:

Ten Things I Enjoy the Most About Work

		Rank
1.	_____	____
2.	_____	____
3.	_____	____
4.	_____	____
5.	_____	____
6.	_____	____
7.	_____	____
8.	_____	____
9.	_____	____
10.	_____	____

Fifth, you should also identify the types of interpersonal environments you prefer working in. Do this by specifying the types of people you like and dislike associating with:

Interpersonal Environments

Characteristics of people I like working with:	Characteristics of people I dislike working with:
_____	_____
_____	_____
_____	_____
_____	_____
_____	_____
_____	_____
_____	_____
_____	_____
_____	_____

Computer Programs and Online Services

Several computerized self-assessment programs and online assessment services identified in Chapter 6 (page 130) largely focus on career interests and values. Again, you may be able to get access to such computerized assessment programs through your local community college, career center, or library. The testing and assessment websites identified on pages 130-131 include instruments for measuring interests and values.

Your Future as Objectives

All of these exercises are designed to explore your past and present work-related values. At the same time, you need to project your values into the **future**. What, for example, do you want to do over the next 10 to 20 years? We'll return to this type of value question in Chapter 9 when we address the critical objective-setting stage of the job search process.

8

Know Your Motivated
Skills and Abilities (MAS)

ONCE YOU KNOW WHAT YOU really do well and enjoy doing, your next task should be to analyze those interests, values, abilities, and skills that form a **recurring motivated pattern**. This "pattern" is the single most important piece of information you need to know about yourself in the whole self-assessment process. Knowing your skills and abilities alone without knowing how they relate to your interests and values will not give you the necessary direction for finding the job you want. You simply **must** know your pattern. Once you do, your job search may take on a whole new direction that will produce amazing results.

What's Your MAS?

The concept of motivated abilities and skills (MAS) enables us to relate your interests and values to your skills and abilities. But how do we identify your MAS beyond the questions and exercises outlined thus far?

Your pattern of motivated abilities and skills becomes evident once you analyze your **achievements or accomplishments**. For it is your achievements that tell us what you both did well and enjoyed doing. If we analyze and synthesize many of your achievements, we are likely to identify a **recurring pattern** that most likely goes back to your childhood and which will continue to characterize your achievements in the future.

An equally useful exercise would be to identify your weaknesses by analyzing your failures. These, too, would fall into recurring patterns. Understanding what your weaknesses are might help you avoid jobs and work situations that bring out the worst in you. Indeed, you may learn more about yourself by analyzing your failures than by focusing solely on your accomplishments.

For now, let's focus on your positives rather than identify your negatives. After you complete the strength exercises in this chapter, you may want to reverse the procedures to identify your weaknesses.

Numerous self-directed exercises can assist you in identifying your pattern of motivated abilities and skills. The basic requirements for making these exercises work for you are **time and analytical ability**. You must spend a great deal of time detailing your achievements by looking at your history of accomplishments. Once you complete the historical reconstruction task, you must comb through your "stories" to identify recurring themes and patterns. This requires a high level of analytical ability which you may or may not possess. If analysis and synthesis are not two of your strong skills, you may want to seek assistance from a friend or professional who is good at analyzing and synthesizing information presented in narrative form. Career management firms such as BH Careers International (60+ offices, www.bhcareers. com) and People Management, Inc. (www.jobfit-pmi.com) are known for their use of this type of motivated pattern approach. Their versions of this assessment technique are presented in *Haldane's Best Resumes for Professionals* (Impact Publications) and *The Truth About You* (Ten Speed Press).

Several paper-and-pencil exercises are designed to help identify your pattern of motivated abilities and skills. We outline some of the most popular and thorough such exercises that have proved useful to thousands of people.

The Skills Map

Richard Bolles's "Quick Job Hunting Map" has become a standard self-assessment tool for thousands of job seekers and career changers who are willing to spend the time and effort necessary for discovering their pattern of motivated abilities and skills. Offering a checklist of over 200 skills organized around John Holland's concept of *The Self-Directed Search* for defining work environments (realistic, investigative, artistic, social, enterprising, and conventional), the "Map" requires you to identify seven of your most satisfying accomplishments, achievements, jobs, or roles. After detailing each achievement, you analyze the details of each in relation to the checklist of skills. Once you do this for all seven achievements, you should have a comprehensive picture of what skills you (1) use most frequently and (2) enjoy using in satisfying and successful settings. This exercise not only yields an enormous amount of information on your interests, values, skills, and abilities, it also assists you in the process of analyzing the data. If done properly, the "Map" should also generate a rich "skills" vocabulary which you should use in your resumes and letters as well as in interviews. For information on this "Map", see page 129.

We highly recommend using the "Map" because of the ease in which it can be used. If you will spend the six to 20 hours necessary to complete it properly, the "Map" will give you some important information about yourself. Unfortunately, many people become overwhelmed by the exercise and either decide not to complete it, or they try to save time by not doing it according to the directions. You simply must follow the directions and spend the time and effort necessary if you want the maximum benefits from this exercise.

Keep in mind that like most self-assessment devices, there is nothing magical about the "Map". Its basic organizing principles are simple. Like other exercises designed to uncover your pattern of motivated abilities and skills, this one is based on a theory of historical determinism and probability. In other words, once you uncover your pattern, get prepared to acknowledge it and live with it in the future.

> *Once you uncover your pattern, get prepared to acknowledge it and live with it in the future.*

Autobiography of Accomplishments

Less structured than the "Map" device, this exercise requires you to write a lengthy essay about your life accomplishments. Your essay may run anywhere from 20 to 200 pages. After completing it, go through it page by page to identify what you most enjoyed doing (working with different kinds of data, people, processes, and objects) and what skills you used most frequently as well as enjoyed using. Finally, identify those skills you wish to continue using. After analyzing and synthesizing this data, you should have a relatively clear picture of your strongest skills.

This exercise requires a great deal of self-discipline and analytic skill. To do it properly, you must write as much as possible, and in as much detail as possible, about your accomplishments. The richer the detail, the better will be your analysis.

Motivated Skills Exercise

Our final exercise is one of the most complex and time-consuming self-assessment exercises. However, it yields some of the best data on motivated abilities and skills, and it is especially useful for those who feel they need a more thorough analysis of their past achievements. This device is widely used by career counselors. Initially developed by Bernard Haldane, this exercise is variously referred to as "Success Factor Analysis," "System to Identify Motivated Skills," or "Intensive Skills Identification."

This technique helps you identify which skills you **enjoy** using. While you can use this technique on your own, it is best to work with someone else. Since you will need six to eight hours to properly complete this exercise, divide your time into two or three work sessions.

The exercise consists of six steps. The steps follow the basic pattern of generating raw data, identifying patterns, analyzing the data through reduction techniques, and synthesizing the patterns into a transferable skills vocabulary. You need strong analytical skills to complete this exercise on your own. The six steps include:

1. **Identify 15-20 achievements:** While ideally you should inventory over 100-150 achievements, let's start by focusing on a minimum of 15-20 achievements. These consist of things you enjoyed doing, believe you did well, and felt a sense of satisfaction, pride, or accomplishment in doing. You can see yourself performing at your best and enjoying your experiences when you analyze your achievements. This information reveals your motivations since it deals entirely with your voluntary behavior. In addition, it identifies what is right with you by focusing on your positives and strengths. Identify achievements throughout your life, beginning with your childhood. Your achievements should relate to specific experiences – not general ones – and may be drawn from work, leisure, education, military, or home life. Put each achievement at the top of a separate sheet of paper. For example, your achievements might appear as follows:

Sample Achievement Statements

"When I was 10 years old, I started a small paper route and built it up to the largest in my district."

———————————————

"I started playing chess in ninth grade and earned the right to play first board on my high school chess team in my junior year."

———————————————

"Learned to play the piano and often played for church services while in high school."

———————————————

"Designed, constructed, and displayed a dress for a 4-H demonstration project."

———————————————

"Although I was small compared to other guys, I made the first string on my high school football team."

_____

"I graduated from high school with honors even though I was very active in school clubs and had to work part-time."

_____

"I was the first in my family to go to college and one of the few from my high school. Worked part-time and summers. A real struggle, but I made it."

_____

"Earned an 'A' grade on my senior psychology project from a real tough professor."

_____

"Finished my master's degree while working full-time and attending to my family responsibilities."

_____

"Proposed a chef's course for junior high boys. Got it approved. Developed it into a very popular elective."

_____

"Designed the plans for our house and had it constructed within budget."

_____

2. Prioritize your seven most significant achievements.

Your Most Significant Achievements

1. _____

2. _____

3. _____

4. _____

5. _____

6. _____

7. _____

3. **Write a full page on each of your prioritized achievements.**
   You should describe:

   - How you initially became involved.
   - The details of **what you did** and **how you did it.**
   - What was especially enjoyable or satisfying to you.

   Use copies of the "Detailing Your Achievements" form on page 149 to outline your achievements.

4. **Elaborate on your achievements:** Have one or two other people interview you. For each achievement have them note on a separate sheet of paper any terms used to reveal your skills, abilities, and personal qualities. To elaborate details, the interviewer(s) may ask:

   - What was involved in the achievement?
   - What was your part?
   - What did you actually do?
   - How did you go about that?

   Clarify any vague areas by providing an example or illustration of what you actually did. Probe with the following questions:

   - Would you elaborate on one example of what you mean?
   - Could you give me an illustration?
   - What were you good at doing?

   This interview should clarify the details of your activities by asking only "what" and "how" questions. It should take 45 to 90 minutes to complete. Make copies of the "Strength Identification Interview" form on page 150 to guide you through this interview.

5. **Identify patterns by examining the interviewer's notes:**
   Together identify the recurring skills, abilities, and personal

Detailing Your Achievements

ACHIEVEMENT # ___: _____

_____

_____

1. How did I initially become involved? _____

_____

_____

_____

2. What did I do? _____

_____

_____

_____

_____

3. How did I do it? _____

_____

_____

_____

_____

4. What was especially enjoyable about doing it?

_____

_____

_____

_____

Strength Identification Interview

Interviewee _____   Interviewer _____

INSTRUCTIONS: For each achievement experience, identify the **skills** and **abilities** the achiever actually demonstrated. Obtain details of the experience by asking **what** was involved with the achievement and **how** the individual made the achievement happen. Avoid "why" questions which tend to mislead. Ask for examples or illustrations of what and how.

Achievement #1:

Achievement #2:

Achievement #3:

Recurring abilities and skills:

qualities **demonstrated** in your achievements. Search for patterns. Your skills pattern should be clear at this point; you should feel comfortable with it. If you have questions, review the data. If you disagree with a conclusion, disregard it. The results must accurately and honestly reflect how you operate.

6. **Synthesize the information by clustering similar skills into categories:** For example, your skills might be grouped in the following manner:

Synthesized Skill Clusters

Investigate/Survey/Read	Teach/Train/Drill
Inquire/Probe/Question	Perform/Show/Demonstrate
Learn/Memorize/Practice	Construct/Assemble/Put together
Evaluate/Appraise/Assess	
Compare	Organize/Structure/Provide
	definition/Plan/Chart course
Influence/Involve/Get	Strategize/Coordinate
participation/Publicize	
Promote	Create/Design/Adapt/Modify

This exercise yields a relatively comprehensive inventory of your skills. The information will better enable you to use a **skills vocabulary** when identifying your objective, writing your resume and letters, and interviewing. Your self-confidence and self-esteem should increase accordingly.

Other Alternatives

Several other techniques also can help you identify your motivated abilities and skills:

1. List all of your hobbies and analyze what you do in each, which ones you like the most, what skills you use, and your accomplishments.

2. Conduct a job analysis by writing about your past jobs and identifying which skills you used in each job. Cluster the skills into related categories and prioritize them according to your preferences.

3. Acquire a copy of Arthur F. Miller and Ralph T. Mattson's *The Truth About You* and work through the exercises found in the Appendix. While its overt religious message, extreme deterministic approach, and laborious exercises may turn off some users, you may find this book useful nonetheless. This is an abbreviated version of the authors' SIMA (System for Identifying Motivated Abilities) technique used by their career counseling firm, People Management, Inc. (www.jobfit-pmi.com). If you need professional assistance, contact this firm directly. They can provide you with several alternative services consistent with the career planning philosophy and approach outlined in this chapter.

4. Complete John Holland's *The Self-Directed Search (SDS)*. You'll find it in his book, *Making Vocational Choices: A Theory of Vocational Personalities and Work Environments* or in a separate publication entitled *The Self-Directed Search – A Guide to Educational and Vocational Planning*. Also, check out the publisher's (Psychological Assessment Resources) website for an online version of the SDS: www.self-directed-search.com.

Benefit From Redundancy

The self-directed MAS exercises generate similar information. They identify interests, values, abilities, and skills you already possess. While aptitude and achievement tests may yield similar information, the self-directed exercises have three major advantages over the standardized tests: less expensive, self-monitored and evaluated, and measure motivation **and** ability.

Each exercise demands a different investment of time. Writing your life history and completing the Motivated Skills Exercise and Bolles's "Map" are the most time consuming. On the other hand, Holland's *Self-Directed Search* can be completed in a few minutes. But the more time you invest with each technique, the more useful information you will generate.

We recommend creating redundancy by using at least two or three different techniques. This will help reinforce and confirm the validity of your observations and interpretations. If you have a great deal of work experience, we recommend using the more thorough exercises. The more you put into these techniques and exercises, the greater the benefit to other stages of your job search. You will be well prepared to target your job search toward specific jobs that fit your MAS as well as communicate your qualifications loudly and clearly to employers. A carefully planned career or career change should not do less than this.

Bridging Your Past and Future

Many people want to know about their future. If you expect the self-assessment techniques in Chapters 6, 7, and 8 to spell out your future, you will be disappointed. Fortune tellers, horoscopes, and various forms of mysticism may be what you need.

These are historical devices which integrate past achievements, abilities, and motivations into a coherent framework for projecting future performance. They clarify past strengths and recurring motivations for targeting future jobs. Abilities and motivations are the **qualifications** employers expect for particular jobs. Qualifications consist of your past experience **and** your motivated abilities and skills.

The assessment techniques provide a bridge between your past and future. They treat your future preferences and performance as functions of your past experiences and demonstrated abilities. This commonsense notion – **past performance is the best predictor of future performance** – is shared by employers, especially among those who increasingly conduct behavior-based interviews that are designed to uncover such patterns.

Yet, employers hire a person's **future** rather than their past. And herein lies an important problem you can help employers overcome. Getting the job that is right for you entails communicating to prospective employers that you have the necessary qualifications.

Employers rightfully believe that past performance is the best predictor of future performance. Accordingly, you need to clearly communicate your predictable "pattern of performance" to employers.

Indeed, employers will look for signs of your future productivity **for them**. Since you are an unknown and risky quantity for prospective employers, you must communicate evidence of your past productivity so they can better predict your future performance. This evidence is revealed clearly in your past achievements as outlined in our assessment techniques.

The overall value of using these assessment techniques is that they should enhance your occupational mobility over the long run. The major thrust of all these techniques is to identify abilities and skills which are **transferable** to different work environments. This is particularly important if you are making a career change. You must overcome employers' negative expectations and objections toward career changers by clearly communicating your transferable abilities and skills in the most positive terms possible. These assessment techniques are designed to do precisely that.

9

Develop a Powerful and Realistic Objective

ONCE YOU'VE IDENTIFIED YOUR interests, skills, and abilities, you should be well prepared to develop a clear and purposeful objective for targeting your job search toward specific jobs, organizations, and employers. With a renewed sense of direction and versed in an appropriate language, you should be able to communicate to employers that you are a talented and purposeful individual who **achieves results**. Your objective must tell employers what you will **do for them** rather than what you want from them. It targets your accomplishments around employers' needs. In other words, your objective should become employer-centered rather than self-centered.

Goals and Objectives

Goals and objectives are statements of what you want to do in the future. When combined with an assessment of your interests, values, abilities and skills and related to specific jobs, they give your job search needed direction and meaning for the purpose of targeting specific employers. Without them, your job search may founder as you present an image of uncertainty and confusion to potential employers.

When you identify your strengths, you also create the necessary database and vocabulary for developing your job objective. Using this vocabulary, you should be able to communicate to employers that you are a talented and purposeful individual who achieves results.

If you fail to do the preliminary self-assessment work necessary for developing a clear objective, you will probably wander aimlessly in a highly decentralized, fragmented, and chaotic job market looking for interesting jobs you might fit into. Your goal, instead, should be to find a job or career that is compatible with your interests, motivations, skills, and talents as well as related to a vision of your future. In other words, try to find a job fit for you and your future rather than try to fit into a job that happens to be advertised and for which you think you can qualify.

Examine Your Past, Present, and Future

Depending on how you approach your job search, your goals can be largely a restatement of your past MAS patterns (Chapter 8) or a vision of your future. If you base your job search on an analysis of your motivated abilities and skills, you may prefer restating your past patterns as your present and future goals. On the other hand, you may want to establish a vision of your future and set goals that motivate you to achieve that vision through a process of self-transformation.

The type of goals you choose to establish will involve different processes. However, the strongest goals will be those that combine your motivated abilities and skills with a realistic vision of your future.

Orient Yourself to Employers' Needs

Your objective should be a concise statement of what you want to do and what you have to offer to an employer. The position you seek is "what you want to do"; your qualifications are "what you have to offer." Your objective should state your strongest qualifications for meeting employers' needs. It should communicate what you have to offer an employer without emphasizing what you expect the employer to do for you. In other words, your objective should be **work-centered**, not self-centered; it should not contain trite terms which emphasize what you want, such as give me a(n) "opportunity for advancement," "position working with people," "progressive company," or "creative position." Such terms are viewed as "canned" job search language which say little of value about you. Above all, your objective should reflect your honesty and integrity; it should not be "hyped."

> *Your objective should be employer- or work-centered rather than self-centered. Above all, it should reflect your honesty and integrity; it should not be "hyped."*

Identifying what it is you want to do can be one of the most difficult job search tasks. Indeed, most job hunters lack clear objectives. Many engage in a random, and somewhat mindless, search for jobs by identifying available job opportunities and then adjusting their skills and objectives to fit specific job openings. While you can get a job using this approach, you may be misplaced and unhappy with what you find. You will fit into a job rather than find a job that is fit for you.

Knowing what you want to do can have numerous benefits. First, you define the job market rather than let it define you. The inherent fragmentation and chaos of the job market should be advantageous for you, because it enables you to systematically organize job opportunities around your specific objectives and skills. Second, you will communicate professionalism to prospective employers. They will receive a precise indication of your interests, qualifications, and purposes, which places you ahead of most other applicants. Third, being purposeful means being able to communicate to employers what

> *The strongest goals will be those that combine your motivated abilities and skills with a realistic vision of your future.*

you really want to do. Employers are not interested in hiring indecisive and confused individuals who will probably have difficulty taking initiative because they really don't know what they should be doing in the first place. Employers want to know what it is you can and will do **for them**. With a clear objective – based upon a thorough understanding of your motivated skills and interests – you can take control of the situation as you demonstrate your value to employers.

Finally, few employers really know what they want in a candidate. Like most job seekers, employers lack clear employment objectives and knowledge about how the job market operates. If you know what you want and can help the employer define his or her "needs" as your objective, you will have achieved a tremendously advantageous position in the job market.

Be Purposeful and Realistic

Your objective should communicate that you are a **purposeful individual who achieves results**. It can be stated over different time periods as well as at various levels of abstraction and specificity. You can identify short-, intermediate-, and long-range objectives and very general to very specific objectives. Whatever the case, it is best to know your prospective audience before deciding on the type of objective. Your objective should reflect your career interests as well as employers' needs.

Objectives also should be **realistic**. You may want to become president of the United States or solve all the world's problems. However, these objectives are unrealistic. While they may represent your ideals and fantasies, you need to be more realistic in terms of what you can personally accomplish in the immediate future given your particular skills, pattern of accomplishments, level of experience, and familiarity with the job market. What, for example, are you prepared to deliver to prospective employers over the next few months? While it is good to set challenging objectives, you can overdo it. Refine your objective by thinking about the next major step or two you would like to make in your career advancement. Develop a realistic action plan that focuses on the details of progressing your career one step at a time. By all means avoid making a grandiose leap outside reality!

Project Yourself Into the Future

Even after identifying your abilities and skills, specifying an *objective* can be the most difficult and tedious step in the job search process; it can stall the resume writing process indefinitely. This simple one-sentence, 25-word statement can take days or weeks to formulate and clearly define. Yet, it must be specified prior to writing the resume and engaging in other job search steps. An objective gives meaning and direction to all other activities.

Your objective should be viewed as a function of several influences. Since you want to build upon your strengths and you want to be realistic, your abilities and skills will play a central role in formulating your work objective. At the same time, you do not want your objective to become a function solely of your past accomplishments and skills. You may be very skilled in certain areas, but you may not want to use these skills in the future. As a result, your values and interests filter which skills you will or will not incorporate into your work objective.

Overcoming the problem of historical determinism – your future merely reflecting your past – requires incorporating additional components into defining your objective. One of the most important is your ideals, fantasies, or dreams. Everyone engages in these, and sometimes they come true. Your ideals, fantasies, or dreams may include making $1,000,000 by age 40; owning a Mercedes-Benz and a Porsche; taking trips to Rio, Hong Kong, and Rome; owning your own business; developing financial independence; writing a best-selling novel; solving major social problems; or winning the Nobel Peace Prize. If your fantasies require more money than you are now making, you will need to incorporate monetary considerations into your work objective. For example, if you have these fantasies, but your sense of realism tells you that your objective is to move from a $40,000 a year position to a $42,000 a year position, you will be going nowhere – unless you can fast-track in your new position. Therefore, you will need to set a higher objective to satisfy your fantasies.

You can develop realistic objectives many different ways. We don't claim to have a new or magical formula, only one which has worked for many individuals. We assume you are capable of making intelligent career decisions if given sufficient data. Using redundancy once again, our approach is designed to provide you with sufficient corroborating data from several sources and perspectives so that you can make preliminary decisions. If you follow our steps in setting a realistic objective, you should be able to give your job search clear direction.

Four major steps are involved in developing a work objective. Each step can be implemented in a variety of ways:

STEP 1: Develop or obtain basic data on your functional/transferable skills, which we discussed in Chapter 6.

STEP 2: Acquire corroborating data about yourself from others, tests, and yourself. Several resources are available for this purpose:

A. **From others:** Ask three to five individuals whom you know well to evaluate you according to the questions in the "Strength Evaluation" form on page 159. Explain to these people that you believe their candid appraisal will help you gain a better understanding of your strengths and weaknesses from the perspectives of others. Make copies of this form and ask your evaluators to complete and return it to a designated third party who will share the information – but not the respondent's name – with you.

B. **From vocational tests:** Although we prefer self-generated data, vocationally oriented tests can help clarify, confirm, and translate your understanding of yourself into occupational directions. If you decide to use vocational tests, contact a professional career counselor who can administer and interpret the tests. We suggest several of the following tests:

- *Myers-Briggs Type Indicator®*
- *Strong Interest Inventory®*
- *Self-Directed Search (SDS)*
- *Campbell Interest and Skill Survey*
- *Keirsey Character Sorter*
- *Birkman Method*
- *Enneagram*
- *FIRO-B*
- *California Psychological Inventory (CPI)*

Strength Evaluation

TO: _____

FROM: _____

I am going through a career assessment process and thought you would be an appropriate person to ask for assistance. Would you please candidly respond to the questions below? Your comments will be given to me by the individual designed below; s/he will not reveal your name. Your comments will be used for advising purposes only. Thank you.

What are my strengths?

What weak areas might I need to improve?

In your opinion, what do I need in a job or career to make me satisfied?

Please return to: _____

- *16 Personality Factors Profile*
- *Edwards Personal Preference Schedule*
- *Kuder Occupational Interest Survey*
- *APTICOM*
- *Jackson Vocational Interest Survey*
- *Ramak Inventory*
- *Vocational Interest Inventory*
- *Career Assessment Inventory*
- *Temperament and Values Inventory*

C. **From yourself:** Numerous alternatives are available for you to practice redundancy. Refer to the exercises in Chapter 7 that assist you in identifying your work values, job frustrations and dissatisfactions, things you love to do, things you enjoy most about work, and your preferred interpersonal environments.

STEP 3: Project your values and preferences into the future by completing simulation and creative thinking exercises:

A. **Ten Million Dollar Exercise:** First, assume that you are given a $10,000,000 gift; now you don't have to work. Since the gift is restricted to your use only, you cannot give any part of it away. What will you do with your time? At first? Later on? Second, assume that you are given another $10,000,000, but this time you are required to give it all away. What kinds of causes, organizations, charities, etc. would you support? Complete the following form in which you answer these questions:

What Will I Do With Two $10,000,000 Gifts?

First gift is restricted to my use only:

_____

_____

_____

Second gift must be given away:

_____

_____

_____

B. **Obituary Exercise:** Make a list of the most important things you would like to do or accomplish before you die. Two alternatives are available for doing this. First, make a list in response to this lead-in statement: *"Before I die, I want to..."*

Before I Die, I Want to . . .

1. _____

_____

2. _____

_____

3. _____

_____

4. _____

_____

5. _____

_____

6. _____

_____

7. _____

_____

8. _____

_____

9. _____

_____

10. _____

_____

Second, write a newspaper article which is actually your obituary for 10 years from now. Stress your accomplishments over the coming 10-year period.

My Obituary

Obituary for Mr./Ms. _____ to appear in the
_____ Newspaper in 2_____.

_____

_____

_____

_____

_____

_____

_____

_____

_____

_____

_____

_____

_____

_____

C. **My Ideal Work Week:** Starting with Monday, place each day
   of the week as the headings of seven sheets of paper. Develop a
   daily calendar with 30-minute intervals, beginning at 7am and
   ending at midnight. Your calendar should consist of a 118-hour
   week. Next, beginning at 7am on Monday (sheet one), identify
   the **ideal activities** you would enjoy doing, or need to do for
   each 30-minute segment during the day. Assume you are capable
   of doing anything; you have no constraints except those you
   impose on yourself. Furthermore, assume that your work
   schedule consists of 40 hours per week. How will you fill your
   time? Be specific.

My Ideal Work Week

Monday

am		pm	
7:00	_____	4:00	_____
7:30	_____	4:30	_____
8:00	_____	5:00	_____
8:30	_____	5:30	_____
9:00	_____	6:00	_____
9:30	_____	6:30	_____
10:00	_____	7:00	_____
10:30	_____	7:30	_____
11:00	_____	8:00	_____
11:30	_____	8:30	_____
Noon	_____	9:00	_____
12:30	_____	9:30	_____
p.m.		10:00	_____
1:00	_____	10:30	_____
1:30	_____	11:00	_____
2:00	_____	11:30	_____
2:30	_____	12:00	_____
3:00	_____	Continue for Tuesday, Wednesday, Thursday, and Friday	
3:30	_____		

D. **My Ideal Job Description:** Develop your ideal future job. Be sure you include:

- Specific interests you want to build into your job
- Work responsibilities
- Working conditions
- Earnings and benefits
- Interpersonal environment
- Working circumstances, opportunities, and goals

Description of My Ideal Job

_____

_____

_____

_____

_____

_____

_____

_____

_____

_____

_____

_____

_____

_____

_____

_____

_____

_____

_____

_____

Use "My Ideal Job Specifications" on page 165 to outline your ideal job. After completing this exercise, synthesize the job and write a detailed paragraph which describes the kind of job you would most enjoy:

My Ideal Job Specifications

Job Interests	Work Responsibilities	Working Conditions	Earnings/Benefits	Circumstances/Opportunities/Goals

STEP 4: Test your objective against reality. Evaluate and refine it by conducting market research, a force field analysis, library research, and informational interviews.

A. Market Research: Four steps are involved in conducting this research:

1. **Products or services:** Based upon all other assessment activities, make a list of what you **do** or **make**:

Products/Services I Do or Make

1. _____

2. _____

3. _____

4. _____

5. _____

6. _____

7. _____

8. _____

9. _____

10. _____

2. **Market:** Identify who needs, wants, or buys what you do or make. Be very specific. Include individuals, groups, and organizations. Then, identify **what** specific **needs** your products or services fill. Next, assess the **results** you achieve with your products or services.

The Market for My Products/Services

Individuals, groups, and organizations needing me:

1. _____

2. _____

3. _____

4. _____

5. _____

Needs I fulfill:

1. _____
2. _____
3. _____
4. _____
5. _____

Results/outcomes/impacts of my products/services:

1. _____
2. _____
3. _____
4. _____
5. _____

3. **New Markets:** Brainstorm a list of **who else** needs your products or services. Think about ways of expanding your market. Next, list any new needs your current or new market has which you might be able to fill:

Developing New Needs

Who else needs my products/services?

1. _____
2. _____
3. _____
4. _____
5. _____

New ways to expand my market:

1. _____
2. _____
3. _____
4. _____
5. _____

New needs I should fulfill:

1. _____
2. _____
3. _____
4. _____
5. _____

4. **New products and/or services:** List any new products or services you can offer and any new needs you can satisfy:

New Products/Services I Can Offer

1. _____
2. _____
3. _____
4. _____
5. _____

New Needs I Can Meet

1. _____
2. _____
3. _____
4. _____
5. _____

B. **Force Field Analysis:** Once you develop a tentative or firm objective, force field analysis can help you understand the various internal and external forces affecting the achievement of your objective. Force field analysis follows this sequence of activities:

■ **Clearly state your objective or course of action.** Make sure it's based upon your MAS and is employer-oriented rather than self-centered.

■ **List the positive and negative forces affecting your objective.** Specify the internal and external forces working **for** and

against you in terms of who, what, where, when, and how much. Estimate the impact of each on your objective.

- **Analyze the forces.** Assess the importance of each force upon your objective and its probable effect upon you. Some forces may be irrelevant to your goal. You may need additional information to make a thorough analysis.

- **Maximize positive forces and minimize negative ones.** Identify actions you can take to strengthen positive forces and to neutralize, overcome, or reverse negative forces. Focus on real, important, and probable key forces.

- **Assess the feasibility of attaining your objective** and, if necessary, modifying it in light of new information.

C. **Conduct Online and Library Research:** This research should strengthen and clarify your objective. Consult various reference materials on alternative jobs and careers. Most of these resources are available in print form at your local library or bookstore. Some are available in electronic versions online. If you explore the numerous company profiles and career sites available on the Internet, you should be able to tap into a wealth of information on alternative jobs and careers. Two good resources for initiating online research are Margaret Riley Dikel, *The Guide to Internet Job Search* (McGraw-Hill) and Pam Dixon, *Job Searching Online for Dummies* (IDG Books). For directories to key employment websites, see Ron and Caryl Krannich, *America's Top Internet Job Sites* and *The Directory of Websites for International Jobs* (Impact Publications); Bernard Haldane Associates, *Haldane's Best Employment Websites for Professionals* (Impact Publications); and Gerry Crispin and Mark Mehler, *CareerXroads* (MMC Group). Many of the resources traditionally found in libraries are available online. The following websites function as excellent gateway sites, online databases, and research tools:

- **CEO Express**   www.ceoexpress.com
- **Hoover's Online**   www.hoovers.com
- **Dun and Bradstreet's Million Dollar Database**   www.dnbmdd.com/mddi
- **Corporate Information**   www.corporateinformation.com
- **BizTech Network**   www.brint.com

- **AllBusiness**   www.allbusiness.com
- **BizWeb**   www.bizweb.com
- **Business.com**   www.business.com
- **America's CareerInfoNet**   www.acinet.org
- **Newspapers USA**   www.newspapers.com
- **Salary.com**   www.salary.com
- **Annual Report Service**   www.annualreportservice.com
- **Bloomberg**   www.bloomberg.com
- **Chamber of Commerce**   www.chamberofcommerce.com
- **CNN Money**   http//money.cnn.com
- **Daily Stocks**   www.dailystocks.com
- **The Corporate Library**   www.thecorporatelibrary.com
- **Forbes Lists**   www.forbes.com/lists
- **Fortune 500**   www.fortune.com
- **Harris InfoSource**   www.harrisinfo.com
- **Inc. 500**   www.inc.com/500
- **Moodys**   www.moodys.com
- **Motley Fool**   www.fool.com
- **NASDAQ**   www.nasdaq.com
- **One Source Corp Tech**   www.onesource.com
- **Standard & Poors**   www.standardandpoors.com
- **The Street**   www.thestreet.com
- **Thomas Regional**   www.thomasregional.com
- **Thomas Register**   www.thomasregister.com

Career and Job Alternatives

- *25 Jobs That Have It All*
- *50 Cutting Edge Jobs*
- *Almanac of American Employers*
- *Almanac of American Employers Mid-Size Firms*
- *America's Top 100 Jobs for People Without a Four-Year Degree*
- *Best Jobs for the 21st Century*
- *Enhanced Guide for Occupational Exploration*
- *Guide to Occupational Exploration*
- *Quick Prep Careers*
- *Occupational Outlook Handbook*
- *Occupational Outlook Quarterly*
- *O*NET Dictionary of Occupational Titles*

Industrial Directories

- _Dun and Bradstreet's Middle Market Directory_
- _Dun and Bradstreet's Million Dollar Directory_
- _Encyclopedia of Business Information Sources_
- _Geography Index_
- _Poor's Register of Corporations, Directors, and Executives_
- _Standard Directory of Advertisers_
- _The Standard Periodical Directory_
- _Standard and Poor's Industrial Index_
- _Standard Rate & Data Business Publications Directory_
- _Thomas' Register of American Manufacturers_

Associations

- _Encyclopedia of Associations_
- _National Trade and Professional Associations_
- Access thousands of associations online through: www.Ipl. org/ref/ AON and www.asaenet.org.

Government Sources

- _The Book of the States_
- _Congressional Directory_
- _Congressional Staff Directory_
- _Congressional Yellow Book_
- _Federal Directory_
- _Federal Yellow Book_
- _Municipal Yearbook_
- _Taylor's Encyclopedia of Government Officials_
- _United Nations Yearbook_
- _United States Government Manual_
- _Washington Information Directory_

Newspapers

- Major city newspapers and trade newspapers. Many are available online through these gateway sites: www.Ipl.org/reading/news, www.newsdirectory.com, www.newspaperlinks.com, and www. newspapers.com.
- Your targeted city newspaper – the Sunday edition.

Business Publications

- *Business 2.0, Business Week, Economist, Fast Company, Inc., Forbes, Fortune, Harvard Business Review, Newsweek, Smart Money, Time, U.S. News and World Report, Wired.* Many of these and other business-oriented publications can be viewed online through this terrific website: www.CEO Express.com.

- Annual issues of publications surveying the best jobs and employers for the year: *Money, Fortune, Forbes,* and *U.S. News and World Report.* Several of these reports and publications are available online: www.money.com, www.fortune. com, and www.forbes.com/lists.

Other Library Resources

- Trade journals
- Publications of Chambers of Commerce; state manufacturing associations; and federal, state, and local government agencies
- Telephone books – the Yellow Pages
- Trade books on "how to get a job" (see order form at the end of this book and www.impactpublications.com)

D. **Conduct Informational Interviews:** This may be the most useful way to clarify and refine your objective. We'll discuss this procedure in Chapters 12 and 13.

After completing these steps, you will have identified what it is you **can** do (abilities and skills), enlarged your thinking to include what it is you would **like** to do (aspirations), and probed the realities of implementing your objective. Thus, setting a realistic work objective is a function of the diverse considerations outlined on page 173.

Your work objective is a function of both subjective and objective information as well as combines idealism with realism. We believe the strongest emphasis should be placed on your competencies and should include a broad database. Your work objective is realistic in that it is tempered by your past experiences, accomplishments, skills, and current research. An objective formulated in this manner permits you to think beyond your past experiences.

Objective Setting Process

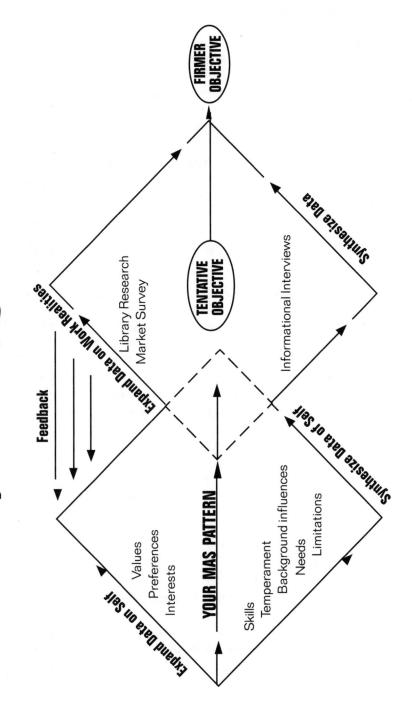

State a Functional Objective

Your job objective should be oriented toward skills and results or outcomes. You can begin by stating a functional job objective at two different levels: a general objective and a specific one for communicating your qualifications to employers both on resumes and in interviews. Thus, this objective-setting process sets the stage for other key job search activities. For the general objective, begin with the statement:

Stating Your General Objective

I would like a job where I can use my ability to _____which will result in
_____.

The objective in this statement is both a **skill** and an **outcome**. For example, you might state:

Skills-Based and Results-Oriented Objective

I would like a job where my experience in program development, supported by innovative decision-making and systems engineering abilities, will result in an expanded clientele and a more profitable organization.

At a second level you may wish to re-write this objective in order to target it at various consulting firms. For example, on your resume it becomes:

Job-Targeted Objective

An increasingly responsible research position in consulting, where proven decision-making and systems engineering abilities will be used for improving organizational productivity.

The following are examples of weak and strong objective statements. Various styles are also presented:

Weak Objectives

Management position which will use business administration degree and will provide opportunities for rapid advancement.
_____

A position in social services which will allow me to work with people in a helping capacity.

A position in Human Resources with a progressive firm.

Sales Representative with opportunity for advancement.

Stronger Objectives

To use computer science training in **software development** for designing and implementing operating systems.

A public relations position which will maximize opportunities to develop and implement programs, to organize people and events, and to communicate positive ideas and images. Effective in public speaking and in managing a publicity/promotional campaign.

A position as a General Sales Representative with a pharmaceutical house which will use chemistry background and ability to work on a self-directed basis in managing a marketing territory.

A position in data analysis where skills in mathematics, computer programming, and deductive reasoning will contribute to new systems development.

Retail Management position which will use sales/customer service experience and creative abilities for product display and merchandising. Long term goal: Progression to merchandise manager with corporate-wide responsibilities for product line.

Responsible position in investment research and analysis. Interests and skills include securities analysis, financial planning, and portfolio management. Long range goal: to become a Chartered Financial Analyst.

It is important to relate your objective to your audience. While you definitely want a good job that pays well, your audience wants to know what you can do for them in exchange for a good paying job. Remember, your objective should be work-centered, not self-centered.

We will return to this discussion when we examine how to develop the objective section on your resume. Your objective will become the key element for organizing all other elements on your resume. It gives meaning and direction to your job search. Your objective says something very important about how you want to conduct your life with the employer. It gives them an important indicator of the value you will bring to this job. Most important of all, it tells them who you really are in terms of your key values and accomplishments – a short answer to the big question of *"Why should I hire you?"*

10

Write Effective Resumes and Letters

NOW THAT YOU KNOW (1) what you do well, (2) what you enjoy doing, and (3) what you want to do in the future – based on your assessment and objective-setting work in the previous four chapters – you have the basic information necessary for communicating your key qualifications to employers. But what will you do with this information? What messages do you want to send to employers about yourself? How will you convey these messages – by telephone, letter, e-mail, fax, or in face-to-face meetings? What's the best way to the next step in your job search?

Communicating Positive Images

At every stage in the job search you must communicate a positive image to potential employers. The initial impression you make on an employer through applications, resumes, letters, telephone calls, or informational interviews will determine whether the employer is interested in interviewing you and offering you a position.

Developing and managing effective job search communication should play a central role in everything you do related to finding employment. While this communication will take several verbal and nonverbal forms, your first communication with employers will most likely be by letter, e-mail, fax, or telephone. Job search letters often include your calling card – the resume. Essentially nonverbal forms of communication, these documents should be written and distributed with impact.

Writing Resumes

Resumes are important tools for communicating your purpose and capabilities to employers. While many jobs only require a completed application form, you definitely should prepare a resume for influencing the hiring process. Application forms do not substitute for resumes.

Many myths surround resumes and letters. Some people still believe a resume should summarize one's history. Others believe it will get them a job. And still others believe a resume should be mailed or e-mailed in response to classified ads, job listings, or resume databases. The reality is closer to this: A resume advertises your qualifications to prospective employers. It is your calling card for getting interviews that lead to job offers. It should be used at any time to enhance your employability.

A resume advertises your qualifications to prospective employers. It is your calling card for getting interviews.

Ineffective Resumes

Most people write ineffective resumes. Misunderstanding the purpose of resumes, they make numerous mistakes commonly associated with weak resumes and poor advertising copy. Their resumes often lack an objective, include unrelated categories of information, are too long, and appear unattractive. Other common pitfalls identified by employers include:

- Poor layout
- Misspellings and punctuation errors
- Poor grammar
- Unclear purpose
- Too much jargon
- Irrelevant data
- Negative comments about employers
- Poorly typed and reproduced
- Unexplained time gaps
- Too boastful
- Deceptive or dishonest
- Difficult to understand or interpret

Your resume, instead, should incorporate the characteristics of strong and effective resumes. It should:

- Clearly communicate your purpose and competencies in relation to employers' needs.
- Be concise and easy to read.
- Outline a pattern of success highlighted with examples of key accomplishments.
- Motivate the reader to read it in-depth.
- Tell employers that you are a responsible and purposeful individual – a doer who can quickly solve their problems.

Keep in mind that most employers are busy people who normally glance at a resume for only 20 to 30 seconds. Your resume, therefore, must sufficiently catch their attention to pass the 20- to 30-second evaluation test. Above all, it must motivate the reader to take action. When writing your resume, ask yourself the same question asked by employers: *"Why should I read this or contact this person for an interview?"* Your answer should result in an attractive, interesting, unique, and skills-based resume.

Types of Resumes

You have four basic types of resumes to choose from: chronological, functional, combination, or resume letter. Each form has various advantages and disadvantages, depending on your background and purpose. For example, someone first entering the job market or making a major career change should use a functional resume. On the other hand, a person who wants to target a particular job may choose to use a powerful resume letter that may also

> *Employers are busy people who normally only glance at a resume for 20 or 30 seconds.*

function as a "T" letter or Focus Piece. Examples of these different types of resumes and letters are included at the end of this chapter. Further assistance in developing each section of your resume is found in our three comprehensive resume development books, *High Impact Resumes and Letters*, *Dynamite Resumes*, and *The Savvy Resume Writer*.

The **chronological resume** is the standard resume used by most applicants who are not very job search savvy. It often comes in two forms: traditional and improved. The **traditional chronological resume** is also known as the "obituary resume," because it both "kills" your chances of getting a job and is a good source for writing your obituary. Summarizing your work history, this resume lists dates and names first and duties and responsibilities second; it includes extraneous information such as height, weight, age, marital status, gender, and hobbies. While relatively easy to write, this is the most ineffective resume you can produce. Its purpose at best is to inform people of what you have done in the past as well as where, when, and with whom. It tells employers little or nothing about what you want to do, can do, and will do for them.

The **improved chronological resume** better communicates to employers your purpose, past achievements, and probable future performance. This resume works best for individuals who have extensive experience directly related to a position. This resume should include a clear work objective. The work experience section should include the names and locations of former employers followed by a brief description of relevant accomplishments, skills, and responsibilities; inclusive employment dates should appear at the end. It should stress **accomplishments** and **skills** rather than formal duties and responsibilities – that you are a productive and responsible person who gets things done, a doer. While this resume performs better than the traditional chronological resume, it still has major limitations because of its chronological format. It simply doesn't highlight very well major accomplishments and a pattern of success.

Functional resumes should be used by individuals making a significant career change, first entering the workforce, or re-entering the job market after a lengthy absence. This resume should stress your accomplishments and transferable skills regardless of previous work settings and job titles. This could include accomplishments as a housewife, volunteer worker, or Sunday school teacher. Names of employers and dates of employment should not appear on this resume.

> *Functional resumes should be used by individuals making a significant career change.*

Functional resumes have certain weaknesses. While they are important bridges for the inexperienced and for those making a career change, some employers dislike these resumes. Since many employers still look for names, dates, and direct job experience, this resume does not meet their expectations. You should use a functional resume only if you have limited work experience or your past experience doesn't strengthen your objective when making a career change.

Combination resumes, also known as hybrid resumes, combine the best features of both chronological and functional resumes. Having more advantages than disadvantages, this resume best communicates accomplishments to employers. It's an ideal resume for experienced professionals who are advancing in their careers as well as for those making a career change.

Combination resumes have the potential to both **meet** and **raise** the expectations of employers. You should stress your accomplishments and skills as well as include your work history. Your work history should appear as a separate section immediately following your presentation of accomplishments and skills in the "Areas of Effectiveness," "Experience," or "Achievements" section. It is not necessary to include dates unless they enhance your resume. This is the perfect resume for someone with work experience who wishes to change to a job in a related career field.

Resume letters are substitutes for resumes. Appearing as a job inquiry or application letter, resume letters highlight various sections of your resume, such as work history, experience, areas of effectiveness, objective, or education, in relation to employers' needs. These letters are used when you prefer not sending your more general resume. Resume letters have one major weakness: they give employers insufficient information and thus may prematurely eliminate you from consideration.

Structuring Resume Content

After choosing an appropriate resume format, you should generate the necessary information for structuring each category of your resume. You developed much of this information when you identified your motivated abilities and skills and specified your objective in Chapters 6 through 9. Include the following information on separate sheets of paper:

Contact Information: Name, street address, and telephone/fax numbers, e-mail address.

Work Objective: Refer to your data in Chapter 9 on writing an objective.

Education: Degrees, schools, dates, highlights, special training.

Work Experience: Paid, unpaid, civilian, military, and part-time employment. Include job titles, employers, locations, dates, skills, accomplishments, duties, and responsibilities. Use the functional language outlined in Chapters 6 and 7.

Achievements: Things you did that provided **benefits** to others, especially initiatives that **resulted** in outcomes for previous employers.

Other Experience:	Volunteer, civic, and professional member-ships. Include your contributions, demon-strated skills, offices held, names, and dates.
Special Skills or Licences/ Certificates:	Computer, Internet, foreign languages, teaching, paramedical, etc., relevant to your objective.
Other Information:	References, expected salary, willingness to relocate/travel, availability dates, and other information supporting your objective.

Producing Drafts

Once you generate the basic data for constructing your resume, your next task is to reduce this data into draft resumes. If, for example, you write a combination resume, the internal organization of the resume should be as follows:

- Contact information
- Work objective
- Qualifications/experience/achievements
- Work history or employment
- Education

Be careful in including any other type of information on your resume. Other information most often is extraneous or negative information. You should only include information designed to strengthen your objective.

While your first draft may run more than two pages, try to get everything into one or two pages for the final draft. Most employers lose interest after reading the first page. If you produce a two-page resume, one of the best formats is to attach a supplemental page to a self-contained one-page resume.

Your final draft should conform to the following rules for creating an excellent resume:

Rules for Effective Resumes
RESUME "DON'TS"

- **Don't** use abbreviations except for your middle name.
- **Don't** create a cramped and crowded look.
- **Don't** make statements you can't document.
- **Don't** use the passive voice.

- **Don't** change tense of verbs.
- **Don't** use lengthy sentences and descriptions.
- **Don't** refer to yourself as "I."
- **Don't** include negative information.
- **Don't** include extraneous information.

RESUME "DO'S"

- **Do** include an employer-centered objective.
- **Do** focus on your major accomplishments as they relate to the needs of the employer.
- **Do** use action verbs and the active voice.
- **Do** include nouns so your resume can be scanned for keywords.
- **Do** be direct, succinct, and expressive with your language.
- **Do** appear neat, well organized, and professional.
- **Do** use ample spacing and highlights (all caps, underlining, bulleting) for different emphases (except if it's an electronic resume).
- **Do** maintain an eye-pleasing balance.
- **Do** check carefully your spelling, grammar, and punctuation.
- **Do** clearly communicate your purpose and value to employers.
- **Do** communicate your strongest points first.

Evaluating the Final Product

You should subject your resume drafts to two types of evaluations. An **internal evaluation** consists of reviewing our lists of "do's" and "don'ts" to make sure your resume conforms to these rules. An **external evaluation** should be conducted by circulating your resume to three or more individuals whom you believe will give you frank, objective, and useful feedback. Avoid people who tend to flatter you. The best evaluator would be someone in a hiring position similar to one you will encounter in the actual interview. Ask these people to critique your draft resume and suggest improvements in both form and content. This will be your most important evaluation. After all, the only evaluation that counts is the one that helps get you an interview. Asking someone to critique your resume is one way to spread the word that you are job hunting. As we will see in Chapter 12, this is one method for getting invited to an interview!

Final Production

Your final resume can be typed, word-processed, or typeset. If you produce it the old fashioned way – type it on a typewriter – make the final product look as professional as possible. But being old technology, a typewriter doesn't yield a top professional look. Furthermore, producing a resume in this manner communicates that you are probably a generation behind with your communication skills – still using a typewriter rather than a computer. Typeset resumes are largely a waste of time and money since you can achieve the same print quality using a computer and printer.

It's best to word-process your resume and print it on a laser printer (600 dpi or higher preferred). Dot matrix and near letter quality printers make your resume look both unprofessional and mass produced. Word-processed resumes give you the greatest flexibility to custom design your resume for individual employers. If you lack good word-processing skills, take your resume to a printer or quick copy center, such as Kinkos, which should be able to give you first-class production for under $50.00.

Be sure to proofread the final copy. Don't spend good money on production only to later find typing errors. Better still, have someone else proofread your resume. You may be too close to your subject to catch all errors.

Remember, your resume is your calling card – it should represent your best professional image.

When reproducing the resume, you must consider the quality and color of paper as well as the number of copies you need. By all means use good quality paper. You should use 20-pound or heavier bond paper. Costing 3¢ to 7¢ per sheet, this paper can be purchased through stationery stores and printers. It is important not to cut corners at this point by purchasing cheap paper or using copy machine paper. You may save $5 on 100 copies, but you also will communicate an unprofessional image to employers.

Use one of the following paper colors: white, cream, light tan, light gray, or light blue. Avoid blue, yellow, green, pink, orange, red, or any other bright or pastel colors. Conservative, light, neutral colors are the best. Any of these colors can be complemented with black ink. In the case of light gray – our first choice – a navy blue ink looks best. Dark brown ink is especially attractive on light tan paper. However, be very careful in using any color other than white since more and more employers electronically scan resumes. Resumes printed on colored papers do not scan well.

Your choices of paper quality and color say something about your personality and professional style. They communicate nonverbally your potential strengths and weaknesses. Employers will use these as indicators for screening you in or out of an interview. At the same time, these choices may make your resume stand out from the crowd of standard black-on-white resumes.

Whatever your choices, do not try to cut costs when it comes to producing your resume. It simply is not worth it. Remember, your resume is your calling card – it should represent your best professional image. Put your best foot forward at this stage. Go in style; spend a few dollars on producing a first-class resume.

Job Search Letters

Regardless of how you send your resume, it should be accompanied by a cover letter. Indeed, certain types of cover letters – especially powerful "T" letters and Focus Pieces – are often more important than resumes. After interviewing for information or a position, you should send a thank you letter. Other occasions will arise when it is both proper and necessary for you to write different types of job search letters. Numerous examples of job search letters are presented in our *High Impact Resumes and Letters, Dynamite Cover Letters*, and *201 Dynamite Job Search Letters*. For a unique set of powerful "T" letters and Focus Pieces, see *Haldane's Best Cover Letters for Professionals*. All of these resources are published by Impact Publications.

Your letter writing should follow the principles of good resume and business writing. Job hunting letters are like resumes – they advertise you for interviews. Like good advertisements, these letters should follow four basic principles for effectiveness:

1. Catch the reader's attention.
2. Persuade the reader of your benefits or value.
3. Convince the reader with evidence.
4. Move the reader to acquire the product – you!

In addition, the content of your letters should be the basis for conducting screening interviews as well as a face-to-face interviews.

Basic Preparation Rules

Before you begin writing a job search letter, ask yourself several questions to clarify the content of your letter:

- What is the **purpose** of the letter?
- What are the **needs** of my audience?
- What **benefits** will my audience gain from me?
- What is a good opening sentence or paragraph for grabbing the **attention** of my audience?
- How can I maintain the **interest** of my audience?

- How can I best end the letter so that the audience will be **persuaded** to contact me?
- If accompanied by a resume, how can my letter best **advertise the resume?**
- Have I spent enough *time* revising and proofreading the letter?
- Does the letter represent my **best professional effort?**

Since your letters are a form of business communication, they should conform to the rules of good business correspondence:

Principles of Good Business Communication

- Organize what you will say by outlining the content of your letter.
- Know your purpose and structure your letter accordingly.
- Communicate your message in a logical and sequential manner.
- State your purpose immediately in the first sentence and paragraph; main ideas always go first.
- End by stating what your reader can expect next from you.
- Use short paragraphs and sentences; avoid complex sentences.
- Punctuate properly and use correct grammar and spelling.
- Use simple and straightforward language; avoid jargon.
- Communicate your message as directly and briefly as possible.

The rules stress how to both **organize and communicate** your message with impact. At the same time, you should always have a specific purpose in mind as well as know the needs of your audience.

Types of Letters

Cover letters provide cover for your resume. You should avoid overwhelming a one-page resume with a two-page letter or repeating the contents of the resume in the letter. A short and succinct one-page letter which highlights one or two points in your resume is sufficient. Three paragraphs will suffice. The first paragraph should state your interests and purposes for writing. The second paragraph should highlight your possible value to the employer. The third paragraph should state that you will call the individual at a particular time to schedule an interview.

However, do not expect great results from cover letters. Many professional job search firms use computers and mailing lists to flood the job market with thousands of unsolicited resumes and cover letters each day. Other job seekers use "canned" job search letters produced by computer software programs, such as *WinWay Resumes*, designed to generate model job search letters. As a result, employers are increasingly suspicious of the authenticity of such letters. To cope with the sheer volume of communications, many employers use resume management software to scan, store, and retrieve such communications – or they throw away most of the unsolicited resumes and letters they receive.

Approach letters are written for the purpose of developing job contacts, leads, or information as well as for organizing networks and getting interviews – the subjects of Chapter 12. Your primary purposes should be to get employers to engage in the 5R's of informational interviewing:

- **Reveal** useful information and advice.
- **Refer** you to others.
- **Read** your resume.
- **Revise** your resume.
- **Remember** you for future reference.

These letters help you gain access to the hidden job market by making important networking contacts that lead to those all-important informational interviews.

Approach letters can be sent out en masse to uncover job leads, or they can target particular individuals or organizations. It is better to target these letters since they have maximum impact when personalized in reference to a position.

> *Approach letters should get employers to engage in the 5R's of informational interviewing.*

The structure of approach letters is similar to other letters. The first paragraph states your purpose. In so doing, you may want to use a personal statement for openers, such as *"Mary Tillis recommended that I write to you..."* or *"I am familiar with your..."* State your purpose, but do not suggest that you are asking for a job – only career advice or information. In your final paragraph, request a meeting and indicate you will call to schedule such a meeting at a mutually convenient time.

Thank you letters may well become your most effective job search letters. They especially communicate your thoughtfulness. These letters come in different forms and are written for various occasions. The most common thank you letter is written after receiving assistance, such as job search information and advice or a critique of your resume. Other occasions include:

- **Immediately following an interview:** Thank the interviewer for the opportunity to interview for the position. Repeat your interest in the position.

- **Receive a job offer:** Thank the employer for his or her faith in you and express your appreciation.

- **Rejected for a job:** Thank the employer for the "opportunity" to interview for the job. Ask to be remembered for future reference.

- **Terminate employment:** Thank the employer for the experience and ask to be remembered for future reference.

- **Begin a new job:** Thank the employer for giving you this new opportunity and express your confidence in producing the value he or she is expecting from you.

Being remembered by employers is the closest thing to being invited to an interview and offered a job.

Examples of these letters are included at the end of this chapter.

Several of these thank you letters are unusual, but they all have the same goal – to be remembered by potential employers in a positive light. In a job search, being remembered by employers is the closest thing to being invited to an interview and offered a job.

Distribution and Management

The only good resumes are the ones that get read, remembered, referred, and result in a job interview. Therefore, after completing a first-rate resume, you must decide what to do with it. Are you planning to only respond to classified ads with a standard mailing piece consisting of your conventional or electronic resume and a formal cover letter? Do you prefer posting your resume online with resume databases or e-mailing it to potential employers? But wait a minute; classified ads and resume databases only represent one portion of the job market. What other creative distribution methods might you use, such as sending it to friends, relatives, and former employers; mailing it in a shoe box with a note (*"Now that I've got my foot in the door, how about an interview?"*); gift wrapping it; or having it delivered by a singing messenger? What's the best way to proceed?

Responding to Classified Ads

Most of your writing activities should focus on the hidden job market where jobs are neither announced nor listed. At the same time, you should respond to job listings in newspapers, magazines, human resources offices, and on websites as well as get your resume into online resume databases. While this is largely a numbers game, you can increase your odds by the way you respond to the listings.

You should be selective in your responses. Since you know what you want to do, you will be looking for only certain types of positions. Once you identify them, your response entails little expenditure of time and effort – a quick e-mail, fax, or a paper envelope, letter, stamp, resume, and some of your time. You have little to lose. While you have the potential to gain by sending a letter and resume in response to an ad, remember the odds are usually against you.

It is difficult to interpret job listings, regardless of whether they are in print or electronic format. Some employers place blind ads with P.O. Box numbers and e-mail addresses in order to collect resumes for future reference. Others wish to avoid aggressive applicants who telephone or "drop in" for interviews. Many employers work through professional recruiters who place these ads or they post job listings on electronic bulletin boards. While you may try to second guess the rationale behind such ads, it's always best to respond to them as you would to ads with an employer's name, address, or telephone number. Assume there is a real job behind each ad.

> *Keep your letter brief and concise and high-light your qualifications as stated in the employer's ad.*

Most ads request a copy of your resume. Employers increasingly request that it be sent by e-mail or fax. You should respond with a cover letter and resume as soon as you see the ad. Depending on how much information about the position is revealed in the ad, your letter should be tailored to emphasize your qualifications vis-a-vis the ad. Examine the ad carefully. Underline any words or phrases which relate to your qualifications. In your cover letter, you should use similar terminology in emphasizing your qualifications. The most powerful cover letter you can send is the classic "T" letter which literally matches your skills and accomplishments with each of the employer's requirements. Keep the letter brief and to the point.

If the ad asks you to state your salary history or salary requirements, state "negotiable" or "open." Alternatively, you can include a figure by stating a salary range 20 percent above your present salary base or include a total compensation figure. For example, if you are making $40,000 a year, you can state *"My current salary is in the $40,000 to $45,000 range"* or *"My current compensation package is worth $63,000 a year."*

Use your own judgment in addressing the salary question. There is no hard and fast rule on stating a figure or range. We recommend that you **be honest but not stupid**. A figure helps the employer screen out individuals with too high a salary expectation. However, most people prefer to keep salary considerations to the end of the final interview – after they have demonstrated their value and have more information about the position. This may occur during the initial interview but more likely during the second, third, or even fourth interview.

You may be able to increase your odds by sending a second copy of your letter and resume two or three weeks after your initial response. Most applicants normally reply to an ad during the seven-day period immediately after it appears in print. Since employers often are swamped with responses, your letter and resume may get lost in the crowd. If you send a second copy of your resume two or three weeks later, the employer will have more time to give you special attention. By then, he or she also will have a better basis on which to compare you to the others. However, if the employer electronically scans resumes, sending a second copy of your resume and letter will not affect the outcome.

Keep in mind that your cover letter and resume may be screened among 400 other resumes and letters. Thus, you want your cover letter to be eye-catching and easy to read. Keep it brief and concise and highlight your qualifications as stated in the employer's ad. If you know your resume will be electronically scanned, make sure it includes lots of keywords and is formatted properly for scanners. Don't spend a great deal of time responding to an ad or waiting anxiously at your mailbox, telephone, or computer for a reply. Keep moving on to other job search activities.

Self-Initiated Methods

Your letters and resumes can be distributed and managed in various ways. Many people broadcast or "shotgun" hundreds of cover letters and resumes to prospective employers. This is a form of gambling where the odds are always against you. For every 100 people you contact in this manner, expect one or two who might be interested in you. After all, successful direct-mail experts at best expect only a 2-percent return on their mass mailings!

If you choose to use the broadcast method, you can increase your odds by using the **telephone**. Call the prospective employer within a week after he or she receives your letter. This technique will probably increase your effectiveness rate from 1 to 5 percent.

However, many people are broadcasting their resumes today and more and more employers are using automated resume management systems. As more resumes and letters descend on employers, the effectiveness rates may be even lower. This also can be an expensive marketing method. You would be much better off posting an electronic version of your resume on various online employment sites where your exposure rate will be much higher and more targeted to the needs of specific employers. Start by surveying job listings and posting your resume on these top Internet sites:

- www.directemployers.com
- www.monster.com
- www.careerbuilder.com
- www.careerjournal.com
- www.4work.com
- http://hotjobs.yahoo.com
- www.nationjob.com
- www.flipdog.com
- www.careerflex.com
- www.employment911.com

This electronic form of broadcasting is also the cheapest way to go – it's usually free to job seekers.

Your best distribution strategy will be your own modification of the following procedure:

1. Selectively identify with whom you are interested in working.
2. Send an approach letter.
3. Follow up with a telephone call requesting an informational interview.

In more than 50 percent of the cases, you will get an interview. It is best not to include a copy of your resume with the approach letter. If you include a resume, you communicate the wrong message – you want a job rather than information and advice. Keep your resume for the very end of the interview. Chapter 12 outlines procedures for conducting this informational interview.

Resume Databases and Online Recruiting

The Internet has quickly become the best friend of both employers and headhunters who can recruit personnel much faster and cheaper than through more traditional recruitment channels. Even small companies, with fewer than 10 employees, now use the Internet to advertise jobs and search resume databases for qualified candidates. At the same time, the Internet offers job seekers an important tool to add to their job search arsenal. Make sure you include the Internet in your job search by posting your resume on numerous sites, conducting research, and networking for information, advice, and referrals. Start with the 10 major sites listed above. While you may not get your next job through the Internet, at least you will acquire lots of useful information over the Internet for enhancing your overall job search.

For more information on the use of electronic resume databases and online recruiting, we recommend the following resources:

Adams Internet Job Search Almanac (Michelle Roy Kelly, ed.)

America's Top Internet Job Sites (Ron and Caryl Krannich)

CareerXroads (Gerry Crispin and Mark Mehler)

Career Exploration on the Internet (Facts on File)

Cyberspace Job Search Kit (Fred E. Jandt and Mary B. Nemnich)

The Directory of Websites for International Jobs (Ron and Caryl Krannich)

Electronic Resumes and Online Networking (Rebecca Smith)

e-Resumes (Susan Britton Witcomb and Pat Kendall)

The Everything Online Job Search Book (Steve Graber)

The Guide to Internet Job Searching (Margaret Riley Dikel)

Haldane's Best Employment Websites for Professionals (Bernard Haldane Associates)

Job-Hunting on the Internet (Richard Nelson Bolles)

Job Searching Online for Dummies, with CD-ROM (Pam Dixon)

Weddle's Job-Seeker's Guide to Employment Web Sites (Peter D. Weddle)

Most of these books are available in libraries and bookstores or they can be ordered directly from Impact Publications (see order form at the end of this book or visit www.impactpublications.com).

Recordkeeping

Once you begin distributing letters and resumes, you also will need to keep good records for managing your job search writing campaign. You can do this the old fashioned way by purchasing file folders for your correspondence and notes. Be sure to make copies of all letters you write since you may need to refer to them over the telephone or before interviews. Record your activities with each employer – letters, resumes, telephone calls, interviews – on a 4x6 card and file it according to the name of the organization or individual. These files will help you quickly access information and evaluate your job search progress.

If you're computer savvy, you may want to electronically organize your recordkeeping activities using a database program. Check your current software programs for a contact manager, calendar, or tracking/follow-up program. Several software programs are now available for networking and tracking activities. Some, such as *WinWay Resume, ResumeMaker, Sharkware, You're Hired!,* and *Finding and Following Up Job Leads,* are designed specifically for tracking job leads and following up specific job search activities. Many of the large employment websites, such as www.monster.com, allow you to manage your resume and track applications online.

Always remember the purpose of resumes and letters – **advertise you for interviews**. They do not get jobs. Since employers know nothing about you and your accomplishments – you're a stranger at their door – **you must effectively communicate your value in writing prior to meeting them in person for the critical job interview**. While you should not overestimate the importance of this written communication, neither should you underestimate it. After all, in the eyes of most employers, you essentially are what you write.

Traditional Chronological Resume
(Obituary Type)

RESUME

James C. Astor	Weight:	190 lbs.
4921 Tyler Drive	Height:	6'0"
Washington, D.C. 20011	Born:	June 2, 1970
	Health:	Good
	Marital Status:	Divorced

EDUCATION
1997-1998:   M.A., Vocational Counseling, Virginia Commonwealth University, Richmond, Virginia.

1986-1990:   B.A., Psychology, Roanoke College, Salem, Virginia.

1984-1986:   High School Diploma, Richmond Community High School, Richmond, Virginia.

WORK EXPERIENCE
6/13/98 to 2/22/2003: Supervisory Trainer, GS-12, U.S. Department of Labor, Washington, D.C. Responsible for all aspects of training. Terminated because of budget cuts.

9/10/96 to 11/21/97: Bartender, Johnnie's Disco, Richmond, Virginia. Part-time while attending college.

4/3/94 to 6/2/96: Counselor, Virginia Employment Commission, Richmond, Virginia. Responsible for interviewing unemployed for jobs. Resigned to work full-time on master's degree.

8/15/91 to 6/15/93: Guidance counselor and teacher, Petersburg Junior High School, Petersburg, Virginia.

2/11/89 to 10/6/89: Cook and waiter, Big Mama's Pizza Parlor, Roanoke, Virginia. Part-time while attending college.

PROFESSIONAL AFFILIATIONS
American Personnel and Guidance Association
American Society for Training and Development
Personnel Management Association
Phi Delta Pi

HOBBIES
I like to play tennis, bicycle, and hike.

REFERENCES
David Ryan, Chief, Training Division, U.S. Department of Labor, Washington, D.C. 20012, (212) 735-0121.

Dr. Sara Thomas, Professor, Department of Psychology, George Washington University, Washington, D.C. 20030, (201) 621-4545.

Thomas V. Grant, Area Manager, Virginia Employment Commission, Richmond, Virginia 26412, (804) 261-4089.

Improved Chronological Resume

_____ JAMES C. ASTOR _____
4921 Tyler Drive
Washington, DC 20011   212/422-8764
astorc@mymail.com

OBJECTIVE: A training and counseling position with a computer firm, where strong administrative, communication, and planning abilities will be used for improving the work performance and job satisfaction of employees.

EXPERIENCE: U.S. Department of Labor, Washington, D.C.
Planned and organized counseling programs for 5,000 employees. Developed training manuals and conducted workshops on interpersonal skills, stress management, and career planning; resulted in a 50-percent decrease in absenteeism. Supervised team of five instructors and counselors. Conducted individual counseling and referrals to community organizations. Advised government agencies and private firms on establishing in-house employee counseling and career development programs. Consistently evaluated as outstanding by supervisors and workshop participants. 1998 to present.

Virginia Employment Commission, Richmond, Virginia.
Conducted all aspects of employment counseling. Interviewed, screened, and counseled 2,500 job seekers. Referred clients to employers and other agencies. Coordinated job vacancy and training information for businesses, industries, and schools. Reorganized interviewing and screening processes which improved the efficiency of operations by 50 percent. Cited in annual evaluation for "outstanding contributions to improving relations with employers and clients." 1990-1997.

Petersburg Junior High School, Petersburg, Virginia.
Guidance Counselor for 800 students. Developed program of individualized and group counseling. Taught special social science classes for socially maladjusted and slow learners. 1987-1989.

EDUCATION: M.A., Vocational Counseling, Virginia Commonwealth University, Richmond, Virginia, 1994.

B.A., Psychology, Roanoke College, Salem, Virginia, 1986.

REFERENCES: Available upon request.

Functional Resume

JAMES C. ASTOR

| 4921 Tyler Drive | Washington, D.C. 20011 | 212/422-8764 |
| | | astorc@mymail.com |

OBJECTIVE   A training and counseling position with a computer firm, where strong administrative, communication, and planning abilities will be used for improving the work performance and job satisfaction of employees.

EDUCATION   Ph.D. in process, Industrial Psychology, George Washington University, Washington, D.C.

M.A., Vocational Counseling, Virginia Commonwealth University, Richmond, Virginia, 1997.

B.A., Psychology, Roanoke College, Salem, Virginia 1989.

AREAS OF   Administration
EFFECTIVENESS   Supervised instructors and counselors. Coordinated job vacancy and training information for businesses, industries, and schools.

Communication
Conducted over 100 workshops on interpersonal skills, stress management, and career planning. Frequent guest speaker to various agencies and private firms. Experienced writer of training manuals and public relations materials.

Planning
Planned and developed counseling programs for 5,000 employees. Reorganized interviewing and screening processes for public employment agency. Developed program of individualized and group counseling for community school.

PERSONAL   Enjoy challenges and working with people. . .interested in productivity. . .willing to relocate and travel.

REFERENCES   Available upon request.

Combination Resume

_____ JAMES C. ASTOR _____
4921 Tyler Drive
Washington, D.C. 20011   212/422-8764
astorc@mymail.com

OBJECTIVE: A training and counseling position with a computer firm, where strong administrative, communication, and planning abilities will be used for improving the work performance and job satisfaction of employees.

AREAS OF EFFECTIVENESS

ADMINISTRATION: Supervised instructors and counselors. Coordinated job vacancy and training information for businesses, industries, and schools.

COMMUNICATION: Conducted over 100 workshops on interpersonal skills, stress management, and career planning. Frequent guest speaker to various agencies and private firms. Experienced writer of training manuals and public relations materials.

PLANNING: Planned and developed counseling programs for 5,000 employees. Reorganized interviewing and screening processes for public employment agency. Developed program of individualized and group counseling for community school.

WORK HISTORY: Supervisory Trainer, U.S. Department of Labor, Washington, D.C., 1997 to present.

Counselor, Virginia Employment Commission, Richmond, Virginia, 1993-1996.

Guidance counselor and teacher, Petersburg Junior High School, Petersburg, Virginia, 1990-1992.

EDUCATION: M.A., Vocational Counseling, Virginia Commonwealth University, Richmond, Virginia, 1997.

B.A., Psychology, Roanoke College, Salem, Virginia, 1982.

PERSONAL: Enjoy challenges and working with people. . .interested in productivity. . .willing to relocate and travel.

Combination Resume – continued

<u>SUPPLEMENTAL INFORMATION</u>   JAMES C. ASTOR

<u>Continuing Education and Training</u>

- Completed 12 semester hours of computer science courses.
- Attended several workshops during past three years on employee counseling and administrative methods:

> "Career Development For Technical Personnel," Professional Management Association, 3 days, 1999.

> "Effective Supervisory Methods For Training Directors," National Training Associates, 3 days, 1998.

> "Training the Trainer," American Society For Training and Development, 3 days, 1996.

> "Time Management," U.S. Department of Labor, 3 days, 1995.

> "Career Development For Technical Personnel," Professional Management Associates, 3 days, 1994.

> "Counseling the Absentee Employee," American Management Association, 3 days, 1994.

<u>Training Manuals Developed</u>

- "Managing Employee Stress," U.S. Department of Labor, 1998.
- "Effective Interpersonal Communication in the Workplace," U.S. Department of Labor, 1994.
- "Planning Careers Within the Organization," U.S. Department of Labor, 1993.

<u>Research Projects Completed</u>

- "Employee Counseling Programs for Technical Personnel," U.S. Department of Labor, 1999. Incorporated into agency report on "New Directions in Employee Counseling."
- "Developing Training Programs for Problem Employees," M.A. thesis, Virginia Commonwealth University, 1997.

<u>Professional Affiliations</u>

- American Personnel and Guidance Association
- American Society for Training and Development
- Personnel Management Association

<u>Educational Highlights</u>

- Completing Ph.D. in Industrial Psychology, George Washington University, Washington, DC, 2005.
- Earned 4.0/4.0 grade point average as a graduate student.

Resume Letter

4921 Tyler Drive
Washington, D.C. 20011
March 15, 20 ____

Doris Stevens
STR Corporation
179 South Trail
Rockville, Maryland 21101

Dear Ms. Stevens:

STR Corporation is one of the most dynamic computer companies in the nation. In addition to being a leader in the field of small business computers, STR has a progressive employee training and development program which could very well become a model for other organizations. This is the type of organization I am interested in joining.

I am seeking a training position with a computer firm which would utilize my administrative, communication, and planning abilities to develop effective training and counseling programs. My experience includes:

<u>Administration</u>: Supervised instructors and counselors. Coordinated job vacancy and training information for businesses, industries, and schools.

<u>Communication</u>: Conducted over 100 workshops on interpersonal skills, stress management, and career planning. Frequent guest speaker to various agencies and private firms. Experienced writer of training manuals and public relations materials.

<u>Planning</u>: Planned and developed counseling programs for 5,000 employees. Reorganized interviewing and screening processes for public employment agency. Developed program of individualized and group counseling for community school.

In addition, I am completing my Ph.D. in industrial psychology with emphasis on developing training and counseling programs for technical personnel.

Could we meet to discuss your program as well as how my experience might relate to your needs? I will call your office on Tuesday morning, March 23, to arrange a convenient time to meet with you.

I especially want to show you a model employee counseling and career development program I recently developed. Perhaps you may find it useful for your work with STR.

Sincerely yours,

James C. Astor

James C. Astor
astorc@mymail.com

Cover Letter

2842 South Plaza
Chicago, Illinois 60228
March 12, 20 _____

David C. Johnson
Director of Personnel
Bank of Chicago
490 Michigan Avenue
Chicago, Illinois 60222

Dear Mr. Johnson:

The accompanying resume is in response to your listing in the Chicago Tribune for a loan officer.

I am especially interested in this position because my experience with the Small Business Administration has prepared me for understanding the financial needs and problems of the business community from the perspectives of both lenders and borrowers. I wish to use this experience with a growing and community-conscious bank such as yours.

I would appreciate an opportunity to meet with you to discuss how my experience will best meet your needs. My ideas on how to improve small business financing may be of particular interest to you. Therefore, I will call your office on the morning of March 17 to inquire if a meeting can be scheduled at a convenient time.

I look forward to meeting you.

Sincerely yours,

Joyce Pitman

Joyce Pitman
pitmanj@mymail.com

Approach Letter
Referral

821 Stevens Point
Boston, MA 01990
April 14, 20 ____

Terri Fulton
Director of Personnel
TRS Corporation
6311 W. Dover
Boston, MA 01991

Dear Ms. Fulton:

Alice O'Brien suggested that I contact you about my interest in personnel management. She said you are one of the best people to talk to in regard to careers in personnel.

I am leaving government after seven years of increasingly responsible experience in personnel. I am especially interested in working with a large private firm. However, before I venture further into the job market, I want to benefit from the experience and knowledge of others in the field who might advise me on opportunities for someone with my qualifications.

Perhaps we could meet briefly sometime during the next two weeks to discuss my career plans. I have several questions which I believe you could help clarify. I will call your office on Tuesday, April 22, to schedule a meeting time.

I look forward to discussing my plans with you.

Sincerely yours,

Katherine Kelly

Katherine Kelly
kellyk@mymail.com

Approach Letter
Cold Turkey

2189 West Church Street
New York, NY 10011
May 3, 20 ____

Patricia Dotson, Director
Northeast Association for
  the Elderly
9930 Jefferson Street
New York, NY 10013

Dear Ms. Dotson:

I have been impressed with your work with the elderly. Your organization takes a community perspective in trying to integrate the concerns of the elderly with those of other community groups. Perhaps other organizations will soon follow your lead.

I am anxious to meet you and learn more about your work. My background with the city Volunteer Services Program involved frequent contacts with elderly volunteers. From this experience I decided I preferred working primarily with the elderly.

However, before I pursue my interest further, I need to talk to people with experience in gerontology. In particular, I would like to know more about careers with the elderly as well as how my background might best be used in the field of gerontology.

I am hoping you can assist me in this matter. I would like to meet with you briefly to discuss several of my concerns. I will call next week to see if your schedule permits such a meeting.

I look forward to meeting you.

Sincerely,

Carol Timms

Carol Timms
timmsc@mymail.com

Thank You Letter
Post-Informational Interview

9910 Thompson Drive
Cleveland, Ohio 43382
June 21, 20 ____

Jane Evans, Director
Evans Finance Corporation
2122 Forman Street
Cleveland, Ohio 43380

Dear Ms. Evans:

Your advice was most helpful in clarifying my questions on careers in finance. I am now reworking my resume and have included many of your thoughtful suggestions. I will send you a copy next week.

Thanks so much for taking time from your busy schedule to see me. I will keep in contact and follow through on your suggestion to see Sarah Cook about opportunities with the Cleveland-Akron Finance Company.

Sincerely,

Daryl Haines

Daryl Haines
hainesd@mymail.com

Thank You Letter
Post-Job Interview

2962 Forrest Drive
Denver, Colorado 82171
May 28, 20 ____

Thomas F. Harris
Director, Personnel Department
Coastal Products Incorporated
7229 Lakewood Drive
Denver, Colorado 82170

Dear Mr. Harris:

Thank you again for the opportunity to interview for the marketing position. I appreciated your hospitality and enjoyed meeting you and members of your staff.

The interview convinced me of how compatible my background, interest, and skills are with the goals of Coastal Products Incorporated. My prior marketing experience with the Department of Commerce has prepared me to take a major role in developing both domestic and international marketing strategies. I am confident my work for you will result in increased profits within the first two years.

For more information on the new product promotion program I mentioned, call David Garrett at the Department of Commerce; his number is 202/726-0132. I talked to Dave this morning and mentioned your interest in this program.

I look forward to meeting you again.

Sincerely,

Jim Potter

Tim Potter
pottert@mymail.com

Thank You Letter
Job Rejection

564 Court Street
St. Louis, MO 53167
April 29, 20 ___

Ralph Ullman, President
S.T. Ayer Corporation
6921 Southern Blvd.
St. Louis, MO 53163

Dear Mr. Ullman:

I appreciated your consideration for the Research Associate position. While I am disappointed in not being selected, I learned a great deal about your corporation, and I enjoyed meeting with you and your staff. I felt particularly good about the professional manner in which you conducted the interview.

Please keep me in mind for future consideration. I have a strong interest in your company. I believe we would work well together. I will be closely following the progress of your company over the coming months. Perhaps we will be in touch with each other at some later date.

Best wishes.

Sincerely,

Martin Tollins

Martin Tollins
tollinsm@mymail.com

Thank You Letter
Job Offer Acceptance

7694 James Court
San Francisco, CA 94826
June 7, 20 ____

Judith Greene
Vice President
West Coast Airlines
2400 Van Ness
San Francisco, CA 94829

Dear Ms. Greene:

I am pleased to accept your offer, and I am looking forward to joining you and your staff next month.

The customer relations position is ideally suited to my background and interests. I assure you I will give you my best effort in making this an effective position within your company.

I understand I will begin work on July. If, in the meantime, I need to complete any paper work or take care of any other matters, please contact me.

I enjoyed meeting with you and your staff and appreciated the professional manner in which the hiring was conducted.

Sincerely,

Joan Kitner

Joan Kitner
kitnerj@mymail.com

11

Research Alternative Jobs and Communities

THE OLD ADAGE THAT "knowledge is power" is especially true when conducting a job search. Your job search is only as good as the knowledge you acquire and use for finding the job you want.

Gathering, processing, and using information is the lifeblood of any job search. Research integrates the individual job search activities and provides feedback for adapting strategies to the realities of the job market. Given the numerous individuals and organizations involved in your job search, you must develop an information gathering strategy that will help you gain knowledge about, as well as access to, those individuals and organizations that will play the most important role in your job search.

Research Purposes

Research is the key to gathering, processing, and using information in your job search. It is a skill that will point you in fruitful directions for minimizing job search frustrations and maximizing successes. Be sure to make research one of your top priorities.

However, most people are reluctant to initiate a research campaign which involves using libraries and computers, telephoning, and meeting new people. Such reluctance is due in part to the lack of knowledge on how to conduct research and where to find resources, and in part to a certain cultural shyness which inhibits individuals from initiating contacts with strangers. However, research is not a difficult process. After all, most people conduct research daily as they read and converse with others about problems. This daily research process needs to be specified and focused on your job search campaign.

Research serves several purposes when adapted to your job search. First, knowing the who, what, when, and where of organizations and individuals is essential for targeting your resume and conducting informational and job interviews. Second, the research component should broaden your perspective on the job market in relation to your motivated abilities and skills and job objective. Since there are over 1,100 different job titles as well as thousands and thousands of job markets, even a full-time research campaign will uncover only a small segment of the job market relevant to your interests and skills.

A third purpose of research is to better understand how to relate your motivated abilities and skills to specific jobs and work environments. Once you research and understand the critical requirements of a given job in a specific work environment, you can assess the appropriateness of that job for you vis-a-vis your pattern of motivated abilities and skills (MAS).

Fourth, researching organizations and individuals should result in systematically uncovering a set of contacts for developing your job search network. One of your major research goals should be to compile names, addresses, and telephone numbers of individuals who may become important resources in your new network of job contacts.

A fifth purpose of research is to learn the **languages** (jargon) of alternative jobs and careers. You can learn to better converse in these languages by reading trade journals, annual reports, pamphlets, and other organizational literature as well as talking with people in various occupational fields. Knowing these languages – especially asking and answering intelligent questions in the language of the employer – is important for conducting successful referral and job interviews as well as using the right keywords on your resume.

Finally, research should result in bringing some degree of structure, coherence, and understanding to the inherently decentralized, fragmented, and chaotic job market. Without research, you place yourself at the mercy of chance and luck; thus, you become a subject of your environment. Research best enables you to take control of your situation. It is power.

Your research activities should focus on four major targets: occupational alternatives, organizations, individuals, and communities. If you give equal time to each, you will be well on your way to getting job interviews and offers.

Investigate Alternative Jobs and Careers

Your initial research should help familiarize you with **job and career alternatives**. For example, the U.S. Department of Labor now identifies over 1,100 job titles (condensed from over 13,000 job titles a few years ago). Most individuals are occupationally illiterate; they are unaware of the vast array of available jobs and careers. Therefore, it is essential to investigate occupational alternatives in order to broaden your perspective on the job market.

You should start your research by examining several key directories that provide information on alternative jobs and careers:

- _Occupational Outlook Handbook_
- _Encyclopedia of Careers and Vocational Guidance_
- _Enhanced Guide to Occupational Exploration_
- _Guide to Occupational Exploration_
- _O*NET Dictionary of Occupational Titles_

The latest version of the _Occupational Outlook Handbook_, most data related to the _O*NET_, and other useful career exploration information are now available online by visiting these three websites operated by the U.S. Department of Labor:

- _OOH_   www.bls.gov/oco
- _O*NET_   www.onetcenter.org
- **America's CareerInfoNet**   www.acinet.org

You will also find several books that focus on alternative jobs and careers. McGraw-Hill, for example, produces one of the most comprehensive series of books on alternative jobs and careers. Their books address nearly 100 different job and career fields. Representative titles in their _"Opportunities in..."_ series include:

- _Opportunities in Acting_
- _Opportunities in Aerospace_
- _Opportunities in Banking_
- _Opportunities in Business Management_
- _Opportunities in Cable Television_
- _Opportunities in Computer Systems_
- _Opportunities in Electronics Careers_
- _Opportunities in Eye Care Careers_
- _Opportunities in Health and Medical Careers_
- _Opportunities in Interior Design and Decorating_
- _Opportunities in Laser Technology_
- _Opportunities in Medical Imaging_
- _Opportunities in Occupational Therapy_
- _Opportunities in Pharmacy Careers_
- _Opportunities in Public Relations_
- _Opportunities in Teaching_
- _Opportunities in Visual Arts_

This company also publishes two other useful sets of books in a *"Careers in..."* and a *"Careers for You"* series. Titles in the *"Careers in..."* series include:

- *Careers in Accounting*
- *Careers in Advertising*
- *Careers in Business*
- *Careers in Child Care*
- *Careers in Communications*
- *Careers in Computers*
- *Careers in Education*
- *Careers in Engineering*
- *Careers in Environment*
- *Careers in Finance*
- *Careers in Government*
- *Careers in Health Care*
- *Careers in High Tech*
- *Careers in Horticulture and Botany*
- *Careers in International Business*
- *Careers in Journalism*
- *Careers in Law*
- *Careers in Marketing*
- *Careers in Medicine*
- *Careers in Nursing*
- *Careers in Science*
- *Careers in Social and Rehabilitation Services*
- *Careers in Travel, Tourism, and Hospitality*

The nearly 50 books in the *"Careers for You"* series include such titles as:

- *Careers for Animal Lovers*
- *Careers for Bookworms*
- *Careers for Car Buffs*
- *Careers for Caring People*
- *Careers for Computer Buffs*
- *Careers for Class Clowns & Other Engaging Types*
- *Careers for Color Connoisseurs & Other Visual Types*
- *Careers for Computer Buffs & Other Technological Types*
- *Careers for Courageous People*
- *Careers for Crafty People*
- *Careers for Culture Lovers and Other Artsy Types*
- *Careers for Cybersurfers*
- *Careers for Environmental Types*
- *Careers for Fashion Plates*
- *Careers for Film Buffs*
- *Careers for Financial Mavens & Other Money Movers*
- *Careers for Foreign Language Aficionados*
- *Careers for Good Samaritans*
- *Careers for Gourmets*
- *Careers for Health Nuts*
- *Careers for High Energy People*
- *Careers for History Buffs*
- *Careers for Introverts & Other Solitary Types*

- *Careers for Kids at Heart*
- *Careers for Legal Eagles*
- *Careers for Music Lovers*
- *Careers for Mystery Lovers*
- *Careers for Nature Lovers*
- *Careers for Night Owls*
- *Careers for Number Crunchers*
- *Careers for Perfectionists & Other Meticulous Types*
- *Careers for Plant Lovers*
- *Careers for Self Starters*
- *Careers for Shutterbugs*
- *Careers for Sports Nuts*
- *Careers for Talkative Types*
- *Careers for Travel Buffs*
- *Careers for Writers*

Facts on File publishes 15 volumes on alternative jobs and careers in various industries, including such titles as:

- *Career Opportunities in Advertising and Public Relations*
- *Career Opportunities in Art*
- *Career Opportunities in Computers and Cyberspace*
- *Career Opportunities in Food and Beverage Industry*
- *Career Opportunities in Health Care*
- *Career Opportunities in the Music Industry*
- *Career Opportunities in Theater and Performing Arts*
- *Career Opportunities in Travel and Tourism*
- *Career Opportunities in Writing*

Impact Publications publishes 23 volumes on international, public service, and nonprofit careers as well as a nontraditional career series for girls:

- *Directory of Federal Jobs and Employers*
- *Directory of Websites for International Jobs*
- *Complete Guide to International Jobs and Careers*
- *Complete Guide to Public Employment*
- *Cool Careers for Girls as Crime Solvers*
- *Cool Careers for Girls as Environmentalists*
- *Cool Careers for Girls in Air and Space*
- *Cool Careers for Girls in Computers*
- *Cool Careers for Girls in Construction*
- *Cool Careers for Girls in Cybersecurity and National Safety*

- *Cool Careers for Girls in Engineering*
- *Cool Careers for Girls in Food*
- *Cool Careers for Girls in Health*
- *Cool Careers for Girls in Law*
- *Cool Careers for Girls in Performing Arts*
- *Cool Careers for Girls in Sports*
- *Cool Careers for Girls in Travel and Hospitality*
- *Cool Careers for Girls With Animals*
- *Federal Applications That Get Results*
- *Federal Jobs in Law Enforcement*
- *International Jobs Directory*
- *Jobs and Careers With Nonprofit Organizations*
- *Jobs for Travel Lovers*
- *Jobs in Russia and the Newly Independent States*

Many other books examine a wide range of jobs and careers. Some are annual or biannual reviews of today's most popular jobs. You should find several of these books particularly helpful:

- *50 Coolest Jobs in Sports*, David Fischer (Arco)
- *100 Best Careers For the 21st Century*, Shelly Fields (Arco)
- *101 Careers*, Michael Markavy (Wiley & Sons)
- *Adams Jobs Almanac* (Adams Media)
- *American Almanac of Jobs and Salaries*, John W. Wright (Avon)
- *America's Top 100 Jobs for People Without a Four-Year Degree*, Ron and Caryl Krannich (Impact)
- *Best Jobs for the 21st Century*, Ron and Caryl Krannich (Impact)
- *Careers Encyclopedia*, Craig T. Norback, ed. (McGraw-Hill)
- *Cool Careers for Dummies*, Nemko and Edwards (IDG)
- *High-Tech Careers for Low-Tech People*, William Schaffer (Ten Speed)
- *Jobs Rated Almanac*, Les Krantz (St. Martin)

If you are unable to find these books in your local library or bookstore, they can be ordered directly from Impact Publications. Order information is found at the end of this book as well as through Impact's online career bookstore: www.impactpublications.com.

Target Organizations

After completing research on occupational alternatives, you should identify specific organizations which you are interested in learning more about. Next compile lists of names, addresses, and telephone numbers of important individuals in each organization. Also, explore the home pages of various companies on the World Wide Web and write or telephone them for information, such as an annual report and recruiting literature.

The most important information you should be gathering concerns the organizations' goals, structures, functions, problems, and projected future opportunities and development. Since you invest part of your life in such organizations, treat them as you would a stock market investment. Compare and evaluate different organizations.

Several directories will assist you in researching organizations. Most are available in the reference sections of libraries:

- *Directory of American Firms Operating in Foreign Countries*
- *The Directory of Corporate Affiliations: Who Owns Whom*
- *Dun & Bradstreet's Middle Market Directory*
- *Dun & Bradstreet's Million Dollar Directory*
- *Dun & Bradstreet's Reference Book of Corporate Managements*
- *Encyclopedia of Business Information Sources*
- *Fitch's Corporation Reports*
- *MacRae's Blue Book*
- *Moody's Manuals*
- *The Multinational Marketing and Employment Directory*
- *Standard & Poor's Industrial Index*
- *Standard Rate and Data Business Publications Directory*
- *Thomas' Register of American Manufacturers*

Many of the business research websites we identified on pages 169-170 are "must surfing" sites for job seekers. If you have only time to visit a few of these sites, make sure they include our top five:

- **CEO Express**   www.ceoexpress.com
- **Hoover's Online**   www.hoovers.com
- **Dun and Bradstreet's**
  Million Dollar Database   www.dnbmdd.com/mddi
- **Corporate Information**   www.corporateinformation.com
- **BizTech Network**   www.brint.com

If you are interested in jobs with a particular organization, you should visit their website for employment information and/or contact the human resources office for information on the types of jobs offered within the organization. Many companies include an extensive and relatively sophisticated employment section on their home page that allows individuals to enter their resumes into a company database or apply online for specific positions. Indeed, companies are increasingly recruiting online for all types of positions, from entry level to top management. Good examples include Cisco Systems (www. cisco.com), Motorola (www.motorola.com), Microsoft (www. microsoft.com), and the Boston Consulting Group (www.bcg.com). You may be able to examine vacancy announcements which describe the duties and responsibilities of specific jobs as well as survey the profiles of key company personnel. Some companies even include information about the company culture and tips on conducting an effective job search with the company! If you are interested in working for federal, state, or local governments, each agency will have a personnel office which can supply you with descriptions of their jobs. To gain quick Internet access to **federal government** agencies, including vacancy announcements, go to the following websites:

- FedWorld   www.fedworld.gov
- USA Jobs   www.usajobs.opm.gov
- FederalJobsCentral   www.fedjobs.com
- Federal Jobs Digest   www.jobfed.com

If you wish to work in **law enforcement**, visit these websites:

- Law Enforcement Jobs   www.lawenforcementjobs.com
- Cop Career.com   www.copcareer.com
- Job Cop   www.jobcop.com

Individuals oriented toward working in the **nonprofit sector** should visit these useful gateway websites:

- GuideStar   www.guidestar.org
- Action Without Borders   www.idealist.org
- Foundation Center   www.fdncenter.org
- Independent Sector   www.independentsector.org
- Internet Nonprofit Center www.nonprofits.org

Contact Individuals

While examining websites and directories and reading books on alternative jobs and careers will provide you with useful job search information, much of this material may be too general for specifying the right job for you. In the end, the best information will come directly from people in specific jobs in specific organizations. To get this information you must interview people. You especially want to learn more about the people who make the hiring decisions.

You might begin your investigations by contacting various professional and trade associations for detailed information on jobs and careers relevant to their members. Since most of these organizations have home pages on the Internet, you should be able to locate their websites by using one of the standard search engines, such as www.google.com and www.yahoo.com, or by visiting these two gateway websites to trade and professional associations:

- **Associations on the Net**   www.ipl.org/ref/AON
- **AssociationCentral**   www.associationcentral.com

For names, addresses, telephone numbers, websites, e-mails, and publications of such associations, consult the following key directories, which are available in most libraries:

- *Associations USA* (Omnigraphics)
- *The Encyclopedia of Associations* (Thomson Learning)
- *National Trade and Professional Associations* (Columbia Books)

Your most productive research activity will be talking to people or networking for information, advice, and referrals. Informal, word-of-mouth communication is still the most effective channel of job search information. In contrast to reading books or surfing the Internet, people have more current, detailed, and accurate information. Ask them about:

- Occupational fields
- Job requirements and training
- Interpersonal environments
- Performance expectations
- Their problems
- Salaries
- Advancement opportunities
- Future growth potential of the organization
- How to acquire more information and contacts in a particular field

You may be surprised how willingly friends, acquaintances, and strangers will give you useful information. But before you talk to people, do your research so that you are better able to ask thoughtful questions.

Ask the Right Questions

The quality of your research will only be as good as the questions you ask. Therefore, you should focus on a few key questions that will yield useful information for guiding your job search. Answers to these questions will help make important job search decisions relevant to informational and job interviews.

Who Has the Power to Hire?

Finding out who has the power to hire may take some research effort on your part. Keep in mind that human resources offices normally do not have the power to hire. They handle much of the paperwork involved in announcing vacancies, taking applications, testing candidates, screening credentials, and placing new employees on the payroll. In other words, personnel offices tend to perform auxiliary support functions for those who do the actual hiring – usually individuals in operating units.

If you want to learn who really has the power to hire, you need to conduct research on the particular organization that interests you. You should ask specific questions concerning who normally is responsible for various parts of the hiring process:

- Who describes the positions?
- Who announces vacancies?
- Who receives applications?
- Who administers tests?
- Who selects eligible candidates?
- Who chooses whom to interview?
- Who conducts the interview?
- Who offers the jobs?

If you ask these questions about a specific position you will quickly identify who has what powers to hire. Chances are the power to hire is **shared** between the human resources office and the operating unit. You should not neglect the personnel office, and in some cases it will play a powerful role in all aspects of the hiring. Your research will reveal to what degree the hiring function is centralized, decentralized, or fragmented within a particular organization.

How Does Organization X Operate?

It's best to know as much as possible about the internal operations of an organization before joining it. Your research may uncover information that would convince you that an organization is not one in which you wish to invest your time and effort. You may learn, for example, that Company X has a history of terminating employees before they become vested in the company retirement system. Or Company X may be experiencing serious financial problems and morale may be extremely low. They may lie to their employees or engage in unethical behavior. Or advancement within Company X may be very political, and company politics are vicious and debilitating.

You can get financial information about most companies by examining their annual reports as well as by talking to individuals who know the organization well. Information on the internal operations, especially company politics and power, must come from individuals who work within the organization. Ask them: *"Is this a good organization to work for?"* and let them expand on specific areas you wish to probe – advancement opportunities, working conditions, relationships among co-workers and supervisors, growth patterns, internal politics, management style, work values, opportunities for taking initiative.

What Do I Need to Do to Get a Job With Organization X?

The best way to find how to get a job in a particular organization is to follow the advice in the next chapter on prospecting, networking, and informational interviewing. This question can only be answered by talking to people who know both the formal and informal hiring practices.

You can get information on the formal hiring system by visiting the company's website or contacting the human resources office. A telephone call should be sufficient for this information.

But you must go beyond the formal system and human resources office in order to learn how best to conduct your job search. This means contacting people who know how one really gets hired in the organization, which may or may not follow the formal procedures. The best sources of information will be individuals who play a major role in the hiring process.

Identify the Right Community

Your final research target is central to all other research targets and it may occur at any stage in your research. Identifying the geographical area where you would like to work will be one of your most important decisions. Once you make this decision, other job search decisions and activities become easier. For example, if you live in a small town, you may need to move in order to change careers. If you are a member of a two-career family, opportunities for both you and your spouse will be greater in a growing metropolitan area. If you decide to move to another community, you will need to develop a long-distance job search campaign which has different characteristics from a local campaign. It involves visiting community websites, writing letters, making long-distance phone calls, and visiting a community for strategic one-to two-week periods during your vacations.

Deciding where you want to live involves researching various communities and comparing advantages and disadvantages of each. In addition to identifying specific job alternatives, organizations, and individuals in the community, you need to do research on other aspects of the community. After all, you will live in the community, buy or rent a residence, perhaps send children to school, and participate in community organizations and events. Often these environmental factors are just as important to your happiness and well-being as the particular job you accept. For example, you may be leaving a $45,000 a year job for a position in your favorite community – San Francisco. But you may quickly find you are worse off with your new $60,000 a year job, because you must pay $700,000 for a home in San Francisco that is nearly identical to the $300,000 home in your small town community. Consequently, it would be foolish for you to take a new job without first researching several facets of the community other than job opportunities.

Research on different communities can be initiated in libraries and over the Internet. While most of this research will be historical in nature, several resources will provide you with a current profile of various communities. Statistical overviews and comparisons of states and cities are found in the *U.S. Census Data, The Book for the States,* and the *Municipal Yearbook.* Many libraries have a reference section of telephone books on various cities. If this section is weak or absent in your local library, contact your local telephone company. They have a relatively comprehensive library of telephone books. In addition to giving you names, addresses, and telephone numbers, the Yellow Pages are invaluable sources of information on the specialized structures of the public and private sectors of individual communities. The library may also have state and community directories as well as subscriptions to some state and community magazines and city newspapers. Research magazine, journal, and newspaper articles on different communities by consulting several print and online references available through your local library.

The Internet has a wealth of information on the best places to live and work. For data and perspectives on the best places to live, visit these websites:

- **Find Your Spot**   www.findyourspot.com
- **Kid Friendly Cities**   www.kidfriendlycities.org
- **Money Magazine**   www.money.cnn.com/real_estate/
                              index.html
- **Real Estate Journal**   www.homes.wsj.com/toolkit_res/
                              bestplaces.html
- **Sperling's BestPlaces**   www.bestplaces.net
- **School Report**   theschoolreport.com

For the best places to work, check out these websites:

- **BestJobsUSA**   www.bestjobsusa.com/sections/
                             CAN-bestplaces2003/index.asp
- **College Grad**   www.collegegrad.com/
                             topemployers
- **EmploymentSpot**   www.employmentspot.com/lists
- **Forbes Magazine**   www.forbes.com/lists
- **Fortune Magazine**   www.fortune.com
                             (see "Rankings")
- **Great Place to Work**   http://greatplacetowork.com
- **JobStar Central**   www.jobstar.org/hidden/
                             bestcos.htm
- **Quintessential Careers** www.quintcareers.com/best_
                             places_to_work.html
- **Working Mother**   www.workingmother.com
                             ("Working Mother Exclusives")

If you want to explore various communities, you should examine several of these gateway community sites:

- **Boulevards**   http://boulevards.com
- **Cities.com**   www.cities.com
- **City Guide Lycos**   www.cityguide.lycos.com/
                             destinations
- **CityGuides.Yahoo**   www.cityguides.local.yahoo.com
- **CitySearch**   www.citysearch.com
- **City Travel Guide**   http://citytravelguide.com
- **DigitalCity**   http://digitalcity.com
- **Insiders' Guides**   http://insiders.com
- **TOWD**   www.towd.com
- **USA City Link**   usacitylink.com
- **Yahoo**   www.list.realestate.yahoo.com/
                             re/neighborhood/main.html

Several relocation websites also provide a wealth of information on communities. Check these sites out for linkages to major communities:

- **Homestore.com**   http://homestore.com
- **Monster.com**   www.monstermoving.monster.com
- **Relocation Central**   http://relocationcentral.com

Most major communities and newspapers have websites. If you have access to the Internet, you'll find a wealth of community-based information and linkages on such home pages, from newspapers and housing information to local employers, schools, recreation, and community services. If you don't have Internet access, check with your local library. Most libraries have computers connected to the Internet for use by their patrons. Several employment sites include relocation information and salary calculators which provide information on the cost of living in, as well as the cost of moving to, different communities. These five websites provide linkages to thousands of newspapers:

- **Internet Public Library**   www.ipl.org/div/news
- **NewsDirectory.com**   http://newsdirectory.com
- **Newslink**   www.newslink.org
- **Newspapers.com**   www.newspapers.com
- **Online Newspapers**   www.onlinenewspapers.com

If you are trying to determine the best place to live, you should start with the latest edition of Bert Sperling's and Peter Sander's *Cities Ranked and Rated* and David Savageau's *Places Rated Almanac* (John Wiley & Sons). These books rank cities by various indicators. Both *Money* magazine and *U.S. News & World Report* publish annual surveys of the best places to live in the U.S.

Andrea Kay's *Greener Pastures: How to Find a Job in Another Place* (St. Martin's) outlines useful strategies for conducting a long-distance job search campaign, including the emotional and financial challenges.

You should also consult several city job banks that will give you contact information on specific employers in major metropolitan communities. Adams Media regularly publishes *The National JobBank* and *The JobBank Guide to Employment Services* as well as several annual job bank guides, which may or may not continue being updated. Some of the most popular titles include:

- *The Atlanta JobBank*
- *The Austin/San Antonio JobBank*
- *The Boston JobBank*
- *The Chicago JobBank*
- *The Dallas/Fort Worth JobBank*
- *The Denver JobBank*
- *The Florida JobBank*
- *The Houston JobBank*
- *The Las Vegas JobBank*
- *The Los Angeles JobBank*
- *The Minneapolis/St. Paul JobBank*

- *The New Jersey JobBank*
- *The New York JobBank*
- *The Ohio JobBank*
- *The Philadelphia JobBank*
- *The Pittsburgh JobBank*
- *The Portland JobBank*
- *The Salt Lake City JobBank*
- *The San Francisco JobBank*
- *The Seattle JobBank*
- *The Upstate New York JobBank*
- *The Virginia JobBank*
- *The Washington D.C. JobBank*
- *The Wisconsin JobBank*

After narrowing the number of communities that interest you, further research them in depth. Start by exploring community home pages on the Internet (search by community name). Then kick off community-based research based on the community network concept outlined at the end of Chapter 16. Ask your relatives, friends, and acquaintances for contacts in the particular community; they may know people whom you can write, telephone, or e-mail for information and referrals. Once you have decided to focus on one community, visit it in order to establish personal contacts with key reference points, such as the local Chamber of Commerce, real estate firms, schools, libraries, churches, 40-Plus Club (if appropriate), government agencies, and business firms and associations. Begin developing personal networks based upon the research and referral strategies in the next chapter. Subscribe to the local newspaper and to any community magazines which help profile the community. Follow the help-wanted, society, financial, and real estate sections of the newspaper – especially the Sunday edition. Keep a list of names of individuals who appear to hold influential community positions; you may want to contact them for referrals. Write letters to set up informational interviews with key people; give yourself two months of lead time to complete your letter writing campaign. Your overall research should focus on developing personal contacts which may assist you in both your job search and your move to the community.

Know What's Really Important

Reviewing online and print resources can be extremely time consuming, if taken to the extreme. While you should examine several such resources, do not spend an inordinate amount of time reading, clicking, taking notes, and responding with e-mail. Embrace the Internet, but don't fall in love with it!

Like working the classified ads in newspapers, the Internet tends to be a passive medium that can give you a false sense of making progress with your job search – because you're keeping yourself busy entering your resume into several online resume databases and periodically reviewing job listings, message boards, and chat groups. There are too many other important pro-active job search actions, such as interpersonal networking, that you need to focus your effort on. Your time will be best spent in gathering information through meetings and conversations with key people. Your primary goals in conducting research should be identifying people to contact, making appointments, and asking the right questions which lead to more information and contacts. If you engage in these activities you will know what is important when conducting research.

> *Embrace the Internet, but don't fall in love with it!*

As you get further into your job search, networking for information, advice, and referrals will become an important element in your overall job search strategy. At that time you will come into closer contact with potential employers who can provide you with detailed information on their organizations and specific jobs. If you have a well defined MAS, specific job objectives, and a clearly focused resume, you should be in a good position to make networking pay off with useful information, advice, and referrals. You will quickly discover that the process of linking your MAS and objectives to specific jobs is an on-going one involving several steps in your job search.

12

Network for Information, Advice, and Referrals

NOW THAT YOU HAVE identified your skills, specified your objective, written your resume, and conducted research, what should you do next? At this point let's examine where you are going, so you don't get preoccupied with the trees and thus lose sight of the larger forest. Let's identify the most effective methods for linking your previous job search activities to job interviews and offers. In so doing, you should be well positioned to land the critical job interview.

Focus on Getting Interviews

Everything you do up to this point in your job search should be aimed at **getting a job interview**. The skills you identified, the goals you set, the resume you wrote, and the information you gathered are carefully related to one another so you can clearly communicate your best qualifications to employers who, in turn, will decide to invite you to a job interview.

But there are secrets to getting a job interview you should know before continuing further with your job search. The most important secret is the **informational interview** – a type of interview which yields useful job search information and **may** lead to job interviews and offers. Based on prospecting and networking techniques, these interviews minimize rejections and competition as well as quickly open the doors to organizations and employers you would not normally know about. If you want a job interview, you first need to understand the informational interview and how to initiate and use it for maximum impact. In so doing, you'll be exploring the **hidden job market** of unadvertised vacancies. You'll begin locating opportunities that are best suited for your particular motivated abilities and skills.

Prospecting and Networking

What do you do after you complete your resume? Most people send cover letters and resumes in response to job listings; they then wait to be called for a job interview. Viewing the job search as basically a direct-mail operation, many are disappointed in discovering the realities of direct mail – a 2-percent response rate is considered successful!

Successful job seekers break out of this relatively passive job search role by orienting themselves toward face-to-face action. Being proactive, they develop interpersonal strategies in which the resume plays a **supportive** rather than a central role in the job search. They first present themselves to employers; the resume appears only at the end of a face-to-face conversation.

> *The most effective means of communication are face-to-face and word-of-mouth.*

Throughout the job search you will acquire useful names and addresses as well as meet people who will assist you in contacting potential employers. Such information and contacts become key building blocks for generating job interviews and offers.

Since the best and most numerous jobs are found on the hidden job market, you must use methods appropriate for this job market. Indeed, research and experience clearly show the most effective means of communication are face-to-face and word-of-mouth. The informal, interpersonal system of communication is the central nervous system of the hidden job market. Your goal should be to penetrate this job market with proven methods for success. Appropriate methods for making important job contacts are **prospecting and networking**. Useful methods for getting these contacts to provide you with useful job information are **informational and referral interviews**.

Clearly Communicate Your Qualifications

Taken together, these interpersonal methods help you clearly **communicate your qualifications to employers**. Although many job seekers may be reluctant to use this informal communication system, they greatly limit their potential for success if they do not.

Put yourself in the position of the employer for a moment, especially one who is not fully staffed nor automated to handle hundreds of resumes and phone, fax, and e-mail inquiries. You have a job vacancy to fill. Even under the best of circumstances, hiring is a challenging process filled with all types of potential problems. Not only is it time consuming, the outcome is often uncertain. Worst of all, you may spend a great deal of time and money and still hire the wrong person for the position! You know if you advertise the position, you may be bombarded with hundreds of resumes, applications, phone calls, faxes, e-mails, and walk-ins. While you do want to hire the best qualified individual for the job, you simply don't have time nor patience to review scores of applications. Even if you use a P.O. Box number, the paperwork may quickly overwhelm you. Furthermore, with limited information from application forms, cover letters, and resumes, you find it hard to identify the best qualified individuals to invite for an interview; many look the same on paper.

So what do you do? You might hire a professional search firm or use the services of a temporary employment agency to take on this additional work. Or you may decide to recruit on the Internet by doing keyword searches of various online resume databases or post a job announcement on your home page. You may even try your luck by spending a few hundred dollars to use a few major commercial recruitment sites, such as www.monster.com or www. careerbuilder.com.

> *There's nothing like a personal reference from someone whose professional judgment you trust.*

On the other hand, you may want to better control the hiring process, especially since it appears to be filled with uncertainty and headaches. You want to minimize your risks and time so you can get back to what you do best – accomplishing the external goals of the organization. So you decide to "put the word out" by doing a little word-of-mouth recruiting. Like many other employers, you begin by calling your friends, acquaintances, and other business associates and ask if they or someone else might know of any good candidates for the position. If they can't help, you ask them to give you a call should they learn of anyone qualified for your vacancy. You, in effect, create your own hidden job market – an informal information network for locating desirable candidates. Best of all, your trusted contacts initially **screen** the candidates in the process of **referring** them to you. This both saves you a great deal of time and minimizes your risks in hiring a stranger. Individuals in your network begin sending you names of people they feel would be ideal for your position. After all, they have either worked with these persons or are familiar with their ability to work with others and do the job. There's nothing like a personal reference from someone whose professional judgment you trust.

Even if you are fully staffed and technically capable to handle the recruitment process, you still may use an informal, interpersonal, and parallel recruitment approach to minimize your risks. Indeed, many large companies encourage **employee referrals** for recruiting personnel. While they may post a vacancy on their website or use a commercial recruitment site to find candidates, they also encourage and reward their employees to refer candidates. The reward may be a $1,500 to $2,500 bonus to anyone whose referral results in a new hire. These employee referral systems encourage networking within the hidden job market.

Let's shift perspectives – from the employer to the job seeker. Based on this understanding of the employer's perspective, what should you, the job seeker, do to best improve your chances of getting an interview and job offer? Networking for information, advice, and referrals should play a central role in your overall job search. Remember, employers need to solve personnel problems. By conducting **informational interviews and networking,** you help employers identify their needs, limit their alternatives, and thus make decisions and save money. Especially for career changers, such interviews and networking activities help relieve employers' anxiety about hiring such risky individuals.

At the same time, you gain several advantages by conducting these interviews:

1. You are less likely to encounter rejections since you are not asking for a job – only information, advice, referrals, and to be remembered.

2. You go after high level positions.

3. You encounter little competition.

4. You go directly to the people who have the power to hire.

5. You are likely to be invited to job interviews based upon the referrals you receive.

Most employers want more information on candidates to supplement the "paper qualifications" represented in application forms, resumes, and letters. Studies show that employers in general seek candidates who have these skills: communication, problem solving, analytical, assessment, and planning. Surprising to many job seekers, technical expertise ranks third or fourth in lists of most desired skills. These findings support a frequent observation made by employers: the major problems with employees relate to communication, problem solving, and analysis; most individuals get fired because of political and interpersonal conflicts rather than for technical incompetence.

Employers seek individuals they **like** both personally and professionally. Therefore, communicating your qualifications to employers entails more than just informing them of your technical competence. You must communicate that you have the requisite personal **and** professional skills for performing the job. Prospecting, networking, and informational interviewing activities are the best methods for communicating such "qualifications" to employers.

Develop Networks

Networking is the process of purposefully developing relations with others. Networking in the job search involves connecting and interacting with other individuals who can possibly help you. Your network consists of you interacting with these other individuals. The more you develop, maintain, and expand your networks, the more successful should be your job search.

Your network is your interpersonal environment. While you know and interact with hundreds of people, on a day-to-day basis you may encounter no more than 20 people. You frequently contact these people in face-to-face situations. Some people are more **important** to you than others. You **like** some more than others. And some will be more **helpful** to you in your job search than others. Your basic network may encompass the following individuals and groups: friends, acquaintances, immediate family, distant relatives, professional colleagues, spouse, supervisor, fellow workers, close friends and colleagues, and local businessmen and professionals, such as your banker, lawyer, doctor, cleric, and insurance agent. You should contact many of these individuals for advice relating to your job search.

You need to **identify everyone in your network** who might help you with your job search. You first need to expand your basic network to include individuals you know and have interacted with over the past ten or more years. Make a list of at least 200 people you know. Include friends and relatives from your Christmas card list, past and present neighbors, former classmates, politicians, business persons, previous employers, professional associates, ministers, insurance agents, lawyers, bankers, doctors, dentists, accountants, and social acquaintances – even your postman and UPS driver.

After identifying your extended network, you should try to **link your network to others' networks**. The figure on page 228 illustrates this linkage principle. Individuals in these other networks also have job information and contacts. Ask people in your basic network for referrals to individuals in their networks. This approach should greatly enlarge your basic job search network.

What do you do if individuals in your immediate and extended network cannot provide you with certain job information and contacts? While it is much easier and more effective to meet new people through personal contacts, on occasion you may need to **approach strangers without prior contacts**.

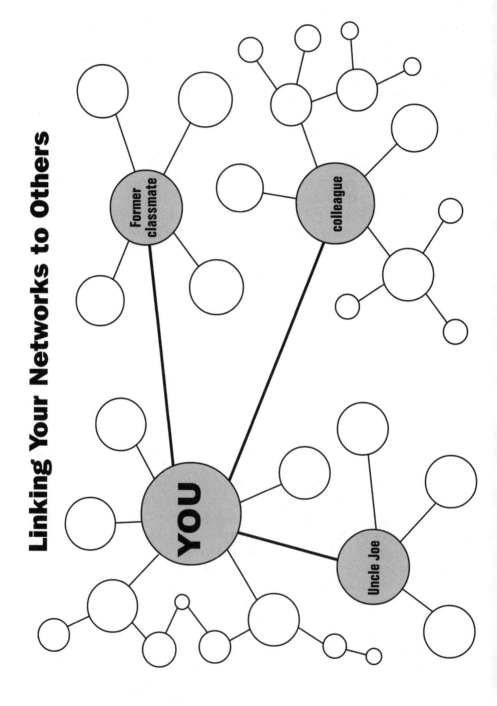

Linking Your Networks to Others

In this situation, try the "cold turkey" approach. Write a letter to someone you feel may be useful to your job search. Research this individual so you are acquainted with their background and accomplishments. In the letter, refer to their accomplishments, mention your need for job information, and specify a date and time you will call to schedule a meeting. Another approach is to introduce yourself to someone by telephone and request a meeting and/or job information. While you may experience rejections in using these approaches, you also will experience successes. And those successes should lead to further expansion of your job search network.

Prospect for Leads

The key to successful networking is an active and routine **prospecting campaign**. Salespersons in insurance, real estate, Amway, Shaklee, and other direct-sales and pyramid businesses understand the importance of prospecting; indeed, many have turned the art of prospecting into a science as well as billion-dollar global businesses! The basic operating principle is **probability**: the number of sales you make is a direct function of the amount of effort you put into developing new contacts and following through. Expect no more than a 10-percent acceptance rate: for every 10 people you meet, nine will reject you and one will accept you. Therefore, the more people you contact, the more acceptances you will receive. If you want to be successful, you must collect many more "no's" than "yeses." In a 10-percent probability situation, you need to contact 100 people for 10 successes.

These prospecting principles are extremely useful for conducting a job search or making a career change. Like sales situations, the job search is a highly ego-involved activity often characterized by numerous rejections accompanied by a few acceptances. While no one wants to be rejected, few people are willing and able to handle more than a few rejections. They take a "no" as a sign of personal failure – and quit prematurely. If they persisted longer, they would achieve success after a few more "no's." Furthermore, if their prospecting activities were focused on gathering information rather than making sales, they would considerably minimize the number of rejections. Therefore, you are well advised to do the following:

- Develop a well organized and active prospecting campaign for uncovering quality job leads.

- Be positive by accepting rejections as part of the game that leads to acceptances.

- Link prospecting to informational interviewing.

- Keep prospecting for more information and "yeses" which will
  eventually translate into job interviews and offers.

A good prospecting pace as you start your search is to make two new contacts each day. Start by contacting people in your immediate network. Let them know you are conducting a job search, but emphasize that you are only doing research. Ask for a few moments of their time to talk about what you are doing. You are only seeking **information and advice** at this time – not a job.

It should take you about 20 minutes to make a contact by letter or telephone. If you make two contacts each day, by the end of the first week you will have 10 new contacts for a total investment of less than seven hours. By the second week you may want to increase your prospecting pace to four new contacts each day or 20 each week. The more contacts you make, the more useful information, advice, and job leads you will receive. If your job search bogs down, you probably need to increase your prospecting activities.

> *The job search is a highly ego-involved activity often characterized by numerous rejections accompanied by a few acceptances.*

Expect each contact to refer you to two or three others who will also refer you to others. Consequently, your contacts should multiply considerably within only a few weeks.

Handle and Minimize Rejections

These prospecting and networking methods are effective, and they can have a major impact on your job search, and your life. While they are responsible for building, maintaining, and expanding multi-million dollar businesses, they work extremely well for job hunters. But they only work for those who have a positive attitude and who are patient and persist. **The key to networking success is to focus on gathering information while also learning to handle rejections.** Learn from rejections, forget them, and go on to more productive networking activities. The major reason direct-sales people fail is because they don't persist. The reason they don't persist is because they either can't take, or they get tired of taking, rejections. This should not happen to you. Always welcome rejections: they will eventually lead to acceptances.

Rejections are no fun, especially in such an ego-involved activity as a job search. But you will encounter rejections as you travel on the road toward job search success. This road is strewn with individuals who quit prematurely because they were rejected four or five times. Don't be one of them!

Our prospecting and networking techniques differ from sales approaches in one major respect: we have special techniques for minimizing the number of rejections. If handled properly, at least 50 percent – maybe as many as 90 percent – of your prospects will turn into "yeses" rather than "no's." The reason for this unusually high acceptance rate is how you introduce and handle yourself before your prospects. Many insurance agents and direct distributors expect a 90-percent rejection rate, because they are trying to sell specific products potential clients may or may not need. Most people don't like to be put on the spot – especially when it is in their own home or office – to make a decision to buy a product.

Be Honest and Sincere

The principles of selling yourself in the job market are similar. People don't want to be put on the spot. They feel uncomfortable if they think you expect them to give you a job. Thus, you should never introduce yourself to a prospect by asking them for a job or a job lead. You should do just the opposite: relieve their anxiety by mentioning that you are not looking for a job from them – only job information and advice. You must be honest and sincere in communicating these intentions to your contact. The biggest turn-off for individuals targeted for informational interviews is insincere job seekers who try to use this as a mechanism to get a job.

Your approach to prospects must be subtle, honest, and professional. You are seeking **information, advice, and referrals** relating to several subjects: job opportunities, your job search approach, your resume, and contacts who may have similar information, advice, and referrals. Most people gladly volunteer such information. They generally like to talk about themselves, their careers, and others. Similar to advice columnists, they like to give advice. This approach flatters individuals by placing them in the role of the expert-advisor. Who doesn't want to be recognized as an expert-advisor, especially on such a critical topic as one's employment?

This approach should yield a great deal of information, advice, and referrals from your prospects. One other important outcome should result from using this approach: people will **remember** you as the person who made them feel at ease and who received their valuable advice. If they hear of job opportunities for someone with your qualifications, chances are they will contact you with the information. After contacting 100 prospects, you will have created 100 sets of eyes and ears to help you in your job search!

Practice the 5R's of Informational Interviewing

The guiding principle behind prospecting, networking, and informational interviews is this: **The best way to get a job is to ask for job information, advice, and referrals; never ask for a job.** Remember, you want your prospects to engage in the 5R's of informational interviewing:

- **Reveal** useful information and advice.
- **Refer** you to others.
- **Read** your resume.
- **Revise** your resume.
- **Remember** you for future reference.

If you network according to this principle, you should join the ranks of thousands of successful job seekers who have experienced the 5R's of informational interviewing. Largely avoiding the advertised job market, you may find your perfect job through such powerful networking activities.

Approach Key People

Whom should you contact within an organization for an informational interview? Contact people who are busy, who have the power to hire, and who are knowledgeable about the organization. The least likely candidate will be someone in the human resources department. Most often the heads of operating units are the most busy, powerful, and knowledgeable individuals in the organization. However, getting access to such individuals may be difficult. Some people at the top may appear to be informed and powerful, but they may lack information on the day-to-day personnel changes, or their influence is limited in the hiring process. It is difficult to give one best answer to this question.

> *The best way to get a job is to ask for job information, advice, and referrals; never ask for a job.*

Therefore, we recommend contacting several types of people. Aim for the busy, powerful, and informed, but be prepared to settle for less. Secretaries, receptionists, and the person you want to meet may refer you to others. From a practical standpoint, you may have to take whomever you can schedule an appointment with. Sometimes people who are less powerful can be helpful. Talk to a secretary or receptionist sometime about their boss or working in the organization. You may be surprised by what you learn!

Nonetheless, you will conduct informational interviews with different types of people. Some will be friends, relatives, or acquaintances. Others will be referrals or new contacts. You will gain the easiest access to people you already know. This can usually be done informally by telephone. You might meet at their home or office or at a restaurant.

You should use a more formal approach to gain access to referrals and new contacts. The best way to initiate a contact with a prospective employer is to **send an approach letter** and follow it up with a phone call. Examples of approach letters are found at the end of Chapter 10. This letter should include the following elements:

OPENERS   If you have a referral, tell the individual you are considering a career in _____. His or her name was given to you by _____who suggested he or she might be a good person to give you useful information about careers in _____.
Should you lack a referral to the individual and thus must use a "cold turkey" approach to making this contact, you might begin your letter by stating that you are aware he or she has been at the forefront of _____ business – or whatever is both truthful and appropriate for the situation. Try to make a personal connection to this person. A subtle form of flattery will be helpful at this stage.

REQUEST   Demonstrate your thoughtfulness and courtesy rather than aggressiveness by mentioning that you know he or she is busy. You hope to schedule a mutually convenient time for a brief meeting to discuss your questions and career plans. Most people will be flattered by such a request and happy to talk with you about their work – if they have time and are interested in you.

CLOSINGS   In closing the letter, mention that you will call the person to see if an appointment can be arranged. Be specific by stating the time and day you will call – for example, Thursday at 2pm. You must take initiative to follow up the letter with a definite contact time. If you don't, you cannot expect to hear from the person. It is **your** responsibility to make the telephone call to schedule a meeting.

ENCLOSURE Do **not** enclose your resume with this approach letter. Take your resume to the interview and present it as a topic of discussion near the **end** of your meeting. If you send it with the approach letter, you communicate a mixed and contradictory message. Remember your purpose for this interview: to gather information and advice. You are not – and never should be – asking for a job. A resume accompanying a letter appears to be an application or a job request.

Many people will meet with you, assuming you are sincere in your approach. On the other hand, many people also are very busy and simply don't have the time to meet with you. If the person puts you off when you telephone for an appointment, clearly state your purpose and emphasize that you are not looking for a job with this person – only information and advice. If the person insists on putting you off, make the best of the situation and try to conduct the informational interview over the telephone. Alternatively, write a nice thank you letter in which you again state your intended purpose; mention your disappointment in not being able to learn from the person's experience; and ask to be remembered for future reference. Enclose your resume with this letter.

While you are ostensibly seeking information and advice, treat this meeting as an important preliminary interview. You need to communicate your qualifications – that you are competent, intelligent, honest, and likable. These are the same qualities you should communicate in a formal job interview. Hence, follow the same advice given for conducting a formal interview and dressing appropriately for a face-to-face meeting (Chapter 13).

Conduct the Interview Well

An informational interview will be relatively unstructured compared to a formal job interview. Since you want the interviewer to advise you, you reverse roles by asking questions which should give you useful information. You, in effect, become the interviewer. You should structure this interview with a particular sequence of questions. Most questions should be open-ended, requiring the individual to give specific answers based upon his or her experience.

The structure and dialogue for the informational interview might go something like this. You plan to take no more than 45 minutes for this interview. The first three to five minutes will be devoted to small talk – the weather, traffic, the office, mutual acquaintances, or an interesting or humorous observation. Since these are the most critical moments in the interview, be especially careful how you communicate nonverbally. Begin your interview by stating your appreciation for the individual's time:

"I want to thank you again for scheduling this meeting with me. I know you're busy. I appreciate the special arrangements you made to see me on a subject which is very important to my future."

Your next comment should be a statement reiterating your purpose as stated in your letter:

"As you know, I am exploring job and career alternatives. I know what I do well and what I want to do. But before I commit myself to a new job, I need to know more about various career options. I thought you would be able to provide me with some insights into career opportunities, job requirements, and possible problems or promising directions in the field of _____."

This statement normally will get a positive reaction from the individual who may want to know more about what it is you want to do. Be sure to clearly communicate your job objective. If you can't, you may indicate that you are lost, indecisive, or uncertain about yourself. The person may feel you are wasting his or her time.

Your next line of questioning should focus on "how" and "what"questions centering on (1) specific jobs and (2) the job search process. Begin by asking about various aspects of specific jobs:

- Duties and responsibilities
- Knowledge, skills, and abilities required
- Work environment relating to employees, work, deadlines, stress
- Advantages and disadvantages
- Advancement opportunities and outlook
- Salary ranges

Your informer will probably take a great deal of time talking about his or her experience in each area. Be a good listener, but make sure you move along with the questions.

Your next line of questioning should focus on your job search activities. You need as much information as possible on how to:

- Acquire the necessary skills
- Best find a job in this field
- Overcome any objections employers may have to you
- Uncover job vacancies which may not be advertised

- Develop job leads
- Approach prospective employers

Your final line of questioning should focus on your resume. Do not show your resume until you focus on this last set of questions. The purposes of these questions are to: (1) get the individual to read your resume indepth, (2) acquire useful advice on how to strengthen it, (3) get reference to prospective employers, and (4) be remembered. With the resume in front of you and your interviewee, ask the following questions:

- Is this an appropriate type of resume for the job I have outlined?

- If an employer received this resume in the mail, how do you think he or she would react to it?

- What do you see as possible weaknesses or areas that need to be improved?

- What about the length, paper quality and color, layout, and type style/size? Are they appropriate?

- What should I do with this resume? Broadcast it to hundreds of employers with a cover letter? Use a "T" letter instead?

- How might I best improve the form and content of the resume?

- Who might be most interested in receiving this resume?

You should receive useful advice on how to strengthen both the content and use of your resume. Most important, these questions force the individual to **read** your resume which, in turn, may be **remembered** for future reference.

Your last question is especially important in this interview. You want to be both **remembered** and **referred**. Some variation of the following question should help:

> *"I really appreciate all this advice. It is very helpful and it should improve my job search considerably. Could I ask you one more favor? Do you know two or three other people who could help me with my job search? I want to conduct as much research as possible, and their advice might be helpful also."*

Before you leave, mention one more important item:

"During the next few months, should you hear of any job opportunities for someone with my interests and qualifications, I would appreciate being kept in mind. And please feel free to pass my name on to others."

Send a nice thank you letter – preferably by mail – within 48 hours of completing this informational interview. Express your genuine gratitude for the individual's time and advice. Reiterate your interests, and ask to be remembered and referred.

Be sure to follow up on any useful advice you receive, particularly referrals. Approach referrals in the same manner you approached the person who gave you the referral. Write a letter requesting a meeting. Begin the letter by mentioning:

"Mr./Ms. _____ suggested that I contact you concerning my research on careers in _____."

If you continue prospecting, networking, and conducting informational interviews, soon you will be busy conducting interviews and receiving job offers. While 100 informational interviews over a two-month period should lead to several formal job interviews and offers, the pay-offs are uncertain because job vacancies are unpredictable. We know cases where the first referral turned into a formal interview and job offer. More typical cases require constant prospecting, networking, and informational interviewing activities. The telephone call or letter inviting you to a job interview can come at any time. While the timing may be unpredictable, your persistent job search activities will be largely responsible for the final outcome.

Telephone for Job Leads

Telephone communication should play an important role in prospecting, networking, and informational interviews. However, controversy centers around how and when to use the telephone for generating job leads and scheduling interviews. Some people recommend writing a letter and waiting for a written or telephone reply. Others suggest writing a letter and following it with a telephone call. Still others argue you should use the telephone exclusively rather than write letters.

How you use the telephone will indicate what type of job search you are conducting. Exclusive reliance on the telephone is a technique used by highly formalized job clubs which operate phone banks for generating job leads. Using the Yellow Pages or Internet phone directories as the guide to employers, a job club member may call as many as 50 employers a day to schedule job interviews. A rather aggressive yet typical dialogue goes something like this:

"Hello, my name is Jim Morgan. I would like to speak to the head of the training department. By the way, what is the name of the training director?"

"You want to talk to Ms. Stevens. Her number is 743-723-8191 or I can connect you directly."

"Hello, Ms. Stevens. My name is Jim Morgan. I have several years of training experience as both a trainer and developer of training materials. I'd like to meet with you to discuss possible openings in your department for someone with my qualifications. Would it be possible to see you on Friday at 2pm?"

Not surprisingly, this telephone approach generates many "no's." If you have a hard time handling rejections, this telephone approach will help you confront your anxieties. The principle behind this approach is **probability**: for every 25 telephone "no's" you receive, you will probably get one or two "yeses." Success is just 25 telephone calls away! If you start calling prospective employers at 9am and finish your 25 calls by 12 noon, you should generate at least one or two interviews. That's not bad for three hours of job search work. It beats a direct-mail approach.

While the telephone is more efficient than writing letters, its effectiveness is questionable. When you use the telephone in this manner, you are basically pitching for a job. You are asking the employer: *"Do you have a job for me?"* There is nothing subtle or particularly professional about this approach. It is effective in uncovering particular types of job leads for particular types of individuals. If you need a job – any job – in a hurry, this is one of the most efficient ways of finding employment. It sure beats standing in line at the state employment office! However, if you are more concerned with finding a job that is right for you – a job you do well and enjoy doing, one that is fit for you – this telephone approach is inappropriate.

You must use your own judgment in determining when and how to use the telephone in your job search. There are appropriate times and methods for using the telephone, and these should relate to your job search goals and needs. We prefer the more conventional approach of writing a letter requesting an informational interview and following it up with a telephone call. While you take the initiative in scheduling an appointment, you do not put the individual on the spot by asking for a job. You are only **seeking information and advice**. This low-keyed approach results in numerous acceptances and has a higher probability of paying off with interviews than the aggressive telephone request. You should be trying to uncover jobs that are right for you rather than any job that happens to pop up from a telephoning blitz.

Use Job Clubs and Support Groups

The techniques outlined thus far are designed for individuals conducting a self-directed job search. Job clubs and support groups are two important alternatives to these techniques.

Job clubs are designed to provide a group structure and support system to individuals seeking employment. These groups consist of about 12 individuals who are led by a trained counselor and supported with telephones, copying machines, and a resource center.

Formal job clubs, such as the 40-Plus Club, organize job search activities for both the advertised and hidden job markets. Job club activities may include:

- Signing commitment agreements to achieve specific job search goals and targets.
- Contacting friends, relatives, and acquaintances for job leads.
- Completing activity forms.
- Using telephones, computers, photocopy machines, postage, and other equipment and supplies.
- Meeting with fellow participants to discuss job search progress.
- Meeting with career counselors or other career specialists.
- Attending job fairs and hiring conferences.
- Telephoning to uncover job leads.
- Using the Internet to research the job market and contact potential employers.
- Researching newspapers, telephone books, and directories.
- Developing research, telephone, interview, and social skills.
- Writing letters and resumes.
- Responding to want ads.
- Completing employment applications.
- Assessing weekly progress and sharing information with fellow group members.

In other words, the job club formalizes many of the prospecting, networking, and informational interviewing activities within a group context and interjects the role of the telephone as the key communication device for developing and expanding networks.

Many job clubs place excessive reliance on using the telephone and Internet for uncovering job leads. Members call prospective employers and ask about job openings. The Yellow Pages and the Internet become the job hunter's best friends. During a two-week period, a job club member might spend most of his or her mornings telephoning for job leads and scheduling interviews. Afternoons are normally devoted to job interviewing.

Many job club methods are designed for individuals who need a job – any job – quickly. Since individuals try to fit into available vacancies, their specific objectives and skills are of secondary concern. Other job club methods are more consistent with the focus and methods outlined in this book, especially those used by 40-Plus Clubs (www.40plus.org/chapters) and Five O'Clock Clubs (www.fiveoclockclub.com).

In lieu of participating in such clubs, you may want to form a support group that adapts some job club methods around our central concept of finding a job fit for you – one appropriate to your objective and in line with your particular mix of skills, abilities, and interests. Support groups are a useful alternative to job clubs. They have one major advantage to conducting a job search on your own: they may cut your job search time in half because they provide an important structure for achieving goals. Forming or joining one of these groups can help direct as well as enhance your individual job search activities.

Your support group should consist of three or more individuals who are job hunting. Try to schedule regular meetings with specific purposes in mind. While the group may be highly social, especially if it involves close friends, it also should be **task-oriented**. Meet at least once a week and include your spouse. At each meeting set **performance goals** for the week. For example, your goal can be to make 20 new contacts and conduct five informational interviews. The contacts can be made by telephone, e-mail, letter, or in person. Share your experiences and job information with each other. **Critique** each other's progress, make suggestions for improving the job search, and develop new strategies together. By doing this, you will be gaining valuable information and feedback which is normally difficult to gain on one's own. This group should provide important psychological supports to help you through your job search. After all, job hunting can be a lonely, frustrating, and exasperating experience. By sharing your experiences with others, you will find you are not alone. You will quickly learn that rejections are part of the game. The group will encourage you, and you will feel good about helping others achieve their goals. Try building small incentives into the group, such as the individual who receives the most job interviews for the month will be treated to dinner by other members of the group.

Explore Online Networks and Networking

Networking is increasingly taking on new communication forms in today's high-tech world. As outlined in Chapter 10, job seekers can take advantage of several websites and electronic databases for conducting a job search, from gathering information on the job market to disseminating resumes to employers. The Internet also allows job seekers to network for information, advice, and job leads. If you belong to one of the major Internet service providers, such as America Online, or have direct access to the Internet's World Wide Web, you can use mailing lists, news groups, bulletin boards, blogs, chat groups, message boards, and e-mail to gather job information and make contacts with potential employers. Using e-mail, you can make personal contacts which give you job leads for further networking via computer or through the more traditional networking methods outlined in this chapter.

Several websites will help you develop networking skills as well as put you in contact with important employment-related networks. These sites include a wealth of information on the networking process:

- **WetFeet**   www.wetfeet.com/advice/
                                   networking.asp
- **Monster.com**   http://networking.monster.com
- **Quintessential Careers**   www.quintcareers.com/
                                   networking.html
- **Riley Guide**   www.rileyguide.com/netintv.html
- **WinningTheJob**   www.winningthejob.com
- **SchmoozeMonger**   www.schmoozemonger.com
- **Susan RoAne**   www.susanroane.com/free.html
- **Contacts Count**   www.contactscount.com/articles.
                                   html

Once you begin the process of developing your networks, you may want to use the following websites to locate long-lost friends, classmates, and others who might be helpful in your networking campaign:

- **Anywho**   www.anywho.com
- **Big Yellow**   www.bigyellow.com
- **Classmates**   www.classmates.com
- **InfoSpace**   www.infospace.com
- **KnowX**   www.knowx.com
- **Reunion** (high school)   www.reunion.com
- **Switchboard**   www.switchboard.com
- **The Ultimate White Pages**   www.theultimates.com/white
- **Whowhere Lycos**   www.whowhere.lycos.com
- **Yahoo**   http://people.yahoo.com

If you have military experience and wish to locate some of your former military buddies, be sure to explore these people finders for locating military personnel:

- GI Search.com   www.gisearch.com
- Military.com   www.military.com
- Military Connections   www.militaryconnections.com
- Military USA   www.militaryusa.com

If you've lost contact with your former classmates, try these websites for locating alumni groups:

- Alumni.net   alumni.net
- Alumniconnections   bcharrispub.com/isd/alumni
                                connections.html

Many women's groups organize networking opportunities among their members for career development purposes. The following organizations are especially relevant to female networkers:

- Advancing Women   www.advancingwomen.com
- American Association of
  University Women   www.aauw.org
- American Business
  Women's Association   www.abwahq.org
- Systers   www.www.systers.org
- Business Women's
  Network Interactive   www.bwni.com
- Federally Employed Women   www.few.org
- iVillage   www.ivillage.com
- Women.com   www.women.com
- Womans.net   www.womans-net.com

Business professionals will find these three networking groups of special interest because they sponsor special online and off-line networking events:

- Company of Friends   http://fastcompany.com/cof
- ExecuNet   www.execunet.com
- Technology Executives
  Networking Group   www.theteng.org

Many of the large Internet employment sites maintain message boards. Two of the largest message board operations, which offer opportunities to network for information and advice, are found at these websites:

- Monster.com   http://networking.monster.com/board
- Vault.com   www.vault.com/community/mb/mb_home.jsp

The latest trend or fad in online networking is based upon the "six degrees of separation theory" – everyone is connected to everyone else in the world by only six other people. A somewhat dubious theory, nonetheless, these networks have been responsible for a great deal of news media hype since 2003 on how to expand one's network of connections for personal and professional purposes. Building electronic communities, these networks are designed to put users into contact with thousands of other people for all types of purposes – from dating to making friends to finding a job to recruiting to developing sales forces to closing business deals. The ultimate soft approach to cold calling, these electronic networks tend to be of questionable value to job seekers who have actually used them. After all, they formalize what is essentially an informal, personal process that works best in one degree removed face-to-face situations. Nonetheless, these new electronic networks offer some interesting online networking opportunities for those who have the time and dedication to make them work. They probably work best for those who need to prospect for new business and potential sales contacts, which is the direction many of the more entrepreneurial such networks now take. The following websites are devoted to promoting this type of networking activity:

- **LinkedIn**   www.linkedin.com
- **Friendster**   www.friendster.com
- **Zerodegrees**   www.zerodegrees.com
- **Ryze**   www.ryze.com
- **Tribe**   www.tribe.net
- **Spoke**   www.spoke.com
- **EntreMate**   www.entremate.com

The first website, www.linkedin.com, tends to be used by more job seekers and recruiters than the other networking sites. If you want to try your luck with this type of online networking in your job search, or if you are a recruiter seeking new talent, we recommend starting with LinkedIn.

The Internet can significantly enhance your job search. It offers new networking possibilities for individuals who are literate in today's digital technology. If you have access to the Internet, we recommend getting your resume into various employment websites. Explore their bulletin boards, chat groups, message boards, resources, and job vacancies. Within just a few minutes of electronic networking, you may pick up important job information, advice, and leads that could turn into a real job. For more information on online networking, see the electronic networking sections of our (Ron and Caryl Krannich) two books on networking and the Internet: *The Savvy Networker* and *America's Top Internet Job Sites* (Impact Publications).

13

Interview for Job Offers

AKE NO MISTAKE – the job interview is **the** most important step in the job search process. All previous job search activities lead to this one. Put simply, no interview, no job offer; no job offer, no negotiations, no salary, and no job.

Your previous job search activities have assisted you in getting this far, but the interview itself will determine whether you will be invited to additional interviews and offered a position. How you approach the interview will make a difference in the outcome of the interview. Therefore, you need to know what best to do and not to do in order to make a good impression on your prospective employer.

New Behavioral and Internet Trends

Within the past few years, the job interview – as well as the whole hiring process – has changed in several important ways. These changes require both interviewees and interviewers to improve their preparation for the job interview. Most changes reflect the need of employers to better define their hiring needs and then make more intelligent and cost-effective hiring decisions. While employers used to hire fast and fire slow, more and more employers see the wisdom of doing just the opposite – hire slow and fire fast. This means more extensive screening of candidates and focusing on **patterns of accomplishments** in order to best **predict** employee behavior. Employers want a perfect "fit." This also means conducting a different style of interview. Rather than call a candidate in for one or two interviews, an employer may interview a single candidate four to seven times before making a job offer. So, how do you handle your fifth interview? Not surprisingly, many candidates have difficulty remaining buoyant after the third interview! Those who have mistakenly prepared canned answers to interview questions have difficulty staying on message after responding to dozens of questions that require them to demonstrate their personality, likability, competence, and ability to make thoughtful decisions.

At the same time, employers are taking more time to screen candidates on everything from drugs, skills, and psychological testing to in-depth background checks. Within the interview itself, more and more employers are asking **behavior-based questions** to ascertain a candidate's ability to make decisions and solve problems relevant to their organization. Consequently, candidates who prepare for interviews with memorized or canned answers to anticipated interview questions do not do well in such interviews; they appear coached and thus lack authenticity and originality of thought. Going beyond behavior-based questions, many employers also seek better indicators of a candidate's decision-making style and pattern of performance by conducting **situational interviews**. Giving interviewees hypothetical or real-work problems to solve, interviewers want to see how a candidate actually behaves, rather than what they say, within the context of the company or organization. Accordingly, employers want to know more about your motivated skills and abilities (Chapter 8) and whether or not your MAS is a good fit for their organization by actually observing you in action.

> *While employers used to hire fast and fire slow, many see the wisdom of doing just the opposite – hire slow and fire fast.*

Within the very near future, the Internet will play a key role in screening candidates, from doing background checks and administering skills and psychological tests to conducting interviews via a videolink. Indeed, the Internet is proving to be the perfect medium for improving both the job search and the hiring processes. For employers, new Internet-based hiring software will enable them to eliminate many of the costly face-to-face steps currently involved in interviewing candidates. In so doing, interviews will be more employer-centered with greater emphasis placed on **what you can do for the employer**.

The overall trend is simple: fewer hiring surprises due to poor hiring skills! Employers want to better predict individual performance within their organizations. They can no longer make costly hiring mistakes that are often attributed to their own lack of good screening and interview skills. They simply want to take the guesswork out of hiring. They want the perfect skills set for the perfect fit.

Prepare for Stressful Interviews

Nearly 95 percent of all organizations require job interviews prior to hiring employees. In fact, employers consider an effective interview to be the most important hiring criterion – outranking grade point average, educational level, related work experience, resumes, letters, and recommendations.

While the job interview is the most important job search activity, it also is the most stressful job search experience. Your application, resume, and letters may get you to the interview, but you must perform well in person in order to get a job offer. Knowing the stakes are high, most people face interviews with dry throats and sweaty palms; it is a time of great stress. You will be on stage, and you are expected to put on a good performance.

How do you prepare for the interview? First, you need to understand the nature and purpose of the interview. Second, you must prepare to respond to different interview situations and interviewers. Make sure whoever assists you in preparing for the interview evaluates your performance. Practice the whole interviewing scenario, from the time you enter the door until you leave. You should sharpen your nonverbal communication skills and be prepared to give positive answers to questions as well as ask intelligent questions. The more you practice, the better prepared you will be for the real job interview.

A Special Communication Focus

An interview is a two-way communication exchange between an interviewer and interviewee. It involves both verbal and nonverbal communication. While we tend to concentrate on the content of what we say, research shows that approximately 65 percent of all communication is nonverbal. Furthermore, we tend to give more credibility to nonverbal than to verbal messages. Regardless of what you say, how you dress, sit, stand, use your hands, move your head and eyes, and listen communicates both positive and negative messages.

Job interviews can occur in many different settings and under various circumstances. You may write job interview letters, schedule interviews by telephone, be interviewed over the phone, and encounter one-on-one as well as panel, group, series, behavioral, and situational interviews. Each encounter requires a different set of communication behaviors. For example, while telephone communication is efficient, it may be ineffective for interview purposes. Only certain types of information can be effectively communicated over the telephone because this medium is only verbal and vocal. Honesty, intelligence, and likability – three of the most important values you want to communicate to employers – are primarily communicated nonverbally. Therefore, you should be very careful of telephone interviews – whether giving or receiving them.

Job interviews have different purposes and can be negative in many ways. From your perspective, the purpose of an initial job interview is to get a second interview, and the purpose of the second interview is to get subsequent interviews as well as a job offer. However, for many employers, the purpose of the interview is to eliminate you from additional interview or a job offer. The interviewer wants to know why he or she should **not** hire you. The interviewer tries to do this by identifying your weaknesses. These conflicting purposes can create an adversarial relationship and contribute to the overall interviewing stress experienced by both the applicant and the interviewer.

Since the interviewer has certain expectations about required personalities and performance in candidates, he or she wants to **identify your weaknesses**. You counter by **communicating your strengths** to lessen the interviewer's fears of hiring you. Recognizing that you are an unknown quantity to the employer, you must raise the interviewer's expectations of you.

Answer Questions

Hopefully your prospecting, networking, informational interviewing, and resume and letter writing activities result in several invitations to interview for jobs appropriate to your objective. Once you receive an invitation to interview, you should prepare for the interview as if it were a $1,000,000+ prize. After all, that may be what you earn during your employment.

> *You should prepare for the interview as if it were a $1,000,000+ prize.*

The invitation to interview will most likely come by telephone. In some cases, a preliminary interview will be conducted by telephone. The employer may want to shorten the list of eligible candidates from ten to three. By calling each individual, the employer can quickly eliminate marginal candidates as well as update the job status of each individual. When you get such a telephone call, you have no time to prepare. You may be dripping wet as you step from the shower or you may have a splitting headache as you pick up the phone. Telephone interviews always seem to occur at bad times. Whatever your situation, put your best foot forward based upon your thorough preparation for an interview. You may want to keep a list of questions near the telephone just in case you receive such a call.

Telephone interviews often result in a face-to-face interview at the employer's office. Once you confirm an interview time and place, you should do as much research on the organization and employer as possible as well as learn to lessen your anxiety and stress levels by practicing the interview situation. **Preparation and practice** are the keys to doing your best.

During the interview, you want to impress upon the interviewer your knowledge of the organization by asking insightful questions and giving intelligent answers. Your library and networking research should yield useful information on the organization and employer. Be sure you know something about the organization. Interviewers are normally impressed by interviewees who demonstrate knowledge of and interest in their organization.

You should practice the actual interview by mentally addressing several questions interviewers ask. Most of these questions will relate to your educational background, work experience, career goals, personality, and related concerns. Frequently asked questions include:

Education

- Describe your educational background.
- Why did you attend _____ University (College or School)?
- Why did you major in _____?
- What was your grade point average?
- What subjects did you enjoy the most? The least? Why?
- What leadership positions did you hold?
- How did you finance your education?
- If you could, what would you change about your education?
- Why were your grades so low? So high?
- Did you do the best you could in school? If not, why not?
- What type of specialized training have you received?
- How do you manage to keep up in your field?

Work Experience

- What were your major achievements in each of your past jobs?
- Why did you change jobs before?
- What is your typical workday like?
- What functions do you enjoy doing the most?
- What did you like about your boss? Dislike?
- Which job did you enjoy the most? Why? Which job did you enjoy the least? Why?
- Have you ever been fired? Why?
- What did you especially like about your last job?

Career Goals

- Why do you want to join our organization?
- Why do you think you are qualified for this position?
- Why are you looking for another job?

- Why do you want to make a career change?
- What ideally would you like to do?
- Why should we hire you?
- How would you improve our operations?
- What do you want to be doing five years from now?
- How much do you want to be making five years from now?
- What are your short-range and long-range career goals?
- If you were free to choose your job and employer, where would you go?
- What other types of jobs are you considering? Companies?
- When will you be ready to begin work?
- How do you feel about relocating, traveling, working overtime, and spending weekends in the office?
- What attracted you to our organization?

Personality and Other Concerns

- Tell me about yourself.
- What are your major weaknesses? Your major strengths?
- What causes you to lose your temper?
- What do you do in your spare time? Any hobbies?
- What types of books do you read?
- What role does your family play in your career?
- How well do you work under pressure? In meeting deadlines?
- Tell me about your management philosophy.
- How much initiative do you take?
- What types of people do you prefer working with?
- How _____ (creative, analytical, tactful, etc.) are you?
- If you could change your life, what would you do differently?

Handle Objections and Negatives With Ease

Interviewers must have a healthy skepticism of job candidates. They expect people to exaggerate their competencies and overstate what they will do for the employer. They sometimes encounter dishonest applicants, and some people they hire fail to meet their expectations. Being realists who have made poor hiring decisions before, they want to know why they should **not** hire you. Although they do not always ask you these questions, they think about them nonetheless:

- Why should I hire you?
- What do you really want?

- What can you really do for me?
- What are your weaknesses?
- What problems will I have with you?

Underlying these questions are specific employers' objections to hiring you:

- You're not as good as you say you are; you probably hyped your resume or lied about yourself.
- All you want is a job and security.
- You have weaknesses like the rest of us. Is it alcohol, sex, drugs, finances, shiftlessness, petty politics?
- You'll probably want my job in another five months.
- You won't stay long with us. Ambitious people like you join the competition or **become** the competition.

Employers raise such suspicions and objections because it is difficult to trust strangers in the employment game and they may have been "burned" before. Indeed, in recent years there has been an alarming rise in the number of individuals lying on their resumes or falsifying their credentials.

How can you best handle employers' objections? You must first recognize their biases and stereotypes and then **raise** their expectations. You do this by stressing your strengths and avoiding your weaknesses. You must be impeccably honest in doing so.

Your answers to employers' questions should be positive and emphasize your **strengths**. Remember, the interviewer wants to know what's wrong with you – your **weaknesses**. When answering questions, both the **substance** and **form** of your answers should be positive. For example, such words as "couldn't," "can't," "won't," and "don't" may create a negative tone and distract from the positive and enthusiastic image you are trying to create. While you cannot eliminate all negative words, at least recognize that the type of words you use makes a difference; try to better manage your word choice. Compare your reactions to the following interview answers:

QUESTION: **Why do you want to leave your present job?**

ANSWER 1:   *After working there three years, I don't feel I'm going anywhere. Morale isn't good, and management doesn't reward us according to our productivity. I really don't like working there anymore.*

ANSWER 2:   *After working there three years, I have learned a great deal about managing people and developing new markets. But*

> *it is time for me to move on to a larger and more progressive
> organization where I can use my marketing experience in
> several different areas. I am ready to take on more respon-
> sibilities. This change will be a positive step in my profes-
> sional growth.*

Which one has the greatest impact in terms of projecting positives and
strengths? The first answer communicates too many negatives. The second
answer is positive and upbeat in its orientation toward skills, accomplishments, and the future.

In addition to choosing positive words, select **content information** which
is positive and **adds** to the interviewer's knowledge about you. Avoid
simplistic "yes/no" answers; they say nothing about you. Instead, provide
information which explains your reasons and motivations behind specific
events or activities. For example, how do you react to these two factual
answers?

QUESTION: I see from your resume that you've been working with Company X for five years. Are you one
of the employees being affected by the recent
budget cuts?

ANSWER 1:   *Yes, that's correct.*

ANSWER 2:   *Yes. Like many others, I've been affected by the recent
cutbacks. However, instead of looking at my situation as a
crisis, I'm approaching it as an opportunity to explore
several other strong interests of mine. I know my talents can
be useful in any number of settings, and I'm particularly
interested in the work your department does.*

Let's try another question reflecting possible objections to hiring you:

QUESTION: Your background bothers me somewhat. You've
been with this organization for 10 years. You
know, it's different working in our organization.
Why should I hire you?

ANSWER 1:   *I can understand that.*

ANSWER 2:   *I understand your hesitation in hiring someone with my
background. I would, too, if I were you. Yes, many people*

*don't do well in different occupational settings. But I don't
believe I have that problem. I'm used to working with
people. I work until the job gets done, which often means
long hours and on weekends. I'm very concerned with achieving results. But most important, I've done a great deal of
thinking about my goals. I've researched your organization
as well as many others. From what I have learned, this is
exactly what I want to do, and your organization is the one
I'm most interested in joining. I know I will do a good job,
as I have always done in the past.*

The first answer is incomplete. It misses an important opportunity to give
evidence that you have resolved this issue in a positive manner which is clearly
reflected in the second response.

The most difficult challenge to your positive strategy comes when the
interviewer asks you to describe your negatives or weaknesses. Be careful in
how you answer this sensitive question:

QUESTION: We all have our negatives and weaknesses.
                  What are some of yours?

You can handle this question in any of five different ways, yet still give positive information on yourself:

1. **Discuss a negative which is not related to the job being
    considered:**

    *I don't enjoy accounting. I know it's important, but I find it boring. Even
    at home my wife takes care of our books. Marketing is what I really like
    to do. I'm glad this job doesn't involve any accounting!*

2. **Discuss a negative which the interviewer already knows:**

    *I spent a great deal of time working on advanced degrees, as indicated in
    my resume, and thus I lack extensive work experience. However, I believe
    my education has prepared me well for this job. My leadership experience
    in college taught me how to work with people, organize, and solve
    problems. I write well and quickly. My research experience helped me
    analyze, synthesize, and develop strategies.*

3.　Discuss a negative which you have improved upon:

I used to get over-committed and miss important deadlines. But then I read a book on time management and learned what I was doing wrong. Within three weeks I reorganized my use of time and found I could meet my deadlines with little difficulty. The quality of my work also improved. Now I have time to work out at the gym each day. I'm doing more and feeling better at the same time.

4.　Discuss a "negative" which can also be a positive:

I'm somewhat of a workaholic. I love my work, but I sometime neglect my family because of it. I've been going into the office seven days a week, and I often put in 12-hour days. I'm now learning to better manage my time.

5.　Discuss a negative outside yourself:

I don't feel that there is anything seriously wrong with me. Like most people, I have my ups and downs. But overall I have a positive outlook, feel good about myself and what I've accomplished so far in my life. However, I am somewhat concerned how you might view my wanting to change occupations. I want to assure you that I'm not making this change on a whim. I've taken my time in thinking through the issues and taking a hard look at what I do well and enjoy doing. Like a lot of young people, I guess I didn't have much life experience when I started my career 10 years ago, and I got into sales because I enjoyed that kind of environment. However, as I got more experience and had opportunities to become involved in different areas, my interest in management training developed. I found that I not only enjoyed those activities, but that I had some natural talent for them. While I've enjoyed my years in sales, I am committed to finding work more in line with my interests and abilities.

All of these examples stress the basic point about effective interviewing. Your single best strategy for managing the interview is to **emphasize your strengths and positives**. Questions come in several forms. Anticipate these questions, especially the negative ones, and practice positive responses in order to project your best self in an interview situation.

Encounter Behavior-Based Questions

More and more employers are conducting a different type of interview than they did five or 10 years ago. Known as "behavior-based interviews," these interviews are filled with behavior-based questions designed to elicit clear **patterns of behavior**, which are primarily sets of accomplishments, relevant to the employer's situation. They are specific and challenge interviewees to provide concrete examples of their achievements in different types of situations. Such interviews are based on the simple belief that how a job candidate has responded to certain types of situations in the past is a good predictor of how that person will behave in a similar future situation. Their behavioral "stories" provide clues on how they will solve future problems. Behavior-based questions are likely to begin with some variation of:

- *Give me an example of a time when you . . .*
- *Give me an example of how you . . .*
- *Tell me about how you . . .*

This is an opportunity for you to sell your positives with an example or two. Briefly describe the situation, enthusiastically explain what you did (adding information as to why, if you think this would not be evident), and indicate the outcome.

For example, if the interviewer asks,

"Tell me about a time when you saved an account for your company."

The applicant might respond,

"Just last month I was observing a one-day training session conducted by one of our instructors I supervise. His class evaluations were lower than what we expect of our trainers and my boss told me the client was not happy with the way the training sessions were going. He was afraid we might lose the account.

As I observed the session, it was apparent the instructor knew the material but was having trouble moving the participants through the material in the time allotted. They often broke into small groups to complete an activity, but it was taking a long time as some groups had to wait for others to finish. At the end of the day, Joe and I met with the client who indicated his dissatisfaction and gave us an ultimatum: if the training of future groups couldn't be completed in a day and to his satisfaction, he would get another contractor.

I solved the problem by having Joe develop copies of the end product the participants should have formulated at the end of each activity. At the next training session he was able to pass these out at the end of the allotted time for each phase of the activity.

The seminar participants understood the information and gave the instructor excellent course evaluations and the client was pleased. We not only saved this contract, but got an additional contract from the client as well. My boss and I were both pleased with the outcome."

Obviously you want to select examples that promote your skills and have a positive outcome. Even if the interviewer asks about a time when something negative happened, try to select an example where you were able to turn the situation around and something positive came out of it. For example, if asked, *"Tell me about a time you made a bad decision,"* try to identify an occasion where:

- Even though it wasn't the best decision, you were able to pull something positive out of the situation.

- Though it was a poor decision, you learned from it, and in the next similar situation you made a good decision or know how you will handle it differently the next time a similar situation arises.

- It was bad decision but the negative outcome had only minor impact.

In other words, try to pull something positive – either that you did or that you learned – out of even a negative experience you are asked to relate. As you prepare for your interview, consider situations where you:

- demonstrated leadership
- solved a problem
- increased company profits
- made a good decision/made a poor decision
- handled change (not money, but changing events)
- handled criticism
- met a deadline/missed a deadline
- worked as part of a team

Add to this list other behavioral questions you think of that pertain to the job for which you are applying. For example, if the job includes making presentations, expect questions about a speech where you achieved your goal or conversely about a time when your speech failed miserably.

Ask others who have interviewed with the company, if possible, to find out the types of questions to expect. You may encounter hypothetical questions in which you are asked not what you did, but what you would do if something occurred. With hypothetical questions, the interviewer is less interested in your actual answer – often there is no correct or incorrect response – than in your thought process. The information is revealed in how you would solve a problem or respond to a particular type of situation.

Develop Strong Storytelling Skills

Individuals who do well in behavior-based interviews are those who have a rich background of accomplishments as well as are good storytellers. Indeed, **storytelling** is one of the key communication skills involved in conducting effective interviews. If you want to do well in this type of interview, be sure to **anticipate questions** you might be asked so you can prepare a well thought-out response – a set of revealing stories about your performance – prior to the interview. It is far easier to formulate positive responses to questions in the relaxed setting of your living room than in the stressful and time-constrained setting of the job interview.

Face Situational Interviews

More and more employers also are conducting situational interviews. These revealing interviews enable interviewers to observe the actual behavior of candidates in particular situations. While candidates can prepare for behavioral interviews by focusing on their accomplishments and telling stories about their past performance that communicate a clear pattern of behavior, such interviews are still primarily verbal exchanges. Employers analyze answers to open-ended questions for clues of future performance.

Employers like to conduct situational interviews because they know candidates can't prepare well for the situations in which they may be asked to perform.

Situational interviews may be more predictive of actual future behavior. Interviewers rely less on analyzing verbal cues and more on analyzing observed behavior or performance in key work-related situations. Employers especially like conducting these interviews, because they know candidates can't prepare well for the situations in which they may be asked to perform. These interviews give employers a chance to observe a candidate's decision-making skills in the process of solving problems. Many of these interviews involve mock scenarios in which a candidate is asked to role-play. For example, someone who is interviewing for a customer service position may be asked to play the role of a customer service representative by handling telephone calls from an irate customer. In this scenario the interviewer has a chance to observe how the candidate actually handles such a customer. Does he or she talk down to the customer, get angry, or resolve the problem to the satisfaction of the customer, which they hope will become a repeat customer? The behavior of a competent customer service representative can be readily observed in such a role-playing scenario. Other examples of situational interviews may involve mock negotiation sessions, selling a product, counseling a client, teaching a course, constructing something, or repairing a product.

Face Illegal Questions

Many questions are illegal, but some employers ask them nonetheless. Consider how you would respond to these questions:

- Are you married, divorced, separated, or single?
- How old are you?
- Do you go to church regularly?
- Do you have many debts?
- Do you own or rent your home?
- What social and political organizations do you belong to?
- What does your spouse think about your career?
- Are you living with anyone?
- Are you practicing birth control?
- Were you ever arrested?
- How much insurance do you have?
- How much do you weigh?
- How tall are you?

Don't get upset and say *"That's an illegal question...I refuse to answer it!"* While you may be perfectly right in saying so, this response lacks tact, which may be what the employer is looking for. For example, if you are divorced and the interviewer asks about your divorce, you might respond with *"Does a divorce have a direct bearing on the responsibilities of this position?"* Some employers may ask such questions just to see how you answer or react under stress. Others may do so out of ignorance of the law. Whatever the case, be prepared to handle these questions with tact.

Ask Questions

Interviewers expect candidates to ask intelligent questions concerning the organization and the nature of the work. In fact, many employers indicate that it's often the quality of the questions asked by the candidate that was instrumental in being offered the job. Moreover, you need information and should indicate your interest in the employer by asking questions. Consider asking some of these questions if they haven't been answered early in the interview:

- Tell me about the duties and responsibilities of this job.
- What's the most important thing I should know about this job and company?
- How does this position relate to other positions within this organization?
- How long has this position been in the organization?
- What would be the ideal type of person for this position? Skills? Personality? Working style? Background?
- Can you tell me about the people who have been in this position before? Backgrounds? Promotions? Terminations?
- Whom would I be working with in this position?
- Tell me something about these people? Their strengths? Their weaknesses? Their performance expectations?
- What would I be expected to accomplish during the first year?
- How would I be evaluated?
- Are promotions and raises tied to performance criteria?
- Tell me how this operates.
- What is the normal salary range for such a position?
- Based on your experience, what type of problems would someone new in this position likely encounter?
- I'm interested in your career with this organization. When did you start? What are your plans for the future?
- I would like to know how people get promoted and advance in this organization.
- What is particularly unique about working in this organization?
- What does the future look like for this organization?

You may want to write your questions on a 3x5 card and take it with you to the interview. While it is best to recall these questions, you may need to refer to your list when the interviewer asks you if you have any questions. You might do this by saying: _"Yes, I jotted down a few questions which I want to make sure I ask you before leaving."_ Then pull out your card and refer to the questions.

Dress Appropriately

Appearance is the first thing you communicate to others. Before you have a chance to speak, others notice how you dress and accordingly draw certain conclusions about your personality and competence. Indeed, research shows that appearance makes the greatest difference when an evaluator has little information about the other person. This is precisely the situation you find yourself in at the start of the interview.

Many people object to having their capabilities evaluated on the basis of their appearance and manner of dress. *"But that is not fair,"* they argue. *"People should be hired on the basis of their ability to do the job – not on how they look."* But debating the lack of merit or complaining about the unfairness of such behavior does not alter reality. Like it or not, people do make initial judgments about others based on their appearance. Since you cannot alter this fact and bemoaning it will get you nowhere, it is best to learn to use it to your advantage. If you learn to effectively manage your image, you can convey marvelous messages regarding your authority, credibility, and competence.

Some estimates indicate that as much as 65 percent of the hiring decision may be based on the nonverbal aspects of the interview! Employers sometimes refer to this phenomenon in such terms as "chemistry," "body warmth," or that "gut feeling" the individual is right for the job. This correlates with findings of communication studies that approximately 65 percent of a message is communicated nonverbally.

Rules of the Game

Knowing how to dress appropriately for the interview requires knowing important rules of the game. Like it or not, employers play by these rules. Once you know the rules, you at least can make a conscious choice whether or not you want to play. If you decide to play, you will stand a better chance of winning by using the often unwritten rules to your advantage.

Much has been written on how to dress professionally, especially since John Molloy first wrote his books on dress for success in the 1970s. While this approach has been criticized for promoting a "cookie cutter" or "carbon copy" image, it is still valid for most interview situations. The degree to which employers adhere to these rules, however, will depend on particular individuals and situations. Your job is to know when, where, and to what extent the rules apply to you. When in doubt, follow our general advice on looking professional.

Knowing and playing by the rules does not imply incompetent people get jobs simply by dressing the part. Rather, it means qualified and competent job applicants can gain an extra edge over a field of other qualified, competent individuals by dressing to convey a positive professional image.

Winning the Game

Much advice has been written about how to dress for success – some of it excellent. However, there is a major flaw in most of the advice you encounter. Researchers on the subject have looked at how people in positions of power view certain colors for professional attire. Few have gone beyond this to note that colors do different things on different people. Various shades or clarities of a color or combinations of contrast between light and dark colors when worn together may be unflattering to some individuals and actually diminish that person's "power look."

If you combine the results of research done by John Molloy in *New Women's Dress for Success* and *John Molloy's New Dress for Success* (Warner Books) both on how colors relate to one's power look and that done by JoAnne Nicholson in *Dressing Smart for Men* and *Dressing Smart for Women* (Impact Publications) on how colors relate to people as unique individuals and how to achieve a professional look, you can achieve a win-win situation. You can retain your individuality and look your most enhanced while, at the same time, achieving a look of success, power, and competence.

Your Winning Appearance

A key to effective dressing is to know how to relate the clothing you put on your body to your own natural coloring. Into which category does your coloring fit? Let's find out where you belong in terms of color type:

- **Contrast coloring:** If you are a contrast color type, you have a definite dark-light appearance. You have very dark brown or black hair and light to medium ivory or olive toned skin. Black men and women in this category will have clear light to dark skin tones and dark hair.

- **Light-bright coloring:** If you are of this color type, you have golden tones in your skin and golden tones in your blond or light to medium brown hair. Most of you had blond or light brown hair as children. Black men and women in this category will have clear golden skin in their face and dark hair.

- **Muted coloring:** If you are a muted color type, you have a definite brown-on-brown or red-on-brown appearance. Your skin tone is an ivory-beige, brown-beige, or golden-beige tone – that is, you have a beige skin with a golden-brown cast. Your hair could be red or light to dark brown with camel, bronze, or red highlights. Black men and women in this category will have golden or brown skin tones and dark hair.

- **Gentle coloring:** If you are of this color type, you have a soft, gentle looking appearance. Your skin tone is a light ivory or pink-beige tone and your hair is ash blond or ash brown. You probably had blond or ash brown hair as a child. Black men and women in this category will have pink tones in their skin and dark hair.

There are also some individuals who may be a combination of two color types. If your skin tone falls in one category and your hair color in another, you are a combination color type.

However, if you are not certain which hair or skin tone is yours and are hence undecided as to which color type category you belong to, or want more information on dress and appearance, go to www.dressingsmart.com. You can locate the Color 1 Associate nearest you.

A Color 1 associate can provide you with an individualized color chart that allows you to wear every color in the spectrum, but in your best **shade** and **clarity** as well as written material telling you how you can combine your colors for the best amounts of contrast for your natural coloring (color type).

The color chart is an excellent one-time investment considering the costs of buying the wrong colored suit, shirt, or blouse. It will more than pay for itself if it contributes to an effective interview as you wear your suit in your best shade and put your clothing together to work with, rather than against, your natural coloring. It can help you convey positive images during those crucial initial minutes of the interview – as well as over a lifetime.

Images of Success

John Molloy has conducted extensive research on how individuals can dress effectively. Aimed at working professionals who want to communicate an image of success, his advice is also relevant for anyone interviewing for a job.

Basic attire for men or women interviewing for a position is a suit. Let's look at appropriate suits in terms of color, fabric, and style. The suit color can make a difference in conveying an impression of authority and competence. The suit colors that make the strongest positive statements for you are **your shade** of gray in a medium to charcoal, or **your shade** of blue in a medium to navy. However, you may choose a less authoritative look for some interview settings. Camel or beige are also considered proper colors for men's suits, and women have an even greater color range. Generally even women should select fairly conservative colors for a job interview unless they are interviewing for a job in a field where nonconformity is considered a plus.

When selecting your suit, choose a shade that appears enhancing to you. Should you wear a blue-gray, a taupe-gray, or a shade in between? Do you look better in a somewhat bright navy or a more toned-down navy; a blue navy or a black navy; a navy with a purple or a yellow base to it?

In general, most people will look better in grays with a blue undertone than in grays that are closer to the taupe side of the spectrum. Most people will be enhanced by a navy that is not too bright or contains so much black that it is difficult to distinguish whether the color is navy or black. When selecting a beige or a camel, select a tone that complements your skin color. If your skin has pink tones, avoid beiges and camels that contain gold hues and select pink based beiges/camels that enhance your skin color. Similarly, those of you who have gold/olive tones to your skin should avoid the pink-based camel and beiges.

Your suit(s) should be made of a natural fiber. A good blend of a natural fiber with some synthetic is acceptable as long as it has the "look" of the natural fiber. The very best suit fabrics are wool, wool blends, or fabrics that look like them. Even for the warmer summer months, men can find summer-weight wool suits that are comfortable and look marvelous. They are your best buy. For really hot climates, a linen/silk fabric can work well. Normally a linen will have to be blended with another fiber, often a synthetic, in order to retain a pressed, neat look. The major disadvantage of pure linen is that it wrinkles. Women's suits also should be made of a natural fiber or have the "look" of a natural fiber. The very best winter-weight suit fabrics are wool or wool blends. For the warmer climates or the summer months, women will find few, if any, summer-weight wool suits made for them. Hence linen, blended with a synthetic so it will not look as if it needs constant pressing, or a good silk or silk blend are good choices. Avoid 100 percent polyester materials, or anything that looks like it – especially double-knits – like the plague! It is a definite negative for your look of competence, power, and success.

> *When deciding on your professional wardrobe, always buy clothes to last and buy quality.*

The style of your suit should be classic. It should be well-tailored and well-styled. Avoid suits that appear "trendy" unless you are applying for a job in a field such as the arts or perhaps advertising. A conservative suit that has a timeless classic styling and also looks up-to-date will serve you best not only for the interview, but it will give you several years wear once you land the job.

Men should select a shirt color that is lighter than the color of their suit. JoAnna Nicholson's *Dressing Smart for Men* and *John Molloy's New Dress for Success* go into great detail on shirts, ties, and practically everything you might wear or carry with you. We recommend these books over others because they are based on research rather than personal opinion and promotional fads.

When deciding on your professional wardrobe, always buy clothes to last and buy quality. For women quality means buying silk blouses if you can afford them. Keep in mind not only the price of the blouse itself, but the cleaning bill. There are many polyester blouse fabrics that have the look and feel of silk – this is an exception to the "no polyester" rule. Silk or a polyester that has the look and feel of silk is the fabric for blouses to go with your suits. Choose your blouses in your most flattering shades and clarity of color.

Give your outfit a more "finished and polished" look by accessorizing it effectively. Collect silk scarves and necklaces of semiprecious stones in your suit colors. Wear scarves and necklaces with your suits and blouses in such a way that they repeat the color of the suit. For example, a woman wearing a navy suit and a red silk blouse could accent the look by wearing a necklace of navy sodalite beads or a silk scarf that has navy as a predominate color.

Appear Likable

Remember, most people invited to a job interview have already been "screened in." They supposedly possess the basic qualifications for the job, such as education and work experience. At this point employers will look for several qualities in the candidates, such as honesty, credibility, intelligence, competence, enthusiasm, spontaneity, friendliness, and likability. Much of the message communicating these qualities will be conveyed through your dress as well as through other nonverbal behaviors.

In the end, employers hire people they **like** and who will interact well on an interpersonal basis with the rest of the staff. Therefore, you should communicate that you are a likable candidate who can get along well with others. You can communicate these messages by engaging in several nonverbal behaviors. Four of the most important ones include:

1. **Sit with a very slight forward lean toward the interviewer.** It should be so slight as to be almost imperceptible. If not overdone, it communicates your interest in what the interviewer is saying.

2. **Make eye contact frequently, but don't overdo it.** Good eye contact establishes rapport with the interviewer. You will be perceived as more trustworthy if you will look at the interviewer as you ask and answer questions. To say someone has "shifty eyes" or cannot "look us in the eye" is to imply they may not be completely honest. To have a direct, though moderate eye gaze conveys interest, as well as trustworthiness.

3. **A moderate amount of smiling will also help reinforce your positive image.** You should smile enough to convey your positive attitude, but not so much that you will not be taken seriously. Some people naturally smile often and others hardly ever smile. Monitor your behavior or ask a friend to give you frank feedback on your facial expressions.

4. **Try to convey interest and enthusiasm through your vocal inflections.** Your tone of voice can say a lot about you and how interested you are in the interviewer and the organization.

Close the Interview

Be prepared to end the interview. Many people don't know when or how to close interviews. They go on and on until someone breaks an uneasy moment of silence with an indication that it is time to go.

Thanking you for coming to the interview, interviewers normally will initiate the close by standing and shaking hands. Don't end by saying *"Good-bye and thank you."* As this stage, you should summarize the interview in terms of your interests, strengths, and goals. Briefly restate your qualifications and continuing interest in working with the employer. At this point it is proper to ask the interviewer about selection plans:

"When do you anticipate making your final decision?"

Follow this question with your final one:

"May I call you next week (or an appropriate time in response to the employer's answer about timing of the final decision) to inquire about my status?"

By taking the initiative in this manner, the employer will be prompted to clarify your status soon, and you will have an opportunity to talk further.

Many interviewers will ask you for a list of references. Be sure to prepare such a list **prior to** the interview. Include the names, addresses, and phone numbers of four individuals who will give you positive professional and personal recommendations. If asked for references, you will appear well prepared by presenting a list in this manner. If you fail to prepare this information ahead of time, you may appear at best disorganized and at worst lacking good references. Always anticipate being asked for specific names, addresses, and phone numbers of your references. Remember to ask their permission, in advance, to use them as references

Remember to Follow Up

Once you have been interviewed, be sure to follow through to get nearer to the job offer. One of the best follow-up methods is the thank you letter; you will find examples of these letters at the end of Chapter 10. After talking to the employer over the telephone or in a face-to-face interview, send a thank you letter by e-mail and/or mail. If mailed, which we prefer, this letter should be typed – not handwritten – on good quality bond paper. In this letter express your gratitude for the opportunity to interview. Re-state your interest in the position and highlight any particularly noteworthy points made in your conversation or anything you wish to further clarify. Close the letter by mentioning that you will call in a few days to inquire about the employer's decision. When you do this, the employer should remember you as a thoughtful person.

If you call and the employer has not yet made a decision, follow through with another phone call in a few days. Send any additional information to the employer which may enhance your application. You might also want to ask one of your references to call the employer to further recommend you for the position. However, don't engage in overkill by making a pest of yourself. You want to tactfully communicate two things to the employer at this point: (1) you are interested in the job, and (2) you will do a good job.

Useful Resources

For more information on developing interviewing skills, including follow-up and thank you letters, look for the Krannichs' *Interview for Success, Nail the Job Interview, Savvy Interviewing,* and *201 Dynamite Job Search Letters*; Richard Fein's *111 Dynamite Ways to Ace Your Job Interview* and *101 Dynamite Questions to Ask At Your Job Interview*; Wendy Enelow's *The $100,000+ Interview*; and Bernard Haldane Associates's *Haldane's Best Answers to Tough Interview Questions* (all published by Impact Publications and included in the order form at the end of this book). You also should check out the following websites, which include tips on interviewing. Most sites offer free interview tips and services. A few sites, such as InterviewCoach.com and WSACorp.com, charge consulting fees for assisting individuals in preparing for the job interview.

- Monster.com   www.interview.monster.com
- InterviewPro   www.interviewpro.com
- JobInterview.net   www.job-interview.net
- Interview Coach   www.interviewcoach.com
- Quintessential Careers   www.quintcareers.com/intvres.html
- Wetfeet.com   www.wetfeet.com/advice/interviewing.asp
- Interview Coach   www.interviewcoach.com
- The Riley Guide   www.rileyguide.com/interview.html
- Jobweb   www.jobweb.com/Resumes_Interviews_default.htm
- WinningTheJob   www.winningthejob.com
- WSA Corporation   www.WSACorp.com

14

Negotiate Salary, Benefits, and Your Future

THROUGHOUT YOUR JOB search you need to seriously consider several questions about your financial value and future income. What, for example, are you worth? How much should you be paid for your work? How can you best demonstrate your value to an employer? What dollar value will the employer assign to you? What salary are you willing to accept?

You think you are worth a lot. After impressing upon the employer that you are the right person for the job, the bottom line becomes **money** – your talent and labor in exchange for the employer's cash and benefits. How, then, are you going to deal with these questions in order to get more than the employer may initially be willing to offer?

Most Salaries Are Negotiable

Salary is one of the most important yet least understood considerations in the job search. Many individuals do very well in handling all interview questions except the salary question. They are either too shy to talk about money or they believe you must take what you are offered – because salary is predetermined by employers. As a result, many applicants may be paid much less than they are worth. Over the years, they will lose thousands of dollars by having failed to properly negotiate their salaries. Indeed, many employees are probably underpaid by hundreds of dollars because they failed to properly negotiate their salaries.

Contrary to what many job seekers believe, salary is seldom predetermined. Most employers have some flexibility to negotiate salary or benefits. While most employers do not try to exploit applicants, neither do they want to pay applicants more than what they have to or what a candidate will accept.

Salaries are usually assigned to positions or jobs rather than to individuals. But not everyone is of equal value in performing the job; some are more productive than others. Since individual performance differs, you should attempt to establish your value in the eyes of the employer rather than accept a salary figure for the job. The art of salary negotiation will help you do this.

Today's Salary Influences Your Future Income

We all have financial needs which our salary helps to meet. But salary has other significance too. It is an indicator of our worth to others. It also influences our future income. Therefore, it should be treated as one of the most serious considerations in the job interview.

The salary you receive today will influence your future earnings. Yearly salary increments will most likely be figured as a percentage of your base salary rather than reflect your actual job performance. When changing jobs, expect employers to offer you a salary similar to the one you earned in your last job. Once they learn what you made in your previous job, they will probably offer you no more than a 10% to 15% increase, regardless of your productivity. If you hope to improve your income in the long run, then you must be willing to negotiate your salary from a position of strength.

Always Know What You're Worth

You should be well prepared to deal with the question of salary anytime during your job search but especially during the job interview. Based on your research (Chapter 11) as well as salary information gained from your networking activities (Chapter 12), you should know the approximate salary range for the position you are seeking. If you fail to gather this salary information prior to the screening or job interview, you may do yourself a disservice by accepting too low a figure or pricing yourself out of consideration. It is always best to be informed so you will be in better control to negotiate salary and benefits.

Review Various Compensation Options

At the same time, you need to carefully consider various elements that may be included in compensation packages **before** you consider a job offer and negotiate salary. Base salary, while the most significant and visible element, is only one of many compensation elements, which need to be considered when negotiating salary. Once your job interview begins focusing on compensation questions, consider whether or not many of the following compensation options are included in an offer. Assign dollar amounts to each element, and then add everything to get a total value for the compensation package. Developed by Bernard Haldane Associates (*Haldane's Best Salary Tips for Professionals*, Impact Publications), this checklist will help you identify what you most desire in a compensation package, evaluate a job offer, and compare the value of different job offers:

ELEMENT	VALUE

Basic Compensation Issues

- Base salary — $ _____
- Commissions — $ _____
- Corporate profit sharing — $ _____
- Personal performance bonuses/incentives — $ _____
- Cost of living adjustment — $ _____
- Overtime — $ _____
- Signing bonus — $ _____
- Cash in lieu of certain benefits — $ _____

Health Benefits

- Medical insurance — $ _____
- Dental insurance — $ _____
- Vision insurance — $ _____
- Prescription package — $ _____
- Life insurance — $ _____
- Accidental death and disability insurance — $ _____
- Evacuation insurance (international travel) — $ _____

Vacation and Time Issues

- Vacation time — $ _____
- Sick days — $ _____
- Personal time — $ _____
- Holidays — $ _____
- Flex-time — $ _____
- Compensatory time — $ _____
- Paternity/maternity leave — $ _____
- Family leave — $ _____

Retirement-Oriented Benefits

- Defined benefit plan $ _____
- 401(k) plan $ _____
- Deferred compensation $ _____
- Savings plans $ _____
- Stock-purchase plans $ _____
- Stock bonus $ _____
- Stock options $ _____
- Ownership/equity $ _____

Education

- Professional continuing education $ _____
- Tuition reimbursement for you or your
  family members $ _____

Military

- Compensatory pay during active duty $ _____
- National Guard $ _____

Perquisites

- Cellular phone $ _____
- Company car or vehicle/mileage allowance $ _____
- Expense accounts $ _____
- Liberalization of business-related expenses $ _____
- Child care $ _____
- Cafeteria privileges $ _____
- Executive dining room privileges $ _____
- First-class hotels $ _____
- First-class air travel $ _____
- Upgrade business travel $ _____
- Personal use of frequent-flyer awards $ _____
- Convention participation: professionally related $ _____
- Parking $ _____
- Paid travel for spouse $ _____
- Professional association memberships $ _____
- Athletic club memberships $ _____
- Social club memberships $ _____
- Use of company-owned facilities $ _____
- Executive office $ _____

- Office with a window $ _____
- Laptop computers $ _____
- Private secretary $ _____
- Portable fax $ _____
- Employee discounts $ _____
- Incentive trips $ _____
- Sabbaticals $ _____
- Discounted buying club memberships $ _____
- Free drinks and meals $ _____

Relocation Expenses

- Direct moving expenses $ _____
- Moving costs for unusual property $ _____
- Trips to find suitable housing $ _____
- Loss on sale of present home
  or lease termination $ _____
- Company handling sale of present home $ _____
- Housing cost differential between cities $ _____
- Mortgage rate differential $ _____
- Mortgage fees and closing costs $ _____
- Temporary dual housing $ _____
- Trips home during dual residency $ _____
- Real estate fees $ _____
- Utilities hookup $ _____
- Drapes/carpets $ _____
- Appliance installation $ _____
- Auto/pet shipping $ _____
- Signing bonus for incidental expenses $ _____
- Additional meals expense account $ _____
- Bridge loan while owning two homes $ _____
- Outplacement assistance for spouse $ _____

Home Office Options

- Personal computer $ _____
- Internet access $ _____
- Copier $ _____
- Printer $ _____
- Financial planning assistance $ _____
- Separate phone line $ _____
- Separate fax line $ _____

- CPA/tax assistance $ _____
- Incidental/support office functions $ _____
- Office supplies $ _____
- Furniture and accessories $ _____

Severance Packages (Parachutes)

- Base salary $ _____
- Bonuses/incentives $ _____
- Non-compete clause $ _____
- Stock/equity $ _____
- Outplacement assistance $ _____
- Voice mail access $ _____
- Statement (letter) explaining why you left $ _____
- Vacation reimbursement $ _____
- Health benefits or COBRA reimbursements $ _____
- 401(k) contributions $ _____

TOTAL $ _____

Keep Salary Issues to the Very End

The question of salary may be raised anytime during the job search. Employers may want you to state a salary expectation figure on an application form, in a cover letter, or over the telephone. Most frequently, however, employers will talk about salary during the employment interview. If at all possible, keep the salary question **open** until the very last. Even with application forms, cover letters, and telephone screening interviews, try to delay the discussion of salary by stating "open" or "negotiable." After all, the ultimate purpose of your job search activities is to demonstrate your **value** to employers. You should not attempt to translate your value into dollar figures until you have had a chance to convince the employer of your worth. This is best done near the end of the job interview.

Although employers will have a salary figure or range in mind when they interview you, they still want to know your salary expectations. How much will you cost them? Will it be more or less than the job is worth? Employers prefer hiring individuals for the least amount possible.

You, on the other hand, want to be hired for as much as possible. Obviously, there is room for disagreement and unhappiness as well as negotiation, compromise, and agreement.

One easy way employers screen you in or out of consideration is to raise the salary question early in the interview. A standard question is: *"What are your salary requirements?"* When asked, don't answer with a specific dollar figure. You should aim at establishing your value in the eyes of the employer prior to talking about a figure. If you give the employer a salary figure at this stage, you are likely to lock yourself into it, regardless of how much you impress the employer or what you find out about the duties and responsibilities of the job. Therefore, salary should be the last major item you discuss with the employer.

*Salary should be the last major item you discuss with the employer – **after** you have established your value.*

You should never ask about salary prior to being offered the job, even though it is one of your major concerns. Try to let the employer initiate the salary question. And when he or she does, take your time. Don't appear too anxious. While you may know – based on your previous research – approximately what the employer will offer, try to get the employer to state a figure first. If you do this, you will be in a stronger negotiating position.

Handle Salary Tactfully

When the salary question arises, assuming you do not want to put it off, your first step should be to clearly summarize the job responsibilities/duties as you understand them. At this point you are attempting to do three things:

1. Seek clarification from the interviewer as to the actual job and all it involves.

2. Emphasize the level of skills required in the most positive way. In other words, you emphasize the value and worth of this position to the organization and subtly this may help support the actual salary figure that the interviewer or you later provide.

3. Focus attention on your value in relation to the requirements of the position – the critical linkage for negotiating salary from a position of strength.

You might do this, for example, by saying,

"As I understand it, I would report directly to the vice-president in charge of marketing and I would have full authority for marketing decisions that involve

expenditures of up to $100,000. I would have a staff of five people – a secretary, two copywriters, and two marketing assistants."

Such a summary statement establishes for both you and the interviewer that (1) this position reports to the highest levels of authority; (2) this position is responsible for decision-making involving fairly large sums of money; and (3) this position involves supervision of staff.

Although you may not explicitly draw the connection, you are emphasizing the value of this position to the organization. This position should be worth a lot more than one in which the hiree will report to the marketing manager, be required to get approval for all expenditures over $100, and has no staff – just access to the secretarial pool! By doing this you will focus the salary question (which you have not yet responded to) around the exact work you must perform on the job in exchange for salary and benefits. You have also seized the opportunity to focus on the value of the person who will be selected to fill this vacancy.

Your conversation might go something like this. The employer poses the question:

"What are your salary requirements?"

Your first response should be to summarize the responsibilities of the position. You might begin with a summary statement followed by a question:

"Let me see if I understand all that is involved with this position and job. I would be expected to _____. Have I covered everything or are there some other responsibilities I should know about?"

This response focuses the salary question around the **value** of the position in relation to you. After the interviewer responds to your final question, answer the initial salary expectation question in this manner:

"What is the normal salary range in your company for a position such as this?"

This question establishes the value, as well as the range, for the position or job – two important pieces of information you need before proceeding further into the salary negotiation stage. The employer normally will give you the requested salary range. Once he or she does, depending on how you feel about the figure, you can follow up with one more question.

"What would be the normal salary range for someone with my qualifications?"

This question further establishes the value for the individual versus the position. This line of questioning will yield the salary expectations of the employer without revealing your desired salary figure or range. It also will indicate whether the employer distinguishes between individuals and positions when establishing salary figures.

Reach Common Ground and Agreement

After finding out what the employer is prepared to offer, you have several choices. First, you can indicate that his or her figure is acceptable to you and thus conclude your final interview. Second, you can haggle for more money in the hope of reaching an acceptable compromise. Third, you can delay final action by asking for more time to consider the figure. Finally, you can tell the employer the figure is unacceptable and leave.

The first and the last options indicate you are either too eager or playing hard-to-get. We recommend the second and third options. If you decide to reach agreement on salary in this interview, haggle in a professional manner. You can do this best by establishing a salary range from which to bargain in relation to the employer's salary range. For example, if the employer indicates that he or she is prepared to offer $50,000 to $55,000, you should establish common ground for negotiation by placing your salary range into the employer's range. Your response to the employer's stated range might be:

"Yes, that does come near what I was expecting. I was thinking more in terms of $54,000 to $59,000."

You, in effect, place the top of the employer's range into the bottom of your range. At this point you should be able to negotiate a salary of $55,000 to $57,000, depending on how much flexibility the employer has with salaries. Most employers have more flexibility than they are willing to admit.

Once you have placed your expectations at the top of the employer's salary range, you need to emphasize your value with **supports**, such as examples, illustrations, descriptions, definitions, statistics, comparisons, or testimonials. It is not enough to simply state you were "thinking" in a certain range; you must state why you believe you are worth what you want. Using statistics and comparisons as your supports, you might say, for example:

"The salary surveys I have read indicate that for the position of _____ in this industry and region the salary is between $54,000 and $59,000. Since, as we have discussed, I have extensive experience in all the areas you outlined, I would not need training in the job duties themselves – just a brief orientation to the operating procedures you use here at _____. I'm sure I could be up

and running in this job within a week or two. Taking everything into considera-
tion – especially my skills and experience and what I see as my future contribu-
tions here – I really feel a salary of $58,000 is fair compensation. Is this
possible here at _____?"

Another option is to ask the employer for time to think about the salary offer. You want to sleep on it for a day or two. A common professional courtesy is to give you at least 48 hours to consider an offer. During this time, you may want to carefully examine the job. Is it worth what you are being offered? Can you do better? What are other employers offering for compara-

> *How you negotiate your*
> *salary will affect your*
> *future relations with*
> *the employer.*

ble positions? If one or two other employers are considering you for a job, let this employer know his or her job is not the only one under consideration. Let the employer know you may be in demand elsewhere. This should give you a better bargaining position. Con-

tact the other employers and let them know you have a job offer and that you would like to have your application status with them clarified before you make any decisions with the other employer. Depending on how much flexibility an employer may have to accelerate a hiring decision, you may be able to go back to the first employer with another job offer. With a second job offer in hand, you should greatly enhance your bargaining position.

In both recommended options, you need to keep in mind that you should always negotiate from a position of knowledge and strength – not because of need or greed. Learn about salaries for your occupation, establish your value, discover what the employer is willing to pay, and negotiate in a professional manner. For how you negotiate your salary will affect your future relations with the employer. In general, applicants who negotiate well will be treated well on the job.

Carefully Examine Benefits

Many employers will try to impress candidates with the benefits offered by the company. These might include retirement, bonuses, stock options, medical and life insurance, and cost of living adjustments. If the employer includes these benefits in the salary negotiations, do not be overly impressed. Most benefits are standard – they come with the job. When negotiating salary, it is best to talk about specific dollar figures. But don't neglect to both calculate and negotiate benefits according to the checklist on pages 269-272. Benefits can translate into a significant portion of one's compensation, especially if you are offered stock options, profit sharing, pensions, insurance, and reimbursement accounts. Indeed, recently many individuals in the 1990s who took stock options in lieu of high salaries with start-up high tech firms discovered the importance of benefits when their benefits far outweighed their salaries; making only $30,000 a year, some of them became instant million-aires when their companies went public! In fact, the U.S. Department of Labor estimates that benefits now constitute 43 percent of total compensation for the average worker. For example, a $60,000 offer with Company X may translate into a compensation package worth $80,000; but a $50,000 offer with Company Y may actually be worth more than $100,000 when you examine their different benefits.

If the salary offered by the employer does not meet your expectations, but you still want the job, you might try to negotiate for some benefits which are not considered standard. These might include longer paid vacations, some flex-time, and profit sharing.

Offer a Renegotiation Option

You should make sure your future salary reflects your value. One approach to doing this is to reach an agreement to renegotiate your salary at a later date, perhaps in another six to eight months. Use this technique especially when you feel the final salary offer is less than what you are worth, but you want to accept the job. Employers often will agree to this provision since they have nothing to lose and much to gain if you are as productive as you tell them.

However, be prepared to renegotiate in both directions – up and down. If the employer does not want to give you the salary figure you want, you can create good will by proposing to negotiate the higher salary figure down after six months if your performance does not meet the employer's expectations. On the other hand, you may accept this lower figure with the provision that the two of you will negotiate your salary up after six months if you exceed the employer's expectations. It is preferable to start out high and negotiate down rather than start low and negotiate up.

Renegotiation provisions stress one very important point: you want to be paid on the basis of your performance. You demonstrate your professionalism, self-confidence, and competence by negotiating in this manner. More impor-tant, you ensure that the question of your monetary value will not be closed in the future. As you negotiate the present, you also negotiate your future with this as well as other employers.

Take Time Before Accepting

You should accept an offer only after reaching a salary agreement. If you jump at an offer, you may appear needy. Take time to consider your options.

Remember, you are committing your time and effort in exchange for money and status. Is this the job you really want? Take some time to think about the offer before giving the employer a definite answer. But don't play hard-to-get and thereby create ill-will with your new employer.

While considering the offer, ask yourself several of the same questions you asked at the beginning of your job search:

- What do I want to be doing five years from now?

- How will this job affect my personal life?

- Do I want to travel?

- Do I know enough about the employer and the future of this organization?

- How have previous occupants of this position fared? Why did they have problems?

- Are there other job opportunities that would better meet my goals?

Accepting a job is serious business. If you make a mistake, you could be locked into a very unhappy situation for a long time.

If you receive one job offer while considering another, you will be able to compare relative advantages and disadvantages. You also will have some external leverage for negotiating salary and benefits. While you should not play games, let the employer know you have alternative job offers. This communicates that you are in demand, others also know your value, and the employer's price is not the only one in town. Use this leverage to negotiate your salary, benefits, and job responsibilities.

If you get a job offer but you are considering other employers, let the others know you have a job offer. Telephone them to inquire about your status as well as inform them of the job offer. Sometimes this will prompt employers to make a hiring decision sooner than anticipated. In addition you will be informing them that you are in demand; they should seriously consider you before you get away!

Some job seekers play a bluffing game by telling employers they have alternative job offers even though they don't. Some candidates do this and get away with it. We don't recommend this approach. Not only is it dishonest, it will work to your disadvantage if the employer learns that you were lying. But more important, you should be selling yourself on the basis of your strengths rather than your deceit and greed. If you can't sell yourself honestly, don't expect to get along well on the job. When you compromise your integrity, you demean your value to others and yourself.

Your job search is not over with the job offer and acceptance. You need to set the stage. Be thoughtful by sending your new employer a nice thank you letter. As outlined at the end of Chapter 10, this is one of the most effective letters to write for getting your new job off on the right foot. The employer will remember you as a thoughtful individual whom he looks forward to working with.

The whole point of our job search methods is to clearly communicate to employers that you are competent and worthy of being paid top dollar. If you follow our advice, you should do very well with employers in interviews and negotiating your salary as well as working on the job.

Know Your Value, Emphasize Your Productivity

One final word of advice. Many job seekers have unrealistic salary expectations and exaggerated notions of their worth to potential employers. Given the greater emphasis on productivity and performance in the workplace, many employers are reluctant to negotiate salaries upwards prior to seeing you perform in their organization. Make sure you make a case for justifying your salary expectations. Do you know, for example, what you're really worth in today's job market? Have you researched salary comparables by examining salary surveys found through your professional association, employment firms, and government studies, or revealed on several key websites, such as www. salary.com and www.jobstar.org? In a full employment economy, where your skills and experience are in high demand, you should be better able to negotiate compensation. Your ability to negotiate will in part be a function of such supply and demand factors in the labor market.

You will need to stress your **value** more than ever in employer-centered terms. Your value primarily comes in two forms: income and savings for the organization. For example, if you think you are worth $50,000 a year in salary, will you be productive enough to generate $300,000 of business for the company to justify that amount? Alternatively, are you prepared to save the company $50,000 next year? If you can't translate your salary expectations into dollars and cents profits or savings for the employer, perhaps you should not be negotiating at all!

For more information on salary negotiations for both job seekers and employees, see our *Dynamite Salary Negotiations* and *Get a Raise in 7 Days: 10 Salary Steps to Success* (Impact Publications). Both books outline various steps for calculating your worth and conducting face-to-face negotiations, including numerous sample dialogues. They are available in the "Career Resource" section at the very end of this book (order form) as well as through Impact's online bookstore: www.impactpublications.com. For online assistance with salary information and negotiations, be sure to visit these websites:

- Salary.com   www.salary.com
- JobStar   www.jobstar.org
- Monster.com   http://salary.monster.com
- SalaryExpert   www.salaryexpert.com
- SalarySource   www.salarysource.com
- WageWeb   www.wageweb.com
- Abbott-Langer   www.abbott-langer. com
- BenefitsLink   www.benefitslink.com
- BenefitNews.com   www.benefitnews.com
- Bureau of Labor Statistics   www.bls.gov
- CareerJournal   www.careerjournal.com
- CompGeo Online   www.claytonwallis.com/cxgonl. html

- Employee Benefit
  Research Institute   www.ebri.org
- Homestore.com   www.homefair.com
- Quintessential Careers   www.quintcareers.com/salary_ negotiation.html

- Riley Guide   www.rileyguide.com/netintv.html
- Robert Half International   www.rhii.com
- SalaryMaster   www.salarymaster.com
- Salary Surveys for
  Northwest Employers   www.salarysurveys.milliman. com

Part III

Create Your
Own Opportunities

15

Advance Your Career

THE CAREER DECISIONS YOU make today will affect your career development tomorrow. Indeed, throughout this book we have tried to prepare you for making critical career choices for today and tomorrow. While we cannot predict the future, we do know you will gain greater control over your future when you use our careering and re-careering methods.

After negotiating the job offer, shaking hands, and feeling great for having succeeded in getting a job that is right for you, what's next? How do you get started on the right foot and continue to advance your career? In this chapter we suggest how to best handle your job and career future after congratulating yourself on a job search well done.

Take More Positive Actions

If you managed your interviews and salary negotiations in a professional manner, your new employer should view you in a positive light. Once you've completed the interview, negotiated the salary, and accepted the offer, you should do two things:

1. **Send your new employer a thank you letter.**

    Never underestimate the power of a simple thank you letter. It may be the single most important action you take. Mention your appreciation for the professional manner in which you were hired and how pleased you are to be joining the organization. Reaffirm your goals and your commitment to producing results. This letter should be well received. After all, employers seldom receive such thoughtful letters, and your reaffirmation helps ease the employer's fears of hiring an untested quantity.

2. **Send thank you letters to those individuals who assisted you with your job search, especially those with whom you conducted informational and referral interviews.**

    Tell them of your new position, thank them for their assistance, and offer your assistance in the future. Not only is this a nice and thoughtful thing to do, it also is a wise thing to do for your future.

In both cases, put your best professional foot forward by sending a traditional typed letter by mail. Such a letter means more to the recipient and will more likely be read than a quick and easy e-mail note.

Always remember your network. You work with people who can help you in many ways. Take good care of your network by sending a thank you letter and keeping in contact. In another few years you may be looking for another position. In addition, people in your network may later want to hire you away from your present employer. Since they know what you can do and they like you, they may want to keep you informed of new opportunities. While you will be developing new contacts and expanding your network in your new job, your former contacts should be remembered for future reference. An occasional letter, New Year's card, or telephone call are thoughtful things to do.

Be Alert to Changing Job Requirements

In today's highly competitive and fast-paced work environments, the skills required for the job you have today may change tomorrow. The job you were initially hired to do will often expand into many different directions that can result in a substantial raise or promotion; be open to such changes. Always make sure your on-the-job skills are up-to-date and that you are doing more than what you consider to be "your job." This may mean acquiring new skills and redefining your job in reference to changing organizational requirements. Take initiative and demonstrate your entrepreneurial skills. Treat your boss as if he or she were your client by exceeding performance expectations. Your continuing employment depends on satisfying the needs of your client. Individuals who unexpectedly become victims of downsizing are often ones who did a particular job well but suddenly discover they have the wrong set of skills for an organization undergoing transformation as it attempts to become more competitive. Never assume the skills and experience you have today will be sufficient for the job tomorrow. Always define what you are doing today in terms of the larger organization. Ask yourself, for example, *am I a continuing asset to what may be a rapidly changing organization? Will I be needed as much tomorrow as I am today?*

Beware of Office Politics

After three months on the job, you should know who's who, who has clout, whom to avoid, and how to get things done in spite of people, their positions, and their personal agendas. In other words, you will become inducted into the informal structure of the organization.

You should become aware of this structure and use it to your advantage.

While it goes without saying that you should perform in your job, you need more than just performance. You should understand the informal organization, develop new networks, and use

> *Treat your boss as if he or she were your client by exceeding performance expectations.*

them to advance your career. This means conducting an internal career advancement campaign as well as an annual career check-up.

Don't expect to advance by sitting around and doing your job, however good you may be. Power is distributed in organizations, and politics is often ubiquitous. Learn the power structure as well as how to play positive politics. For sound advice on this subject, see Andres J. DuBrin's *Winning in Office Politics* (Van Nostrand Reinhold) and Marilyn Moats Kennedy's *Office Politics* (Follett).

After a while many organizations appear to be similar in terms of the quality and quantity of politics. Intensely interpersonal jobs are the most political. Indeed, people are normally fired because of politics – not gross incompetence. What do you do, for example, if you find yourself working for a tyrannical or incompetent boss, or a jealous co-worker is out to get you? Some organizational environments can be unhealthy for your professional development.

Conduct an Annual Career Check-Up

We recommend an annual career check-up. Take out your resume and review it. Ask yourself several questions:

- Am I achieving my objective?
- Has my objective changed?
- Is this job meeting my expectations?
- Am I doing what I'm good at and enjoy doing?

- Are my skills up-to-date for this job and organization?
- Am I able to fully use my skills as well as acquire new skills?
- Does this company fully value my contributions?
- Is this job worth keeping?
- How can I best achieve career satisfaction either on this job or in another job or career?
- What other opportunities elsewhere might be better than this job?

Individuals should increasingly ask these questions about their jobs and careers.

Perhaps changing jobs is not the best alternative for you. If you encounter difficulties with your job, you should first assess the nature of the problem. Perhaps the problem can be resolved by working with your present employer. Many employers prefer this approach. They are learning that increased job satisfaction translates into less job stress and absenteeism as well as more profits for the company. Progressive employers want happy workers because they are productive employees. They view job-keeping and job-revitalization as excellent investments in their futures.

Alternatively, you may want to enter your resume into various online resume databases where you can literally keep yourself in the job market 24 hours a day, 365 days a year. Whether you are actively looking for a job or just keeping in touch with potential opportunities, putting your resume online may be a good way to conduct a career check-up on a regular basis. Indeed, we expect more and more individuals will include their resume in such databases as they begin looking at their futures in terms of careering and re-careering. Many Internet recruitment sites offer a new approach to the job search: no longer will you need to start a job search campaign only when you lose your job or decide to change jobs. Putting your resume online with such websites as <u>Monster.com</u>, <u>HotJobs.Yahoo.com</u>, <u>DirectEmployers.com</u>, and <u>CareerBuilder.com</u> allows you to remain constantly active in the job market. In so doing, new and unexpected job opportunities may come your way even though you are perfectly happy with your current job. In other words, participation in such resume databases may result in employers coming to you rather than you seeking out employers by using the job search strategies and techniques outlined in this book.

The concept of an annual career check-up may be replaced with the concept of a lifetime membership in a career health or fitness club. You keep your career healthy and fit by always keeping yourself, via your electronic resume, on the job market.

Use Job-Keeping and Advancement Strategies

Assuming you enjoy your work, how can you best ensure keeping your job as well as advancing your career in the future? What job-keeping skills should you possess for the career environments of today and tomorrow? How can you best avoid becoming a victim of cutbacks, politics, and terminations?

As we noted in Chapter 13, most employers want their employees to perform according to certain expectations associated with today's changing workplace. Hecklinger and Curtin in *Training for Life* (Kendall/Hunt) further expand these expectations into 13 basic job-keeping skills:

Critical Job-Keeping Skills

1. **Ability to do the job well:** develop your know-how and competence.

2. **Initiative:** work on your own without constant direction.

3. **Dependability:** being there when you are needed.

4. **Reliability:** getting the job done.

5. **Efficiency:** being accurate and capable.

6. **Loyalty:** being faithful.

7. **Maturity:** handling problems well.

8. **Cheerfulness:** being pleasant to be with.

9. **Helpfulness:** willing to pitch in and help out.

10. **Unselfishness:** helping in a bind even though it is not your responsibility.

11. **Perseverance:** carrying on with a tedious project.

12. **Responsibility:** taking care of your duties.

13. **Creativity:** finding new ways to solve the employer's problems.

While using these skills will not ensure job security, they will most likely enhance your security and potential for advancement.

A fourteenth job-keeping skill – managing your political environment – is one employers don't like to talk about. It may well be more important than all the other job-keeping skills. Many people who get fired are victims of political assassinations rather than failures at meeting the boss's job performance expectations or scoring well on the annual performance appraisal.

You must become savvy at the game of office politics in order to survive in many jobs. For example, what might happen if the boss you have a good working relationship with today is replaced tomorrow by someone you don't know or by someone you know but don't like? Through no fault of your own – except having been associated with a particular mentor or patron – you may become a victim of the new boss's housecleaning. Accordingly, you get a two-hour notice to clean out your desk and get out. Such political assassinations are common occurrences in the publishing, advertising, media, finance, and other businesses.

Hecklinger and Curtin identify eight survival tactics that can be used to minimize the uncertainty and instability surrounding many jobs today:

Eight Job Survival Tactics

1. **Learn to read danger signals.** Beware of cutbacks, layoffs, and firings before they occur. Adjust to the danger signals by securing your job or by looking for another job.

2. **Document your achievements.** Keep a record of what you accomplish – problems you solve, contributions you make to improving productivity and profits.

3. **Expand your horizons.** Become more aware of other areas in the company and acquire skills for performing other jobs. The more skills you have, the more valuable you should be to the company.

4. **Prepare for your next job.** Seek more training through:

   - apprenticeships
   - community colleges
   - weekend colleges
   - private, trade, or technical schools
   - Internet and correspondence courses
   - industrial training programs

- government training programs – U.S. Department of Agriculture, for example
- military training
- cooperative education
- four-year college or university

5. **Promote yourself.** Talk about your accomplishments with co-workers and supervisors – but don't boast. Keep them informed about your work; let them know you are available for promotion.

6. **Attach yourself to a mentor or sponsor.** Find someone in a position of influence and power whom you admire and who can help you acquire more responsibilities, skills, and advancement. Avoid currying favor.

7. **Continue informational interviewing.** Educate yourself as well as expand your interpersonal network of job contacts by regularly talking to people about their jobs and careers.

8. **Use your motivated abilities and skills.** Success tends to attract more success. Regularly use the abilities and skills you enjoy in different everyday settings.

The most important thing you can do now is to assess your present situation as well as identify what you want to do in the future with your career and life. You may conclude that your job is not worth keeping!

Assess and Change When Necessary

We are not proposing disloyalty to employers or regular job-hopping. Instead, we believe in the great American principle of "self-interest rightly understood"; your first obligation is to yourself. No one owes you a job, and neither should you feel you owe someone your career and life. Jobs and careers should not be life sentences. Periodically assess your career health and feel free to make changes when necessary. You owe it to yourself and others around you to be your very best self.

Since many jobs change for the worse, it may not be worth staying around for headaches and ulcers. Indeed, many people stay around too long; they fail to read signs that say it's time to go. If the organization does not meet your career expectations, use the same job search methods that got you into the organization. Be prepared to bail out for greener pastures by doing your job research and conducting informational and referral interviews. While the grass may not always be greener on the other side, many times it is; you will know by conducting another job search.

Revitalize Your Job

Assuming you know how to survive on your job, what do you do if you experience burnout and high levels of job stress, or are just plain bored with your job? A job change, rather than resolving these problems, may lead to a repetition of the same patterns elsewhere. Techniques for changing the nature of your present job may prove to be your best option.

> *Jobs and careers should not be life sentences. Periodically assess your career health and feel free to make changes when necessary.*

Most people will sometime experience what Marilyn Moats Kennedy (*Career Knockouts*, Follett) calls the "Killer Bs": blockage, boredom, and burnout. What can individuals do to make their jobs less stressful, more interesting, and more rewarding? One answer is found in techniques collectively referred to as "job revitalization."

Job revitalization involves changing work patterns. It requires you to take risks. Again, you need to evaluate your present situation, outline your career and life goals, and develop and implement a plan of action. A job-revitalization campaign may include meeting with your superior to develop an on-the-job career development plan. Set goals with your boss and discuss with him or her how you can best meet these goals on the job. If your boss is not familiar with career development and job-revitalization alternatives, suggest some of these options:

- Rotating jobs
- Redesigning your job
- Creating a new position
- Promotions
- Enlarging your job duties and responsibilities
- Sabbatical or leave of absence
- Part-time work
- Flex-time scheduling
- Job sharing
- Retraining or educational programs
- Internship

Perhaps your supervisor can think of other options which would be acceptable to company policy as well as productive for both you and the organization.

More and more companies recognize the value of introducing career development programs and encourage job revitalization among their employees. They know it is more cost-effective to retain good employees by offering them new job options for career growth within the organization than to see them go. They are especially protective of their star employees, trying to find new ways to keep them happy and productive! Such programs and policies are congruent with the productivity and profit goals of organizations. They are good management practices. As organizations in the coming decade stress greater productivity, hiring right, and retaining star performers, they will place more emphasis on career development and job revitalization. For extended treatments of these subjects within the context of today's workplace, see Dr. Beverly Kaye and Sharon Jordan-Evans, *Love 'Em or Lose 'Em: Getting Good People to Stay* (Barrett-Koehler); Dr. Jim Harris and Joan Brannick, *Finding and Keeping Great Employees* (AMACOM); and Robert E. Kelley, *How to Be a Star At Work* (Time Books).

Prepare for Change

You should prepare yourself for the job realities associated with a society that is undergoing major structural changes. This means avoiding organizations, careers, and jobs that are declining as well as knowing what you do well and enjoy doing. It also means regularly acquiring the necessary training and retraining to function in a turbulent job market. And it means using your career planning skills to effectively career and re-career in the decades ahead. If you do this, you should be well prepared to turn turbulence into new opportunities and to acquire new jobs which will become exciting and satisfying challenges. Above all, you will be fit for the jobs and careers of the future.

16

Relocate to Your Ideal Community

RELOCATION IS AN IMPORTANT job concern for millions of Americans. Most people change residences as frequently as they change jobs. One in every five families moves to a different residence each year; the average person changes addresses 11 times during his life. Each year approximately 7 million Americans move to another state. Relocation often means changing jobs and lifestyles.

People relocate for many reasons. Some are forced to relocate because of a company policy that routinely moves personnel from one branch office to another or from headquarters to field offices, and vice versa. Others choose to relocate when their company closes in one community, consolidates its operations in another community, or opens a new office elsewhere. And still others choose to seek employment in communities that offer better job opportunities or more attractive lifestyles. For them, relocation becomes another strategy in their arsenal of job search techniques.

Whether you are forced to relocate due to company policies or you seek new opportunities in other communities, chances are you will consider relocating sometime in the decade ahead. When you are faced with a relocation decision, you need to deal with new job, community, and lifestyle issues.

Relocate to Career and Re-Career

Where will you be working and living next year, five years, or 10 years from now? If you had the freedom to pick up and move today, where would you love to live? Choosing where you want to live can be just as important as choosing what you want to do. Such a choice involves making career and lifestyle changes.

292

When you conduct a job search, you do so by targeting specific employers in particular communities. In most cases, individuals will conduct their job search in the same community in which they live. For other people, moving to another community is desirable for career and lifestyle purposes. And for others, unemployment may be preferred to leaving their present community.

Whatever your choices, you should weigh the relative costs and benefits of relocating to a new community where job opportunities for someone with your skills may be plentiful. If you live in a declining community or one experiencing little economic growth, job and career opportunities for you may be very limited. You should consider whether it would be better for you to examine job opportunities in other communities which may offer greater long-term career advancement as well as more opportunities for careering and re-careering in the future.

In recent years economic development has shifted toward the West, Southwest, and Southeast as well as to selected metropolitan areas in the East, South, Midwest, and Plains states. Millions of job seekers will continue to migrate to these areas in the decade ahead in response to growing job and lifestyle opportunities. Perhaps you, too, will look toward these areas as you change jobs and careers in the future.

> _Don't ever take to the road until you have done your homework by researching communities, organizations, and individuals as well as created the necessary bridges for contacting employers in a new community_

In this chapter we examine how to conduct both a long-distance and a community-based job search campaign. We use the example of Washington, DC to illustrate the importance of conducting community research as well as for identifying alternative job networks. Nowhere do we recommend that you pull up stakes and take to the road in search of new opportunities. Many people did so in the 1980s as they headed for the reputed promised lands of Houston and Denver. As the booming economies in these communities went bust by the mid-1980s, many of these people experienced a new round of unemployment. This situation could arise in some of today's reputed promised lands in the decade ahead.

Don't ever take to the road until you have done your homework by researching communities, organizations, and individuals as well as created the necessary **bridges** for contacting employers in a new community. Most important, be sure you have the appropriate work-content and networking skills for finding employment appropriate for specific communities.

Target Communities

Many people are attached to their communities. Friends, relatives, churches, schools, businesses, and neighborhoods provide an important sense of identity which is difficult to leave for a community of strangers. Military and diplomatic personnel – the truly transient groups in society – may be the only ones accustomed to moving to new communities every few years. Seasoned movers, many people in these communities readily look forward to each move as a new adventure in living.

The increased mobility of society is partly due to the nature of the job market. Many people voluntarily move to where job opportunities are most plentiful. Thus, Atlanta becomes a boom city with hundreds of additional cars entering its already congested freeways each week. The corporate structure of large businesses, with branches geographically spread throughout the national production and distribution system, requires the movement of key employees from one location to another – much like military and diplomatic personnel.

When you begin your job search, you face two alternative community approaches. You can concentrate on a particular job, regardless of its geographic setting, or you can focus on one or two communities. The first approach, which we term follow-the-job, is widely used by migrant farm workers, cowboys, bank robbers, mercenaries, oil riggers, construction workers, newspaper reporters, college and university professors, and city managers. These people move to where the jobs are in their particular profession. Not surprisingly, many of these job seekers end up in boring communities which may limit their lifestyle options.

If you **follow the job**, you will need to link into a geographically mobile communication system for identifying job opportunities. You can do this by using placement services and job banks of professional associations; subscribing to specialized trade publications; maintaining contacts with fellow professionals in other communities; entering your resume into nationwide and local online job banks and engaging in electronic networking; or creatively advertising yourself to prospective employers through electronic bulletin boards, newspaper ads, or letter blitzes.

On the other hand, you may want to **target a community**. This may mean remaining in your present community or locating a community you find especially attractive because of job opportunities, climate, recreation, or social and cultural environments. Regardless of rumored job opportunities, many people, for instance, would not move to Vermont and South Dakota – the two states with the lowest unemployment rate in June 2004 (3.2-3.3%) – or to the "deep South" where the weather is relatively hot and humid and where the people display marked linguistic, social, and cultural differences. The same is true for Southerners who are not particularly interested in moving to what are reputed to be cold, dreary, and crime-ridden northern cities. At the same time, Washington (DC), Austin, Las Vegas, Atlanta, San Jose, Phoenix, Boulder (CO), Charlottesville (VA), Seattle, Madison (WI), Raleigh-Durham, Minneapolis, Boston, Baltimore, Cincinnati, Nashville, Denver, Ft. Lauderdale, and St. Louis are reputed to be the new promised lands for many people. Seeming oases of prosperity and centers for attractive urban lifestyles, these cities are on the community target list of many job seekers.

We recommend using this second approach of targeting specific communities. The follow-the-job approach is okay if you are young, adventuresome, or desperate; you find yourself in a geographically mobile profession; your career takes precedence over all other aspects of your life; or you have a bad case of wanderlust and thus let others arrange your travel plans. By targeting a community, your job search will be more manageable. Furthermore, moving to another community can be a liberating experience which will have a positive effect on both your professional and personal lives.

Why not find a great job in a community you really love? Fortunately you live in a very large country consisting of numerous communities that offer a terrific range of career and lifestyle opportunities. Let's identify some communities that might be a good "fit" for you as well as eliminate many which you may wish to avoid.

Know the Growing States and Communities

Frictional unemployment – the geographic separation of underemployed and unemployed individuals from high labor demand regions and communities – should present new options for you. Numerous job opportunities may be available if you are willing to relocate to the right communities.

During 2004, unemployment averaged 5.6 percent for the nation as a whole. However, as noted in the following U.S. Department of Labor statistics (www.bls.gov), it was unevenly distributed among the states, with a high of 7.7 percent in the District of Columbia and a low of 3.2 percent in Vermont:

Unemployment By State (June 2004)

State	1000's of Persons	Percentage
District of Columbia	24.5	7.7
Alaska	24.8	7.0
Arizona	141	7.0
Louisiana	143.3	6.9
Michigan	348.1	6.8
Texas	719.8	6.5
New Mexico	59.2	6.5

California	1,110.4	6.3
Washington	196.6	6.1
Ohio	361.6	6.1
Oregon	127.9	6.0
Alabama	129.8	6.0
New York	552.1	5.9
North Carolina	245.3	5.8
South Carolina	145.5	5.7
Pennsylvania	358.6	5.7
Rhode Island	32.6	5.7
Kentucky	113.2	5.6
West Virginia	43.4	5.4
Missouri	167.5	5.4
Massachusetts	184.1	5.3
Colorado	132.4	5.2
Utah	63.0	5.2
Arkansas	84.0	5.1
Florida	425.6	5.1
Wisconsin	162.8	5.1
Oklahoma	86.2	5.0
Kansas	73.1	4.9
New Jersey	214.9	4.8
Tennessee	142.0	4.8
Connecticut	86.4	4.8
Mississippi	81.0	4.7
Indiana	151.2	4.7
Minnesota	140.4	4.7
Georgia	203.2	4.6
Montana	22.6	4.6
Illinois	395.8	4.5
Idaho	32.1	4.5
Nevada	52.9	4.4
Maryland	124.3	4.2
Iowa	69.7	4.2
Maine	28.4	4.0
Delaware	16.9	3.9
New Hampshire	28.8	3.9
Virginia	147.4	3.8
Nebraska	36.9	3.7
Hawaii	21.5	3.5
Wyoming	9.6	3.4
North Dakota	12.3	3.4
South Dakota	14.4	3.3
Vermont	11.3	3.2

Unemployment rates were even more pronounced by cities. At the same time, the following metropolitan areas had the highest and lowest unemployment rates in June 2004 when the average unemployment rate for the country was 5.6 percent:

Highest and Lowest Unemployment By
Metropolitan Area (June 2004)

Metropolitan Area	Percentage Unemployed
Highest Unemployment	
▪ Yuma, AZ	27.6
▪ Visalia-Tulare-Porterville, CA	14.9
▪ Merced, CA	14.1
▪ Yuba City, CA	14.1
▪ Bakersfield, CA	12.7
▪ Fresno, CA	12.5
▪ McAllen-Edinburg, Mission, TX	12.3
Lowest Unemployment	
▪ Bryan-College Station, TX	2.3
▪ Fargo-Moorland, ND	2.5
▪ Columbia, MO	2.5
▪ Bismarck, ND	2.6
▪ Portland, ME	2.6
▪ Enid, OK	2.6
▪ Stamford-Norwalk, CT	2.9

Communities with the highest unemployment rates tend to be in the poorest areas of California, Arizona, and Texas which also have large numbers of seasonal, migrant, and agricultural workers. Unemployment was even higher in many troubled small communities outside these metropolitan areas, especially on poor Indian reservations, such as Pine Ridge, South Dakota (nearly 80 percent in 2004). If you lived in one of these communities, your employment prospects were indeed bleak. Regardless of your job talents and job search skills, these communities simply did not generate enough jobs to go around. To get ahead, one needed to relocate to a more economically viable community, especially one with very low unemployment that had a steady demand for workers. More often than not, this meant relocating to a diversified metropolitan area where opportunities abounded.

Communities with low unemployment rates tend to have a large portion of highly educated and skilled professional workers, many in the high-tech and medical areas, and large higher-education complexes linked to a diversified network of support services. Many of these same communities ranked high on annual lists of the "best" communities to live in because of their combination of attractive economic, educational, and lifestyle opportunities. Many individuals who moved to these communities have had little difficulty finding jobs as well as developing new skills for the 21st century.

In the coming decade we expect Connecticut, Delaware, Georgia, Hawaii, Illinois, Idaho, Indiana, Iowa, Maryland, Minnesota, Nebraska, Nevada, New Hampshire, North Dakota, South Dakota, Tennessee, Vermont, Virginia, and Wyoming to have above-average employment rates. Numerous communities within these states, especially in the 250,000 to 500,000 population range, will offer some of the best job opportunities. However, don't overlook several excellent employment oases (rapidly developing cities and counties) within states that have above average unemployment rates, such as Plano, College Station, and Austin, Texas; Scottsdale, Arizona; and Anaheim, Santa Rosa, and Irvine, California.

Disproportionately found in the West, Southwest, and Southeast, many of the fastest growing communities should continue with medium to high growth rates in the decade ahead. Depending on the extent of another energy crisis, several communities in the energy-rich Rocky Mountain states may once again become boom towns. Communities with large concentrations of high-tech and service industries, supported by a strong higher-education infrastructure – will continue to expand both demographically and economically. Cities with large college and university complexes, such as Boston, Minneapolis-St. Paul, Omaha, Raleigh-Durham-Chapel Hill, Oklahoma City, Salt Lake City, Denver, Madison (WI), Columbia (SC), Knoxville, Atlanta, Austin (TX), Columbus (OH), San Francisco, Seattle, Honolulu, Iowa City, Ann Arbor (MI), and Washington, DC, should experience steady employment growth in the decade ahead. These cities will also generate some of the best paying, high quality jobs.

We foresee continuing population and economic growth in and around several large cities: Las Vegas, Salt Lake City-Ogden, Denver, Minneapolis-St. Paul, Rochester (MN), Milwaukee, Nashville, Dallas-Ft. Worth, Houston, Austin, San Antonio, Gainesville (FL), Fort Lauderdale, Atlanta, Tampa-St. Petersburg, Raleigh-Durham, Pittsburgh, Philadelphia, Washington-Baltimore, Madison, Boston, Indianapolis, Louisville, Atlanta, and Cleveland. Even Southern California – especially the Los Angeles-San Diego corridor – will experience population and job growth in part stimulated by exports to the recovering economies of Mexico and the Pacific Rim.

Even though the overall growth predictions point to the Northwest, Far West, and Southwest, these trends should not deter you from considering older cities in the Northeast and North Central regions. After all, two to three million new jobs are created nationwide each year. New jobs will continue to develop in cities such as Chicago, Philadelphia, and New York; these are still the best places to pursue careers in the fields of banking, publishing, and advertising. Boston is again an attractive employment center. Several communities in the Midwest – especially those with strong educational infrastructures – have transformed their local economies in the direction of high-tech and service industries. Minneapolis-St. Paul, Madison, Chicago, St. Louis, Iowa City, Kansas City, Bloomington-Normal, Indianapolis, Columbus, Cleveland, and Cincinnati in the Midwest, and Philadelphia, Pittsburgh, Baltimore, Washington, DC, Raleigh-Durham-Chapel Hill, and Atlanta in the central to southern Atlantic coast area will remain some of the best cities for jobs and lifestyles in the decade ahead.

Consider the Best Places to Work

If you contemplate relocating to a new community, you should consider communities that are experiencing low unemployment coupled with steady job growth as well as attractive lifestyles. A *Fortune Magazine* survey in 2004 identified 25 cities as the best places for business and work. These cities are considered the top wealth creators which also offer attractive lifestyles and excellent quality of life. The first five cities are especially noted for their higher education institutions and high-tech orientation:

Fortune's Top 25 Metropolitan Area (2004)

Rank	Metro Area	Percent Job Growth (5 years)	Population
1	Madison, WI	32	443,000
2	Raleigh-Durham, NC	52	1,268,000
3	Austin, TX	30	1,349,000
4	Washington, DC	23	5,162,000
5	Atlanta, GA	50	4,386,000
6	Provo, UT	35	388,000
7	Boise, ID	12	465,000
8	Huntsville, AL	46	354,000
9	Lexington, KY	114	490,000
10	Richmond, VA	53	1,023,000
11	Omaha, NE	65	734,000
12	Albuquerque, NM	42	737,000
13	Knoxville, TN	29	704,000
14	Des Moines, IA	90	471,000
15	Houston, TX	55	4,420,000
16	Appleton, WI	78	367,000
17	San Diego, CA	15	2,907,000
18	Albany, NY	68	885,000
19	Minneapolis-St. Paul, MN	74	3,055,000
20	Ann Arbor, MI	54	603,000
21	Little Rock, AR	82	596,000
22	Charleston, SC	33	563,000
23	Fort Worth, TX	58	1,802,000
24	Colorado Springs, CO	47	544,000
25	Reno, NV	28	362,000

Most of these cities are likely to experience solid growth in the decade ahead. The Washington (DC), Atlanta (GA), and Minneapolis/St. Paul (MN) areas are already star performers because of their extensive medical facilities and high-tech infrastructure as well as their attractive lifestyles. These three cities will probably continue to be great growth communities. They will generate a disproportionate number of high-paying jobs due to the high-quality nature of their jobs and workforces. They may well provide models of a new economy and workforce for the next few decades.

Find the Best Place to Live

Community growth and decline trends should be considered as part of your job and career options. If you live in a declining community with few opportunities for your skills and interests, seriously consider relocating to a growth community. Depressed communities simply do not generate enough jobs for their populations. Many communities with populations of 100,000 to 500,000 offer a nice variety of job and lifestyle options.

Except for a few people, one's work should not become one's life. After all, there are more important things in life than one's work. Different communities offer many life choices in addition to jobs. Economic development and job generation are only two of many important community choice concerns. Using several indicators of quality living, a 2004 study of the *American City Business Journals* identified what it considers to be the 20 best counties in the United States in terms of their incomes, education, housing, racial diversity, and short commuting times:

America's Top 20 Counties

Rank	Metro Area	Medium Income	Medium Home Value	Population
1	Los Alamos, NM	$78,993	$214,000	18,343
2	Omsted, MN	$51,316	$114,700	124,277
3	Pitkin, CO	$59,375	$497,000	14,872
4	Douglas, CO	$82,929	$237,600	175,766
5	Loudoun, VA	$80,638	$202,300	169,599
6	Washington, MN	$66,305	$156,200	201,130
7	Johnson, KS	$61,455	$149,300	451,086
8	Hamilton, IN	$71,026	$163,600	182,740
9	Howard, MD	$74,167	$198,600	247,842
10	Fairfax, VA	$81,050	$222,400	969,749
11	Juneau, AK	$62,034	$179,200	30,711
12	Nantucket, MA	$55,522	$583,500	9,520
13	Wake, NC	$54,988	$156,200	627,846
14	Dakota, MN	$61,863	$148,500	355,904

15	Summit, UT	$64,962	$281,600	29,736
16	Dupage, IL	$67,687	$187,600	904,161
17	Chesterfield, VA	$58,537	$119,300	259,903
18	Fayette, GA	$71,227	$170,200	91,263
19	Hennepin, MN	$51,711	$141,100	1,116,200
20	Stafford, VA	$66,809	$155,100	92,446

These rankings have already changed in other surveys; they will undoubtedly change in the coming decade. It is best to consult the latest surveys conducted by _Fortune Magazine_ (www.fortune.com), Sperling (www.bestplaces.net), and City Rating (www.cityrating.com).

Money Magazine's annual survey of the best places to live came up with a different set of conclusions on the lifestyle side of the relocation equation. They found that when considering a community move, respondents most valued these five criteria: clean water, low crime, clean air, good public schools, and low property taxes. Best of all, this survey went beyond the very large metropolitan area focus of most other studies and instead identified "best places" in communities with populations from 100,000 to 249,999, from 250,000 to 999,999, and over 1,000,000. _Money Magazine's_ most recent survey identifies 87 cities and towns as the best places to live. The top 29 include the following:

Money's Best Places to Live

Region/City	Population	Median Household income	Median home price
Eastern Region (over 100,000 population)			
1. Cary NC	104,210	$77,091	$207,000
2. Ramapo, NY	112,684	$64,954	$330,875
3. Coral Springs, FL	128,715	$62,632	$218,500
4. Alexandria, VA	131,918	$59,976	$290,000
5. Sully district, VA	152,169	$92,942	$290,000
Eastern Region (under 100,000 population)			
1. Sugarland Run district, VA	29,115	$103,350	$278,250
2. Manalapan, NJ	34,018	$91,245	$410,000
3. Centreville, VA	50,347	$77,243	$250,000
4. Randolph, NJ	25,643	$104,121	$444,500
5. North Andover, MA	27,725	$79,169	$342,500

Central Region (over 100,000 population)

1. Naperville, IL	139,654	$94,687	$260,000
2. Lawerence, IN	113,967	$52,023	$160,930
3. Overland Park, KS	160,253	$66,674	$191,520
4. Olathe, KS	102,617	$65,111	$175,560

Central Region (under 100,000 population)

1. Woodbury, MN	50,701	$81,592	$219,000
2. Dublin, OH	33,480	$96,828	$355,100
3. Wildwood, MO	33,396	$100,278	$320,000
4. Libertyville, IL	52,147	$79,360	$350,000
5. Chesterfield, MO	55,768	$96,013	$333,000

Western Region (over 100,000 population)

1. Plano, TX	271,090	$82,857	$191,520
2. Anaheim, CA	343,855	$52,196	$340,000
3. Scottsdale, AZ	223,181	$59,596	$263,500
4. Santa Rosa, CA	152,450	$54,537	$349,500
5. Irvine, CA	150,450	$77,662	$430,000

Western Region (under 100,000 population)

1. Rancho Santa Margarita, CA	49,898	$84,159	$350,000
2. Flower Mound, TX	61,579	$99,516	$210,672
3. San Clemente, CA	52,969	$68,799	$555,000
4. Tustin, CA	70,551	$60,250	$391,000
5. Carlsbad, CA	86,511	$68,410	$446,000

For a complete list of *Money's* 87 cities and towns, visit the following website: http://money.cnn.com/best/bplive/cities_table/#analysis. For a complete listing of current data on the 300 largest metropolitan statistical areas, visit *Money's* website: http://money.cnn.com/bestplaces. Designed to be interactive, the site allows you to search for "your best city" by ranking nine factors – from weather and crime rate to health care and transportation.

Seek Out the Best Employers

You might also want to consider some of America's best employers when identifying your ideal community. According to *Fortune Magazine's* most recent survey (2004) of America's most admired companies, these 10 companies ranked at the top:

Fortune's 10 Most Admired Companies, 2004

1. Wal-Mart Stores
2. Berkshire Hathaway
3. Southwest Airlines
4. General Electric
5. Dell Inc.

6. Microsoft
7. Johnson & Johnson
8. Starbucks
9. FedEx
10. IBM

For a complete listing and ranking of all 500 companies in *Fortune's* "best" database, visit this website:

www.fortune.com/fortune/mostadmired

Most of these companies are considered "the best" because they offer excellent employee benefits and perks – from stock options and personal concierge services to on-site child care and sabbaticals – as well as promote a very positive company culture that encourages employee initiative, invests in employee education and training, and are generally fun places to work. The typical company has $1.3 billion in revenues; a workforce that is 44% female and 78.2% Caucasian; low annual personnel turnover; and receives 19,000 applications for 724 jobs. Keep these companies, or at least their characteristics, in mind if and when you make a job change. You may discover a perfect employer as well as a perfect job!

Select a Location Properly

You and your family should take into consideration several factors and questions when deciding on which communities to target your job search. Start by asking yourself these questions:

- What's most important to me/us in making a move – environment, health care, safety, education, employment, economy, culture, taxes, recreation, climate?

- Where would I/we ideally like to live for the next five, 10, or 20 years?

- What is the relative cost of living?

- How attractive are the educational, social, recreational, and cultural opportunities?

- What are the economic and psychological costs of making a move?

- What job and career opportunities are there for me/us?

- How can I/we best conduct a job search in another community?

Many people answer these questions by remaining in their community or by targeting economically growing communities or ones offering excellent lifestyle options. The exodus from the declining industrial cities in the Northeast and North Central regions to the Sunbelt began in the 1960s, expanded in the 1970s, continued into the 1980s with the inclusion of the energy-rich Rocky Mountain states, and further expanded in the 1990s with high-tech industries in the West. Several metropolitan areas in all regions, but especially in the West, will have abundant job opportunities for skilled workers in the decade ahead. Many of these communities also offer attractive lifestyles. Targeting a job search in metropolitan San Francisco, Las Vegas, Denver, Phoenix, Dallas, St. Louis, Minneapolis, Atlanta, Raleigh-Durham, Nashville, Boston, or Washington, DC may be a wise move. While these areas may experience numerous urban problems over the next decade, their problems are ones of growth – traffic congestion, pollution, city planning, crime, and housing shortages – not ones of decline. We believe it is better to experience the problems of growth than of decline, especially since growing economies are more likely to respond to their problems. In a situation of decline, your livelihood becomes threatened. In a situation of growth, your major problem may be fighting the traffic congestion in order to get to a job which offers a promising career.

New frontiers for renewed job and career prosperity abound throughout America if you are willing to pack your bags and move. But most such frontiers require highly skilled individuals, and there can be major financial costs in making such a move, especially if you are a homeowner. If you lack the necessary skills for industries in other communities, consider getting retrained before making a move. Unfortunately, many people making moves today do not have the necessary skills to succeed in many of today's growing communities.

Making a community move on your own involves taking risks. Many people, for example, are locked into financial obligations, such as a mortgaged house that doesn't sell well in what may be a depressed housing market. If you find yourself locked in financially, you may want to consider taking an immediate financial loss in anticipation of renewed prosperity in a community which is experiencing promising growth and prosperity. You may recoup your immediate losses within a year or two. However, you will have to pass through a transition period which can be difficult if you don't approach it in a positive, upbeat manner. The old saying, *"There is no gain without pain,"* is appropriate in many situations involving community moves.

Consider Your Financial Costs

The financial costs of relocating will vary depending on your situation. They can be major, especially if you move to a community with high housing costs. Recent studies conducted by Runzheimer International, for example, found the average costs of relocating to be over $35,000 for homeowners and over $9,000 for non-homeowners. The major costs include:

1. Search for housing – travel, child care, and associated expenses.
2. Closing costs on both the old and new homes.
3. Increases in mortgage payments or apartment rent.
4. Temporary living expenses.
5. Cost of a bridge, equity, or swing loan.
6. Costs of maintaining two residences during the relocation period – very high if the old home does not sell immediately.
7. Shipment of household goods.
8. Final moving expenses.
9. Possible increase in cost of living – property and sales taxes, food, utilities.
10. Travel and job search costs for working spouse.
11. Expenses for marketing a home or subletting an apartment.
12. Miscellaneous costs – deposits, decorating costs, fees, dues.

For information on the latest such costs, see Runzheimer International's website: www.runzheimer.com. They offer detailed reports on hundreds of communities, which include comparative costs of living.

When considering a community move, you should be aware of the relative cost of living in various communities compared to your current cost of living. Several websites include useful cost of living calculators that enable users to compare their current salary with the cost of living in hundreds of other communities. You may, for example, discover your current salary of $50,000 in Atlanta will need to be $70,000 in San Francisco in order to maintain your current cost of living. Some also include lifestyle and moving calculators along with useful information on housing, schools, crime rates, taxes, recreation, and neighborhoods. Try these sites for starters:

- **Homefair**   www.homefair.com
- **MonsterMoving**   www.monstermoving.com

- Relocation Central   www.relocationcentral.com
- Job Relocation   www.jobrelocation.com
- Homescape   www.homescape.com
- 123Relocation.com   www.relo-usa.com
- Employee Relocation Council www.erc.org
- GMAC Relocation Services   www.gmac-relocation.com
- Insiders' Guide   www.insiders.com/relocation
- MoversNet   www.usps.gov/moversnet
- Moving.com   www.moving.com
- MovingCost.com   www.movingcost.com
- Relocate-America   www.relocate-america.com
- Relocation-net.com   www.relocation-net.com
- The Wall Street Journal   www.homes.wsj.com

A Web of Relocation Resources

The Internet includes a wealth of resources to assist you in identifying the best places to work, live, and relocate. For identifying the best places to live and work, be sure to check out the websites we identified on pages 218-219. Assuming you wish to explore various aspects of specific communities, you should include the community websites identified on page 219. For news-papers and magazines on specific communities, check out the gateway websites on page 220.

Conduct a Long-Distance Job Search

How do you target your job search on a particular community? If you decide to remain in your present community, your job search is relatively manageable on a day-to-day basis. If you target another community, you will need to conduct a long-distance job search which requires more extensive use of the mail and telephone as well as carefully planned visits to the community. In fact, you will probably use your job search time more efficiently with a long-distance campaign. In both situations, you need to conduct community research prior to initiating the major communication steps in your job search.

Most of your community research can be conducted in the library or on the Internet. You need names, addresses, and phone numbers of potential employers. Use the major directories we identified in Chapter 11, such as the *Dun & Bradstreet's Middle Market Directory* and *Who's Who in Commerce and Industry*. The annual *Headquarters USA* is an especially useful directory for anyone contemplating a long-distance job search. Search for specific com-munities on the Internet. Many communities maintain home pages that include a wealth of information on housing, education, and employers.

Homefair's website (www.homefair.com) is a good place to start checking out communities.

We particularly recommend starting with the latest edition of *The Sourcebook of ZIP Code Demographics* (CACI Marketing Systems). Found in the reference section of many libraries, this two-volume directory gives detailed information on population, housing, employment, education, income, and transportation in all communities throughout the United States. Organized by zip code, this directory yields a wealth of information on zip coded communities. For example, if you turn to the section on your current zip code, you will discover how your community is structured according to population, housing, employment, language, education, income, and transportation. You can compare your current community to thousands of other zip code communities throughout the country. In some cities with five or more zip codes, you will learn average median family incomes can fluctuate from $13,000 to $65,000, depending on the particular community zip code. We recommend consulting this directory **before** committing yourself to relocating to another community.

As noted in Chapter 11, Adams Media publishers a series of job bank books which identify hundreds of employers and job search services in the following cities and states: Atlanta, Boston, the Carolinas, Chicago, Dallas/Fort Worth, Denver, Detroit, Florida, Houston, Los Angeles, Minneapolis, New York City, Ohio, Philadelphia, Phoenix, Portland, San Diego, San Francisco, Seattle, St. Louis, Tennessee, and Washington, DC. Each book includes annotated descriptions of employers along with addresses and telephone numbers.

The Yellow Pages of telephone directories are especially useful sources for identifying the business and commercial structure of communities as well as for addresses and telephone numbers. The larger the community, the more specialized the businesses. For example, New York City has several businesses specializing in manufacturing manhole covers! At the same time, write to chambers of commerce for information on the community and to companies for annual reports and other organizational literature.

Numerous online resources are available for researching on communities, businesses, and relocation. Most libraries now have access to a variety of online resources relevant to job seekers and those interested in relocating.

Other good sources for conducting a job search include Fran Bastress's comprehensive job search guide for spouses, *The New Relocating Spouse's Guide to Employment* (Impact Publications), and Andrea Kay's *Greener Pastures: How to Find a Job in Another Place* (St. Martin's) which outlines useful strategies for conducting a long-distance job search campaign.

Part of your research may involve narrowing the number of communities you are considering. If you identify 10 alternative communities, outline the criteria by which to evaluate the 10 communities. For example, you may be particularly interested in moving to a community which has a good climate, excellent cultural facilities, unique recreational opportunities, and a sound educational infrastructure in addition to numerous job and career opportunities in your area of interest and skill. Select three communities and initiate a research campaign for more information. If at all possible, schedule a trip to the cities to get an on-site view or feel for the relative environments. Further try to narrow your choices by rank-ordering your preferences among the three communities. Concentrate most of your job search efforts on your top priority community.

Your next step is to develop a strategy for penetrating both the advertised and hidden job markets. If you are conducting a job search outside your present community, the advertised job market will be most accessible to you. However, you need to link into the hidden job market, where most of the good jobs are located. While doing this from a distance is somewhat difficult, nonetheless it can be managed.

Penetrate the Local Job Market

The advertised job market is always the easier to access. Buy a newspaper and read the classified ads. Search online employment sites for job listings. Contact an employment firm and they will eagerly assist you. Walk into a personnel office and they may permit you to fill out an application form.

If you target a community from a distance, begin with the Internet by searching community websites for information. Alternatively, subscribe to a local newspaper; the Sunday edition will most likely meet your needs. This newspaper also will give you other important information on the community – housing market, economics, politics, society, culture, entertainment, and recreation. Survey the help-wanted ads to get a feel for the structure of the advertised job market. Remember, these are not necessarily indicative of the true employment picture in a community – only 20 to 30 percent of the job market. Write letters to various companies and ask about job opportunities. You also may want to contact one or more professional employment agencies or job search firms – preferably fee-paid ones – for job leads. But remember our previous warnings about possible frauds and hucksters!

Efforts to penetrate the advertised job market should be geared toward uncovering the **hidden job market**. For example, in reading the Sunday newspaper, watch for names of important people in the society or living section. You may want to contact some of these people by using an approach letter as outlined in Chapters 11 and 12. The employment agencies may give some indication of the general employment situation in the community – both advertised and hidden job markets. The Chamber of Commerce might be able to give you some job leads other than those advertised. Perhaps you can develop local contacts through membership in an alumni network (see page 242), professional association, or church. Be sure to embrace the Internet: search for information on your targeted community; join news groups; and use message boards – whatever resources that will yield useful information and contacts for conducting a community-based job search.

If you are conducting a long-distance job search, we recommend following the same procedures we outlined in Chapter 12 on networking. Preparation is the key to success. Do your research on potential employers, write letters, make phone calls, and schedule informational and referral interviews. The major difference in this situation is your timing. In addition, you need to give more information to your contacts. In your letter mention that you are planning to move to their community and would appreciate their advice on job opportunities for someone with your qualifications. Mention that you plan to visit the community on such and such a date and would appreciate an opportunity to discuss your job search plan at that time. In this case, enclose your resume with the letter and request a reply to your inquiry. Most people will reply and schedule an interview or refer you to someone else.

You should set aside one or two weeks – preferably more – to literally blitz the community with informational and referral interviews. This requires doing a considerable amount of advance work. For example, use your present community to practice informational and referral interviewing. Contact employers in your area who are in similar positions. Many of them may give you referrals to friends and colleagues in your targeted community.

If you have limited contacts when conducting a long-distance job search, you will probably need to use the "cold turkey" approach more frequently. You should make most of your key contacts at least four weeks before you plan to visit your targeted community. Within two weeks of your visit, you should have scheduled most of your interviews.

Try to schedule at least three interviews each day. You will probably do more because each interview will yield one or two referrals to others. Five interviews a day are manageable if you don't need to spend a lot of time traveling from one site to another. Each day plan to visit sites that are near one another. Within a two-week period, you should be able to conduct 40 to 60 interviews. Use the weekends to research the community further. Contact a realtor who will be happy to show you around the community and inform you of different housing alternatives, neighborhoods, schools, taxes, public services, shopping centers, and a wealth of other community information. You should reserve the last two days for following up on referrals. Scheduling interviews with referrals will have to be made by telephone because of the time factor.

After concluding your one- to two-week visit, follow up your interviews with thank you letters, telephone calls, and letters indicating continuing interest and requesting referrals.

If you receive an invitation to a formal job interview in another city, be sure to clarify the financial question of who pays for the travel. Normally if the employer has requested the interview, the company pays the expense to and from the out-of-town interview. However, if you have invited yourself to an interview by stating that you will be "in town," expect to pay your own expenses. If you are unclear about who initiated the interview, simply ask the employer *"How should we handle the travel expenses?"* This question should clarify the matter so there will be no misunderstanding.

Identify Opportunity Structures

Each community has its own set of social, economic, political, and job market structures. Your job is to understand and use the particular job market structure in your targeted community. Therefore, we outline the case of Washington, DC for illustrative purposes. The principles for identifying and using the institutional and personal networks will remain the same for most communities even though the individuals, groups, and institutions differ for different communities.

The degree of structure differs for every community. However, one thing is relatively predictable: most communities lack a coherent structure for processing job information efficiently and effectively. But communities are made up of networks which enable individuals to network for job information, advice, and referrals. Each community consists of numerous individuals, groups, organizations, and institutions – many of which constitute mutually dependent networks – that are involved in pursuing their own interests in cooperation and competition with one another. The Yellow Pages of your telephone book as well as the membership directory of the local Chamber of Commerce best outline the major actors. Banks, mortgage companies, advertising firms, car dealers, schools, churches, small businesses, industries, hospitals, law firms, governments, and civic and voluntary groups do their "own thing" and have their own internal power structure. No one dominates except in small communities which also are company towns – paper mills, mining companies, universities, or steel mills. At the same time, the groups overlap with each other because of economic, political, and social needs. The bank, for example, needs to loan money to the businesses and churches. The businesses, in turn, need the educational institutions. And the educational institutions need the businesses to absorb their graduates. Therefore, individuals tend to cooperate in seeing that people playing the other games also succeed. Members of school boards, medical boards, and the boardrooms of banks and corporations will overlap and give the appearance of a "power structure" even though power is structured in the loosest sense of the term. The game players compete and cooperate with each other as well as co-op one another. The structures they create are your **opportunity structures** for penetrating the hidden job market. They are **networks** for locating job opportunities.

Examine the case of Washington, DC. The opportunity structures for your job search networks are relatively well defined in this city. While government is the major institution, other institutions are clearly apparent in relation to the government. Within government, both the political and administrative institutions function as alternative opportunity structures in the Washington networks: congressional staffs, congressional committees, congressional sub-committees, congressional bureaucracy, executive staff, departments, independent executive agencies, and independent regulatory agencies. Outside, but clinging to, government are a variety of other groups and networks: interest groups, the media, professional associations, contractors, consultants, law firms, banks, and universities and colleges. As illustrated on page 312, these groups are linked to one another for survival and advancement. Charles Peters (*How Washington Really Works*) calls them "survival networks" which function in the "make believe world" of Washington, DC. Ripley and Franklin (*Congress, Bureaucracy, and Public Policy*) identify the key political dynamics as "subgovernments" – the interaction of interest groups, agencies, and congressional committees.

Washington is the ultimate networking community. For years Washington insiders have used these "survival networks" and "subgovernments" to advance their careers. A frequent career pattern would be to work in an agency for three to four years. During that time, you would make important contacts on Capitol Hill with congressional staffs and committees as well as with private consultants, contractors, and interest groups. Your specialized knowledge on the inner workings of government is marketable to these other people. Therefore, you make a relatively easy job change from a federal agency to a congressional committee or to an interest group. After a few years here, you move to another group in the network. Perhaps you work on your law degree at the same time so that in another five years you can go into the biggest growth industry in the city – law firms. The key to making these moves is the personal contact – whom you know. Particular attention is given to maintaining a current federal application (OF-612) or resume, just in case an opportunity arises for you. Congressional staff members usually last no more than two years; they set their sights on consulting and contracting firms, agencies, or interest groups for their next job move.

Whatever community you decide to focus your job search on, expect it to have its own particular mix of opportunity structures and networks. If you are in a booming high-tech community, such as Seattle or Austin, expect to uncover networks consisting of strong linkages amongst universities, manufacturers, consultants, and a host of small business suppliers, recreational suppliers, and upscale retail operations, from restaurants to department stores. Focus your job search on the key players that define these networks. Do as much research as possible to identify the structure of the networks as well as the key people who can provide access to various elements in the opportunity structures. Washington is not unique in this respect, except for its heavy emphasis on government operations, lawyers, lobbyists, and media; it is just better known, and Washingtonians talk about it more because of their frequent job moves. The mix of players may be different, but the networks and opportunity structures are as ubiquitous as those found in other communities.

Washington Networks

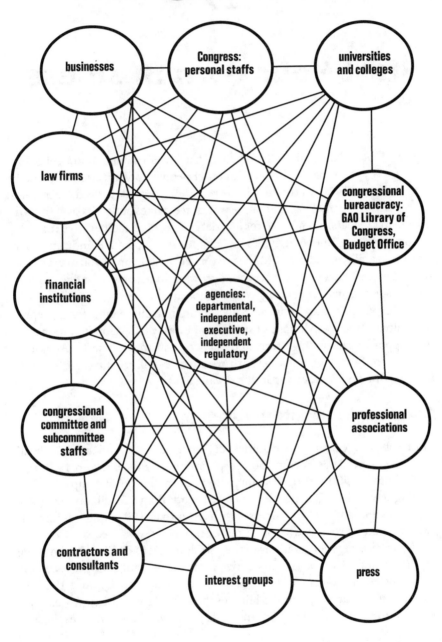

17

Start Your Own Business

WHILE THE PREVIOUS CHAPTERS examined strategies for finding employment in other people's organizations, you may also be interested in working for yourself. Indeed, each year nearly 7 percent of the workforce strikes out on its own to start their own business. They do so for a variety of positive and negative reasons. If your self-assessment activities in Chapters 6, 7, and 8 indicate your motivated abilities and skills (MAS) are very entrepreneurial, you may be best suited for self-employment. You, too, may want to become your own boss as you pursue dreams of operating your own business.

We expect the decade ahead to be another strong period for entrepreneurship in America. Millions of small businesses will develop in response to new opportunities in high-tech and service industries. True to American tradition, self-employment and start-up businesses will remain great frontiers for careering and re-careering in the decade ahead.

Consider Your Alternatives

Most job and career opportunities in America are found among small businesses – not large Fortune 500 corporations. In fact, between 1979 and 1993, Fortune 500 companies eliminated 4.8 million jobs; companies employing fewer than 500 people generated more than 15 million new jobs. Between 1993 and 1999, businesses with fewer than 100 employees hired at twice the rate of those with 500 or more employees.

We expect large corporations in the decade ahead to continue downsizing as they emphasize greater productivity by introducing new cost-cutting technologies, management systems, and e-commerce to improve the efficiency, effectiveness, and profitability of the workplace. In other words, they will continue to cut back on the fastest growing corporate expense –

personnel. The advancement hierarchies of large companies will shorten and career opportunities narrow as these companies further automate as well as shed unwanted personnel. Many of these displaced workers will become entrepreneurs, starting both small and medium-sized businesses – often in competition with their former employers.

Since nearly 90 percent of all new jobs will be created by small businesses employing fewer than 500 individuals, you may wish to target your job search toward opportunities with such businesses; companies with fewer than 100 employees will offer some of the best opportunities. Finding a job with a small business will require a great deal of research because most of these businesses are not well known among job seekers.

One other alternative is to start your own business. The trend toward entrepreneurship is stronger than ever. In 1999, for example, nearly 900,000 new businesses were started – up from 700,000 in 1991. Nearly one in 14 workers attempts to start a business each year, which represents the highest rate of entrepreneurship in the industrialized world. In the decade ahead, millions of individuals will be "pushed" or "pulled" from what were once seen as promising jobs and careers with companies to form their own businesses. As work becomes more centralized, advancement opportunities become more limited, and starting a business becomes easier, millions of individuals will opt for starting their own businesses.

While nearly 900,000 new businesses are started each year, grim and sobering business statistics also discourage many would-be entrepreneurs: another 700,000 to 800,000 businesses fail each year; 50 percent fail within the first 38 months; and nearly 90 percent fail within 10 years. Unfortunately, starting your own business is a risky business; the statistical odds are against anyone becoming a successful entrepreneur.

Nonetheless, owning your business is a viable careering and re-careering alternative to working for someone else – if you approach business intelligently. Many people fail because they lack the necessary ingredients for success. In this chapter we outline the basics for getting started in owning your business and employing yourself.

Examine Risks and Motivations

You will find few challenges riskier and more time-consuming than starting your own business. It involves lots of hard work, long hours, and betting on your financial future. At the same time, you may experience your greatest professional satisfaction in running your own business, especially if you are pursuing your passions.

Starting a business means taking risks. First, while you may have grandiose visions of becoming an overnight success, you will probably go into debt and realize little income during the first two years of building your business. You may be under-capitalized or have overhead costs higher than anticipated. It takes time to develop a regular clientele. What profits you do realize are normally plowed back into the business in order to expand operations and guarantee larger future profits. Second, business is often a trial-and-error process in which it is difficult to predict or ensure outcomes. Due to unforeseen circumstances beyond your control, you may fail even though you work hard and make intelligent decisions. Third, you could go bankrupt and lose more than just your investments of time and money.

At the same time, owning your own business can be tremendously satisfying. It is the ultimate exercise of independence. Being your own boss means you are in control, and no one can fire you – only you and your failures. You are rewarded in direct proportion to your productivity. Your salary is not limited by a boss, nor are your accomplishments credited to others. Unless you decide otherwise, you are not wedded to a 9 to 5 work routine or a two-week vacation each year. Depending on how successful your business becomes, you may be able to retire young and pursue other interests. You can turn what you truly enjoy doing, such as a hobby, into a profitable, rewarding, and fun career.

> *This is the old-fashioned way of making money – hard work, long hours, and lots of hustling.*

But such self-indulgence and gratification have costs which you may or may not be willing to incur. You will probably need at least $30,000 to $50,000 of start-up capital, or perhaps as much as $350,000, depending on the type of business you start. No one will send you a paycheck every two weeks so you can regularly pay your bills. You may work 12- and 14-hour days, seven days a week, and have no vacation during the first few years. And you may become heavily indebted, experience frequent cashflow problems, and eventually have creditors descend on you. In the end, you could go bankrupt and then have to find a job working for someone else.

Why, then, start your own business? If you talk to people who have worked for others and then started their own businesses, they will tell you similar stories. They got tired of drawing a salary while making someone else rich. They got bored with their work and hated coming to an office everyday to engage in a 9 to 5 work routine. They wanted control over what they did. Some worked for jerks; others were victims of organizational politics; and others had difficulty working in an environment structured by others whom they considered less competent than themselves. Many simply couldn't work for others – they had to be in charge of their work. On a more positive note, many started businesses because they had a great idea they wanted to pursue, or they wanted the challenge of independently accomplishing their own goals.

If you decide to go into business for yourself, be sure you know what you want to do, and be willing to take risks and work hard. Don't expect to get rich overnight or sit back and watch your business grow on its own. Starting a business is usually a very sobering experience that tests your motivations, abilities, and skills. Success in a corporate or bureaucratic career may not transfer well to starting your own business which initially requires entrepreneurial skills. Be prepared to work long and hard hours, experience disappointments, and challenge yourself to the limits. You will quickly discover this is the old fashioned way of making money – hard work, long hours, and lots of hustling. But at least you can choose which 18 hours a day you want to work!

There are few things that are more self-actualizing than running your own business. But you must have realistic expectations as well as a motivational pattern which is conducive to taking risks and being an entrepreneur. In Chapters 6, 7, and 8 you identified your motivational patterns and skills. If you like security, predictability, and stability, you probably are a candidate for a position where someone hands you a paycheck each week. If you read and believe in a get-rich-quick book, video, or seminar which tries to minimize your risks and uncertainty, you probably have been ripped off by another enterprising individual who is getting rich writing books, producing videos and audiotapes, and conducting seminars for naive people who respond well to motivational speakers!

Possess the Right Strengths for Success

How can you become self-employed and successful at the same time? No one has a magical success formula for the budding entrepreneur – only advice based on experience. We do know why many businesses fail, and we can identify some basic characteristics for success. Poor management and decision-making lie at the heart of business failures. Many people go into business without doing sufficient market research; they under-capitalize; they select a poor location; they incur extremely high and debilitating overhead costs; they lack commitment; they are unwilling to sacrifice; they can't read or count; and they lack interpersonal and salesmanship skills.

On the positive side, studies continue to identify something called "drive," or the need to achieve, as a key characteristic of successful entrepreneurs. As Kellogg (*Fast Track*, McGraw-Hill) and others have found, young achievers and successful entrepreneurs possess similar characteristics: "A high energy level, restless, a willingness to work hard and take risks, a desire to escape from insecurity."

Successful business people combine certain motivations, skills, and circumstances. Contrary to popular myths, you don't need to be rich or have an

MBA or business experience to get started. If you are willing to gamble and are a self-starter, self-confident, an organizer, and you like people, you should consider this entrepreneurial alternative in your careering and re-careering decisions. These characteristics along with drive, thinking ability, communication and networking skills, technical knowledge, hard work, persistence, and good luck are essential ingredients for business success.

If these are among your strengths, as identified in Chapter 8, you may be a good candidate for starting your own business with a high probability of success. If you feel you have recurring weaknesses in certain areas, you may want to consider finding a business partner who has particular complementary strengths for running a business.

Know Yourself

There are many different ways to get started in business. You can buy into a franchise which can initially cost you $20,000 to $500,000. Advertisements in the *Wall Street Journal* are a good source for hundreds of franchise opportunities from flipping hamburgers to selling animals. You can join someone else's business on a full-time or part-time basis as a partner or employee in order to get some direct business experience. You can try your hand at a direct-sales business such as Amway, Shaklee, or Avon. Hundreds of new direct-sales businesses modeled after Amway's multi-level business methods are now marketing every conceivable product – soap, computers, canoes, motor oil, and milk. You can buy someone else's business or you can start your own business from scratch.

> *Don't be high on motivation but low on knowledge and skills, for "thinking big" is no substitute for doing the work!*

Your decision on how to get started in business should be based upon the data you generated on your skills and goals in Chapters 6, 7, and 8. Do not go into business for negative reasons – get fired, hate your job, can't find work. Unfortunately, many people go into business with totally unrealistic expectations as well as with little understanding of their own goals, skills, and motivations. For example, while it is nice to work around pretty clothes, owning a dress shop requires handling inventory and personnel as well as paying the rent and doing bookkeeping. Getting all those pretty dresses on the rack is hard work! Many people also don't understand how the business world works. It requires a great deal of interpersonal skills to develop and expand personal networks of creditors, clients, colleagues, and competitors.

Therefore, you should do two things before you decide to go into business. First, thoroughly explore your goals and motivations. The questions are familiar:

- What do you want to do?
- What do you do well?
- What do you enjoy doing?

Second, research different types of businesses in order to better understand advantages, disadvantages, procedures, processes, and possible problems. Talk to business owners about their work. Try to learn as much as possible about the reality before you invest your time and money. Surprisingly, few people do this. Many people leap into a business that they think will be great and then later learn it was neither right for them nor did they have realistic expectations of what was involved. This is precisely why so many businesses fail each year.

You should approach business opportunities the same way you approach the job market: do research, develop networks, and conduct informational and referral interviews. Most business people, including your competition, will share their experiences with you and assist you with advice and referrals. Such research is absolutely invaluable. If you fail to do it initially, you will pay later on by making the same mistakes that millions of others have made in starting their own businesses in isolation of others. Don't be high on motivation but low on knowledge and skills, for "thinking big" is no substitute for doing the work!

Look for New Opportunities

Most business people will tell you similar stories of the reality of running your own business. Do your market research, spend long hours, plan, and be persistent. They also will give you advice on what businesses to avoid and what business routines you should be prepared to handle.

Many service and high-tech businesses will be growing in the decade ahead. Given the changing demographic structure – fewer young people, more elderly, the two-career family – numerous opportunities are arising for small personal-service businesses to meet the needs of the elderly and career-oriented families. Businesses relating to restaurants, home maintenance, health care, housing for the elderly, and mortuaries and cemeteries should expand considerably during the next two decades.

Opportunities are also available for inventive business persons who can make more productive use of busy people's time – fast food, financial planning, and mail-order Internet and catalog shopping. The information and high-tech revolutions are taking place at the same time two-career families do not have time to waste standing in lines at banks, grocery stores, and department stores. Mail-order or Internet-based home and office-based shopping should increase dramatically during the next decade.

A service business is especially attractive. It's easy to establish; many require a small initial investment; and the accounting is often simple. You may be able to operate from your home and thus keep your overhead down.

Knowing these trends and opportunities is important, but they should not be the only determining factors in choosing a business. You should start with yourself by again trying to identify a business that is fit for you rather than one you think you might fit into.

Prepare the Basics

You also need to consider several other factors before starting a business. Since a business requires financing, locating, planning, developing customer relationships, and meeting legal requirements, be prepared to address these questions:

1. **How can I best finance the business?** Take out a personal or business loan with a bank? Go into a partnership in order to share the risks and costs? Get a loan from the Small Business Administration?

2. **How much financing do I need?** Many businesses fail because they are under-capitalized. Others fail because of over-spending on rent, furnishings, inventory, personnel, and advertising.

3. **Where is my market?** Just in this community, region, nationwide, or international? Mail-order and Internet-based businesses enable you to expand your market nationwide whereas retail and service businesses tend to be confined to particular communities.

4. **Who are my suppliers?** How many must I work with? What about credit arrangements?

5. **Where is the best location for the business?** Do you need to open a store or operate out of your home? If you need a store or office, is it conveniently located for your clientele? *"Location is everything"* still best summarizes the success of many businesses, especially McDonald's and Wal-Mart, which are noted for their attention to location.

6. **How should the business be legally structured?** Sole proprietorship, partnership, or corporation? Each has certain advantages and disadvantages. For example, a corporation has several tax advantages.

7. **What licenses and permits do I need?** These consist of local business licenses and permits, federal employee identification numbers, state sales tax number, state occupational licenses, federal licenses and permits, and special state and local regulations which vary from state to state and from community to community. What type of insurance do I need? Fire, theft, liability, workers' compensation, and auto?

8. **How many employees do I need and how do I find them?** Can I do without personnel initially until the business expands? Should I use part-time and temporary help? How should I recruit? Should I use the Internet, classified ads, employment firms, headhunters, or network?

9. **What business name should I use?** If incorporated, is anyone else using the name? If a trade name, is it registered?

10. **What accounting system should I use?** Cash or accrual? Can I handle the books or do I need a part-time or full-time accountant? Who will handle the timely calculation and payment of payroll, sales, and corporate taxes as well as insurance, retirement plans, and workers compensation?

11. **Do I need a lawyer?** What type of lawyer? What legal work can I do myself?

12. **How do I develop a business plan?** A business plan should include a definition of the business, a marketing strategy, operational policies, purchasing plans, financial statements, and capital-raising plans.

13. **Show I put together a board of advisors?** It's always good to include respected individuals who can contribute expertise and perspective to your operation.

Get Useful Advice

If you decide to go into business, make sure you choose the right business for your particular skills, abilities, motivation, and interests. A good starting point is Paul and Sarah Edwards's *Finding Your Perfect Work* (Putnam) and Doug Gray's *Have You Got What It Takes? The Entrepreneur's Complete Self-Assessment Guide* (Self-Counseling Press). These books provide useful exercises for assessing your suitability for becoming an entrepreneur. For a good overview of the many decisions you must make in establishing a small business, see Bernard Kamaroff's *Small-Time Operator* (Bell Springs Publishing). This book provides you with all the basic information you need for starting your own business, including ledger sheets for setting up your books. Several other books provide similar how-to advice for the neophyte entrepreneur:

Jan Norman, *What No One Ever Tells You About Starting Your Own Business* (Upstart Publishing Co.)

Bob Adams, *Adams Streetwise™ Small Business Start-Up* (Adams Media)

Peter J. Patsula, *Successful Business Planning in 30 Days* (Patsula Media)

Stephen C. Harper, *McGraw-Hill Guide to Starting Your Own Business* (McGraw-Hill)

National Business Employment Weekly, *NBEW's Guide to Self Employment* (Wiley and Sons)

Gregory and Patricia Kishel, *How to Start, Run, and Stay in Business* (Wiley and Sons)

William J. Stolze, *Start Up* (Career Press)

David E. Gumpert, *How to Really Start Your Own Business* (Inc. Magazine)

Joseph Anthony, *Kiplinger's Working for Yourself* (Kiplinger)

LaVerne Ludden, *Franchise Opportunities Handbook* (JIST Publishing)

Katina Jones, *Adams Businesses You Can Start Almanac* (Adams Media)

Several websites also can provide assistance in starting and running a business:

- **Small Business Administration**　www.sba.gov/starting_business
- **Startup Journal**　www.startupjournal.com
- **BizMove.com**　http://bizmove.com
- **Business Know-How**　http://businessknowhow.com
- **AllBusiness**　www.allbusiness.com

The federal government will help you with several publications available through the Small Business Administration (SBA). Check out the "Library" section of the SBA website, which includes over 200 free e-books and publications as well as numerous resources links related to starting a business:

www.sba.gov/lib/library.html

The Internal Revenue Service (www.irs.gov.gov/businesses/small/article/0,, id=99336,00.html) offers a great deal of tax and accounting information to start-up businesses. The U.S. Chamber of Commerce (www.chamberbiz.com) as well as its local chapters offer useful information. Other useful online resources to help you start a business include:

- **American Express**　http://home2.americanexpress.com/smallbusiness/tool/biz_plan/index.asp
- **Business Gateway**　http://businessgateway.ca
- **Business Owner's Toolkit**　http://toolkit.cch.com
- **CEO Business Express**　www.ceoexpress.com/default.asp
- **Entrepreneur.com**　www.entrepreneur.com
- **Entreworld**　www.entreworld.org
- **eWeb**　http://eweb.slu.edu
- **Home Biz Tools**　http://homebiztools.com
- **Inc.com**　www.inc.com/guides/start_biz
- **Quicken Small Business**　www.quicken.com/smallbusiness
- **SCORE**　www.score.org
- **State Resource Centers**　www.itsimple.biz/resource_center
- **Yahoo Small Business**　http://smallbusiness.yahoo.com

Continue Your Success

The factors for operating a successful business are similar to the 20 principles we outlined in Chapter 5 for conducting a successful job search. Once your initial start-up problems are solved, you must organize, plan, implement, and manage in relation to your goals. Many people lack these abilities. Some people are good at initially starting a business, but they are unable to follow through in managing day-to-day routines once the business is established. And others have the ability to start, manage, and expand businesses successfully.

Be careful about business success. Many business people become obsessed with their work, put in 12- and 14-hour days continuously, and spend seven-day weeks to make the business successful. Unwilling to delegate, they try to do too much and thus become a prisoner to the business. The proverbial "tail wagging the dog" is a common phenomenon in small businesses. For some people, this lifestyle feeds their ego and makes them happy. For others, the 9 to 5 routine of working for someone else on salary may look very attractive only after a few months of self-employment. Therefore, you must be prepared to change your lifestyle when embarking on your own business. Your major limitation will be yourself.

So think it over carefully, do your research, and plan, organize, implement, and manage for success. Even though running your own business is risky and involves hard work, the thrill of independence and success is hard to beat!

Part IV

Take Action to Implement Your Goals

18

Develop a Realistic Plan of Action

U NDERSTANDING WITHOUT ACTION is a waste of time. And buying a how-to book without implementing it is a waste of money. Many people read how-to books, attend how-to seminars, and do nothing other than read more books, attend more seminars, and engage in more wishful thinking. While these activities become forms of therapy for some individuals, they should lead to positive actions for you.

Risk Implementation

From the very beginning of this book we stressed the importance of understanding the job market and developing appropriate job search strategies for getting the job you want. We make no assumptions nor claim any magic is contained in this book. Rather, we have attempted to assemble useful information to help you organize an effective job search which will best communicate your qualifications to potential employers. Individual chapters examined the present and future job markets as well as outlined in how-to terms specific careering and re-careering skills for shaping your own future. We have done our part in getting you to the implementation stage. What happens next is your responsibility.

The methods we outlined in previous chapters have worked for thousands of individuals who have paid thousands of dollars to get similar information from the highly paid professionals. While you may want to see a professional for assistance at certain steps in your job search, if you are self-motivated, you can do everything outlined in this book on your own and with a minimum expenditure of money. The major cost will be your time and effort. However,

327

if you feel you need professional assistance, by all means seek out the best professionals to help you with your job search.

But you must make the effort and take the **risk of implementing** this book. Careering and re-careering take work and are risky businesses. You try something new and place your ego on the line. You subject yourself to the possibility of being rejected several times. And this is precisely the major barrier you will encounter to effective implementation. For many people are unwilling to take more than a few rejections.

Welcome Rejections as Learning Opportunities

Planning is the easiest part of any task. Turning plans into reality is the most difficult challenge. It's relatively simple to set goals and outline a course of action divorced from the reality of actually doing it. But if you don't take action, you will not get your expected results. You must implement if you want desired results.

Once you take action, be prepared for rejections. Employers will tell you *"Thank you – we'll call you,"* but they never do. Other employers will tell you *"We have no positions available at this time for someone with your qualifications"* or *"You don't have the qualifications necessary for this position."* Whatever the story, you may face many disappointments on the road to success.

> *Understanding without action is a waste of time. And buying a how-to book without implementing it is a waste of money.*

Rejections are a normal part of the process of finding employment as well as getting ahead in life. Rejections offer an important learning experience which should help you better understand yourself, employers, and the job-finding process. More important, you must be rejected before you will be accepted. Expect 10 rejections or "nos" for every acceptance or "yes" you receive. If you quit after five or eight rejections, you prematurely end your job search. If you persist in collecting two to five more "no's," you will likely receive a "yes." Most people quit prematurely because their egos are not prepared for more rejections. Therefore, you should welcome rejections as you seek more and more acceptances.

Get Motivated and Work Hard

Assuming you have a firm understanding of each job search step and how to relate them to your goals, what do you do next? The next steps involve **motivation and hard work.** Just how motivated are you to seek a new job or career and thus change your life? Our experience is that individuals need to be sufficiently **motivated** to make the first move and do it properly. If you go about your job search half-heartedly – you just want to "test the waters" to see what's out there – don't expect to be successful. You must be committed to achieving specific goals. Make the decision to properly develop and implement your job search and be prepared to work hard in achieving your goals.

Find Time

Once you've convinced yourself to take the necessary steps to find a job or change and advance your career, you need to find the **time** to properly implement your job search. This requires setting aside specific blocks of time for identifying your motivated abilities and skills, developing your resume, writing letters, making telephone calls, and conducting the necessary research and networking required for success. This whole process takes time. If you are a busy person, like most people, you simply must make the time. As noted in our examination of your time management practices in Chapter 5 (pages 108-109), you should practice your own versions of time management or cut-back management. Get better organized, give some things up, or cut back on all your activities. If, for example, you can set aside one hour each day to devote to your job search, you will spend seven hours a week or 28 hours a month on your search. However, you should and can find more time than this for these activities.

> *Successful job hunters are ones who routinize a job search schedule and keep at it.*

Time and again we find successful job hunters are the ones who routinize specific job search activities. They make contact after contact, conduct numerous informational interviews, submit many applications and resumes, and keep repeating these activities in spite of encountering rejections. They learn that success is just a few more "no's" and informational interviews away. They face each day with a positive attitude fit for someone desiring to change their life – I must collect my 10 "no's" today because each "no" brings me closer to another "yes"!

Commit Yourself in Writing

You may find it useful to commit yourself in writing to achieving job search success. This is a very effective way to get both motivated and directed for action. Start by completing the job search contract on page 330 and keep it near you – in your briefcase or on your desk.

Job Search Contract

1. I'm committed to changing my life by changing my job. Today's date is _____.

2. I will manage my time so that I can successfully complete my job search and find a high quality job. I will complete my time management inventory (pages 104-105) and begin changing my time management behavior on _____.

3. I will begin my job search on _____.

4. I will involve _____ with my job search.
                       (individual/group)

5. I will spend at least one week conducting library research on different jobs, employers, and organizations. I will begin this research during the week of _____.

6. I will complete my skills identification step by _____.

7. I will complete my objective statement by _____.

8. I will complete my resume by _____.

9. Each week I will:

   ■ make _____ new job contacts.

   ■ conduct _____ informational interviews.

   ■ follow up on _____ referrals.

10. My first job interview will take place during the week of _____.

11. I will begin my new job by _____.

12. I will make a habit of learning one new skill each year.

           Signature: _____

           Date: _____

In addition, you should complete weekly performance reports. These reports identify what you actually accomplished rather than what your good intentions tell you to do. Make copies of the performance and planning report form on page 332 and use one each week to track your actual progress and to plan your activities for the next week.

If you fail to meet these written commitments, issue yourself a revised and updated contract. But if you do this three or more times, we strongly suggest you stop kidding yourself about your commitment to find a job. Start over again, but this time consult a professional career counselor who can assist you with your job search. A professional may not be cheap, but if paying for help gets you on the right track and results in the job you want, it's money well spent. Do not be "penny wise but pound foolish" with your future. If you must seek professional advice, be sure you are an informed consumer according to our advice on "shopping for a professional" in Chapter 5.

Career and Re-Career for Your Future

The continuing transformation of the workplace will require millions of individuals to career and re-career in the years ahead. Jobs and careers are changing as the workplace undergoes restructuring due to the impact of new technology and unique events. Not surprisingly, many career fields in demand today may well be glutted tomorrow. The job you have today may well disappear or become transformed into a very different type of job in the coming decade. If you are to survive and prosper in such a rapidly changing environment, you'll need to take action aimed at fireproofing your career.

Throughout this book we have emphasized the importance of **being prepared** for turbulent times. The age of the generalist armed with job search skills alone has passed. The emerging society requires a new type of **generalist-specialist** who is trained for today's technology, **flexible** enough to be retrained in tomorrow's technology, and **adaptive** to new jobs and careers that will arise today and tomorrow. In other words, the society needs more and more generalist-specialists who welcome change by being willing and able to re-career. Knowing and practicing the job search skills outlined in this book, these people also are continuously learning new work-content skills in order to better position themselves in tomorrow's job market. **They transform their careering skills into re-careering competencies**.

If you want to change your life, you should develop and practice re-careering competencies. We recommend two final re-careering actions on your part. First, make an effort to learn one new skill each year; the skill can be related to work, family, community, or a hobby such as building bookcases, operating different computer software programs, repairing appliances, or remodeling your home. If you do this, you will be better prepared for making

Weekly Job Performance and Planning Report

1. The week of: _____.

2. This week I:

   - wrote ____ job search letters.
   - sent ____ resumes and ____ letters to potential employers.
   - completed ____ applications.
   - made ____ job search telephone calls.
   - completed ____ hours of job research.
   - set up ____ appointments for informational interviews.
   - conducted ____ informational interviews.
   - received ____ invitations to a job interview.
   - followed up on ____ contacts and ____ referrals.

3. Next week I will:

   - write ____ job search letters.
   - send ____ resumes and ____ letters to potential employers.
   - complete ____ applications.
   - make ____ job search telephone calls.
   - complete ____ hours of job research.
   - set up ____ appointments for informational interviews.
   - conduct ____ informational interviews.
   - follow up on ____ contacts and ____ referrals.

4. Summary of progress this week in reference to my Job Search Contract commitments:

   _____
   _____
   _____
   _____
   _____
   _____

the career transitions necessary for functioning effectively in turbulent times.

Second, develop your own five-year plan which incorporates yearly career check-ups. At the end of each year, ask yourself: To what degree have I achieved my goals? Which goals do I need to revise? What actions do I need to take to better achieve my goals?

Careers and jobs should not be viewed as life sentences. You should feel free to change jobs and careers when you want to or need to. In fact, millions of people make successful career transitions each year. Some are more successful than others in finding the right job. If you plan your career transition according to the methods outlined in previous chapters and focus on your accomplishments, you should be able to successfully land the job you want – one you do well and really enjoy doing.

Treat yourself right. Take the time and effort to sail into today's job market with a plan of action that links your qualifications to the needs of employers. You are first and foremost an individual with knowledge, abilities, and skills that many employers need and want. If you follow the advice of this book, you will put your best foot forward in communicating your qualifications to employers. You will find a job fit for you. Most important, you can change your life because you are able to change your job.

The Author

RON KRANNICH IS ONE of America's leading career and travel writers who has authored, co-authored, of ghost-written more than 70 books. President of Development Concepts Incorporated, he received his Ph.D. in Political Science from Northern Illinois University. A former Fulbright Scholar, Peace Corps Volunteer, high school teacher, and university professor, he has completed numerous projects on management, career development, local government, population planning, and rural development in the United States and abroad.

Ron's career work began in 1980 as a result of an experimental project he initiated at Old Dominion University in Norfolk, Virginia to introduce students in the liberal arts and humanities to career planning concepts and job search techniques. He collaborated with William Banis, the director of career planning and placement at ODU, in acquiring expertise in the career field. One unexpected result of the project was the publication of his first career book, with William Banis, which also served as Ron's re-careering swan song – *Moving Out of Education*. Shortly thereafter he and his wife, Caryl, established Impact Publications (www.impactpublications.com), which is now a major publisher of career and travel books as well as a center for all types of career resources.

For more than two decades Ron and Caryl have pursued a passion – assisting hundreds of thousands of individuals, from students, the unemployed, and ex-offenders to military personnel, international job seekers, and CEOs, in making critical job and career transitions. Focusing on key job search skills, career changes, and employment fields, their impressive body of work has helped shape career thinking and behavior both in the United States and abroad. Representing one of today's more comprehensive collections of career writing, their work includes such classics as *High Impact Resumes and Letters*, *Interview for Success*, and *Dynamite Salary Negotiations*. With nearly 3 million copies in print, their publications are widely available in bookstores, libraries, and career centers. No strangers to the Internet world, they have written *America's Top Internet Job Sites* and *The Directory of Websites for*

International Jobs and published several Internet recruitment and job search books. They also have developed career-related websites: www.impactpublica tions.com, www.winningthejob.com, www.contentforcareers.com, and www. veteransworld.com. Many of their career tips have appeared on such major websites as www.monster.com, www.careerbuilder.com, www.employment guide.com, and www.campuscareercenter.com.

Ron and Caryl live a double life with travel being their best kept *"do what you love"* career secret. Authors of over 20 travel-shopping guidebooks on various destinations around the world, they continue to pursue their international and travel interests through their innovative *Treasures and Pleasures of...Best of the Best* travel-shopping series and related websites: www.ishop aroundtheworld.com, www.contentfortravel.com, and www.travel-smarter. com. When not found at their home and business in Virginia, they are probably somewhere in Europe, Asia, Africa, the Middle East, the South Pacific, the Caribbean, or the Americas following their other passion – researching and writing about quality antiques, arts, crafts, jewelry, hotels, and restaurants as well as adhering to the career advice they give to others: *"Pursue a passion that enables you to do what you really love to do."*

As both career and travel experts, the Krannichs' work is frequently featured in major newspapers, magazines, and newsletters as well as on radio, television, and the Internet. Available for interviews, consultation, and presentations, Ron can be contacted as follows:

Ron Krannich
krannich@impactpublications.com

Index

Career Resources

THE FOLLOWING CAREER RESOURCES are available directly from Impact Publications. Full descriptions of each title, as well as 10+ downloadable catalogs and 40+ specialty flyers, including videos, software, and posters, can be found on Impact's website: www.impactpublications.com. Complete the following form or list the titles, include shipping (see formula at the end), enclose payment, and send your order to:

IMPACT PUBLICATIONS
9104 Manassas Drive, Suite N
Manassas Park, VA 20111-5211 USA
1-800-361-1055 (orders only)
Tel. 703-361-7300 or Fax 703-335-9486
Email address: info@impactpublications.com
Quick & easy online ordering: www.impactpublications.com

Orders from individuals must be prepaid by check, money order, or major credit card. We accept telephone, fax, and email orders.

Qty.	TITLES	Price	TOTAL
Featured Title			
_____	Change Your Job, Change Your Life	$21.95	_____
Companion Titles By Author			
_____	America's Top Internet Job Sites	$19.95	_____
_____	America's Top 100 Jobs for People Re-Entering the Workforce	$19.95	_____
_____	America's Top 100 Jobs for People Without a Four-Year Degree	$19.95	_____

344

____ Discover the Best Jobs for You	$15.95	____
____ Dynamite Salary Negotiations	$15.95	____
____ Get a Raise in 7 Days	$14.95	____
____ High Impact Resumes and Letters	$19.95	____
____ I Want to Do Something Else, But I'm Not Sure What It Is	$15.95	____
____ Interview for Success	$15.95	____
____ The Job Hunting Guide: College to Career	$14.95	____
____ Job Hunting Tips for People With Not-So-Hot Backgrounds	$17.95	____
____ Job Interview Tips for People With Not-So-Hot Backgrounds	$14.95	____
____ Military Resumes and Cover Letters	$21.95	____
____ Nail the Job Interview	$13.95	____
____ No One Will Hire Me!	$13.95	____
____ Savvy Interviewing: The Nonverbal Advantage	$12.95	____
____ The Savvy Networker	$13.95	____
____ Savvy Resume Writer	$10.95	____

Career Exploration and Job Strategies

____ 5 Patterns of Extraordinary Careers	$17.95	____
____ 25 Jobs That Have It All	$12.95	____
____ 50 Cutting Edge Jobs	$15.95	____
____ 95 Mistakes Job Seekers Make & How to Avoid Them	$13.95	____
____ 100 Great Jobs and How to Get Them	$17.95	____
____ 101 Ways to Recession-Proof Your Career	$14.95	____
____ 300 Best Jobs Without a Four-Year Degree	$16.95	____
____ America's Top 100 Jobs for People Without a Four-Year Degree	$19.95	____
____ Best Jobs for the 21st Century	$19.95	____
____ Career Change	$14.95	____
____ Cool Careers for Dummies	$19.99	____
____ Directory of Executive Recruiters	$49.95	____
____ Five Secrets to Finding a Job	$12.95	____
____ High-Tech Careers for Low-Tech People	$14.95	____
____ How to Get a Job and Keep It	$16.95	____
____ How to Succeed Without a Career Path	$13.95	____
____ Job Hunting Guide: College to Career	$14.95	____
____ Job Search Handbook for People With Disabilities	$17.95	____
____ Knock 'Em Dead	$14.95	____
____ Me, Myself, and I, Inc.	$17.95	____
____ Monster Careers	$18.00	____
____ Occupational Outlook Handbook	$16.90	____
____ O*NET Dictionary of Occupational Titles	$39.95	____
____ Quit Your Job and Grow Some Hair	$15.95	____
____ Rites of Passage at $100,000 to $1 Million+	$29.95	____
____ What Color Is Your Parachute?	$17.95	____
____ Working Identify	$26.95	____

Internet Job Search

____	100 Top Internet Job Sites	$12.95 ____
____	America's Top Internet Job Sites	$19.95 ____
____	CareerXroads	$26.95 ____
____	Career Exploration On the Internet	$24.95 ____
____	Cyberspace Job Search Kit	$18.95 ____
____	Directory of Websites for International Jobs	$19.95 ____
____	Guide to Internet Job Searching	$14.95 ____

Attitude and Motivation

____	100 Ways to Motivate Yourself	$18.99 ____
____	Attitude Is Everything	$14.95 ____
____	Change Your Attitude	$15.99 ____
____	Reinventing Yourself	$18.99 ____

Inspiration and Empowerment

____	101 Secrets of Highly Effective Speakers	$15.95 ____
____	Do What You Love for the Rest of Your Life	$24.95 ____
____	Dream It Do It	$16.95 ____
____	Life Strategies	$13.95 ____
____	Power of Purpose	$20.00 ____
____	Practical Dreamer's Handbook	$13.95 ____
____	Self Matters	$14.00 ____
____	Seven Habits of Highly Effective People	$15.00 ____
____	Who Moved My Cheese?	$19.95 ____

Testing and Assessment

____	Career Tests	$12.95 ____
____	Discover the Best Jobs for You	$15.95 ____
____	Discover What You're Best At	$14.00 ____
____	Do What You Are	$18.95 ____
____	Finding Your Perfect Work	$16.95 ____
____	I Could Do Anything If Only I Knew What It Was	$14.95 ____
____	I Want to Do Something Else, But I'm Not Sure What It Is	$15.95 ____
____	Now, Discover Your Strengths	$27.00 ____
____	What Should I Do With My Life?	$14.95 ____
____	What Type Am I?	$14.95 ____
____	What's Your Type of Career?	$17.95 ____

Resumes and Letters

____	101 Great Tips for a Dynamite Resume	$13.95 ____
____	175 Best Cover Letters	$14.95 ____
____	201 Dynamite Job Search Letters	$19.95 ____

_____ Best KeyWords for Resumes, Cover Letters,
_____ & Interviews $17.95 _____
_____ Best Resumes and CVs for International Jobs $24.95 _____
_____ Best Resumes for $100,000+ Jobs $24.95 _____
_____ Best Resumes for People Without a Four-Year Degree $19.95 _____
_____ Best Cover Letters for $100,000+ Jobs $24.95 _____
_____ Cover Letters for Dummies $16.99 _____
_____ Cover Letters That Knock 'Em Dead $12.95 _____
_____ Cyberspace Resume Kit $18.95 _____
_____ e-Resumes $14.95 _____
_____ Gallery of Best Cover Letters $18.95 _____
_____ Gallery of Best Resumes $18.95 _____
_____ Haldane's Best Cover Letters for Professionals $15.95 _____
_____ Haldane's Best Resumes for Professionals $15.95 _____
_____ High Impact Resumes and Letters $19.95 _____
_____ Resume Shortcuts $14.95 _____
_____ Resumes for Dummies $16.99 _____
_____ Resumes for the Health Care Professional $14.95 _____
_____ Resumes That Knock 'Em Dead $12.95 _____
_____ The Savvy Resume Writer $12.95 _____

Networking

_____ Dynamite Telesearch $12.95 _____
_____ A Foot in the Door $14.95 _____
_____ How to Work a Room $14.00 _____
_____ Masters of Networking $16.95 _____
_____ Power Networking $14.95 _____
_____ The Savvy Networker $13.95 _____

Dress, Image, and Etiquette

_____ Dressing Smart for Men $16.95 _____
_____ Dressing Smart for the New Millennium $15.95 _____
_____ Dressing Smart for Women $16.95 _____
_____ Power Etiquette $14.95 _____
_____ Professional Impressions $14.95 _____

Interviews

_____ 101 Dynamite Questions to Ask
At Your Job Interview $13.95 _____
_____ Haldane's Best Answers to Tough
Interview Questions $15.95 _____
_____ Interview for Success $15.95 _____
_____ Job Interview Tips for People With
Not-So-Hot Backgrounds $14.95 _____
_____ Job Interviews for Dummies $16.99 _____
_____ KeyWords to Nail Your Job Interview $17.95 _____

_____ Nail the Job Interview! $13.95 _____
_____ The Savvy Interviewer $10.95 _____

Salary Negotiations

_____ Better Than Money $18.95 _____
_____ Dynamite Salary Negotiations $15.95 _____
_____ Get a Raise in 7 Days $14.95 _____
_____ Haldane's Best Salary Tips for Professionals $15.95 _____

Military in Transition

_____ Jobs and the Military Spouse $17.95 _____
_____ Military Resumes and Cover Letters $21.95 _____

Ex-Offenders in Transition

_____ 9 to 5 Beats Ten to Life $15.00 _____
_____ 99 Days and a Get Up $9.95 _____
_____ Ex-Offender's Job Search Companion $9.95 _____
_____ Man, I Need a Job $7.95 _____
_____ Putting the Bars Behind You (6 books) $64.70 _____

Government and Nonprofit Jobs

_____ Complete Guide to Public Employment $19.95 _____
_____ Federal Applications That Get Results $23.95 _____
_____ Federal Personnel Guide $12.00 _____
_____ FBI Careers $18.95 _____
_____ Ten Steps to a Federal Job $39.95 _____

International and Travel Jobs

_____ Back Door Guide to Short-Term Job Adventures $21.95 _____
_____ Careers in International Affairs $24.95 _____
_____ Careers in International Business $14.95 _____
_____ Directory of Websites for International Jobs $19.95 _____
_____ Inside Secrets to Finding a Career in Travel $14.95 _____
_____ International Jobs $19.00 _____
_____ International Job Finder $19.95 _____
_____ Jobs for Travel Lovers $19.95 _____
_____ Teaching English Abroad $15.95 _____

VIDEOS

_____ Build a Network for Work and Life $129.00 _____
_____ Common Mistakes People Make in Interviews $79.95 _____
_____ The Complete Job Application $99.00 _____
_____ Down But Not Out $129.00 _____

_____	Exceptional Interviewing Tips	$79.00 _____
_____	Extraordinary Answers to Interview Questions	$79.95 _____
_____	Extreme Interview	$69.00 _____
_____	Looking for Work With Attitude Plus	$129.00 _____
_____	Make a First Good Impression	$129.00 _____
_____	Mastering the Interview	$98.00 _____
_____	Seizing the Job Interview	$79.00 _____
_____	Quick Interview Video	$149.00 _____
_____	Quick Salary Negotiations Video	$149.00 _____
_____	Resumes, Cover Letters, and Portfolios	$98.00 _____
_____	Ten Commandments of Resumes	$79.95 _____
_____	Tips and Techniques to Improve Your Total Image	$98.00 _____
_____	Why Should I Hire You?	$129.00 _____

SUBTOTAL   _____

Virginia residents add 5% sales tax   _____

POSTAGE/HANDLING ($5 for first
product and 8% of SUBTOTAL)   _$5.00_

8% of SUBTOTAL --- _____

TOTAL ENCLOSED ---------------------- _____

SHIP TO:

NAME _____

ADDRESS: _____

_____

_____

PAYMENT METHOD:

❑   I enclose check/money order for $ _____ made payable to
IMPACT PUBLICATIONS.

❑   Please charge $ _____ to my credit card:

❑ Visa   ❑ MasterCard   ❑ American Express   ❑ Discover

Card # _____ Expiration date: ____/____

Signature _____

Keep in Touch . . .
On the Web!

www.impactpublications.com
www.ishoparoundtheworld.com
www.travel-smarter.com
www.contentfortravel.com
www.winningthejob.com
www.veteransworld.com
www.contentforcareers.com